AP Chinese

LANGUAGE AND CULTURE

SIMULATED TESTS

By Bih Hsya Hsieh, Sunny X. Yu

编著：谢碧霞　于晓华

CLERC PUBLISHING

CLERC Publishing
510 Broadway, Suite 200
Millbrae, CA 94030
U.S.A.

Executive Editor: John Zhang
Marketing Director: Doroteo Ng
Editor and Proofread: Xiangyan Liu
Layout & Cover Design: Jiaqing Fang, Tyler Chen
Recordings: Bih Hsya Hsieh, Sunny X. Yu, May Hom, Meng Zhang, Xiangyan Liu

C 2010 CLERC Publishing

Printed in USA

2nd Edition

Exclusive Distributor:

Nan Hai Books
510 Broadway, Suite 200
Millbrae, CA 94030
www.nanhaibooks.com
Tel.: (650) 259 - 2100
Fax.: (650) 259 - 2108

ISBN13: 978-1-61617-001-1
ISBN10:   1-61617-001-8

Publisher's Note for 2nd Edition

The trial edition of *AP Chinese Language and Culture Simulated Tests* has garnered many constructive suggestions and feedbacks. Incorporating the many remarks, the official edition of the *AP Chinese Language and Culture Simulated Tests* is currently available.

修订版声明

《AP中文综合测试模拟试题集》试用版推出之后，我们收到了使用者不少有益的反馈意见。我们尽可能地吸收他们的宝贵意见，推出了正式版《AP中文综合测试模拟试题集》。

Foreword

Since May 2007, when the College Board conducted the AP Chinese Language and Culture Examination for the first time, a number of US schools have established new Chinese language programs, while some high schools with existing Chinese programs have added AP courses to their curricula. The increase in the number of students enrolled in these programs, coupled with rising interest in studying Chinese as well as the steady improvement in the levels of attainment among these students, have all spurred the enthusiasm and dedication of those of us engaged in Chinese language pedagogy. Through our experiences in the classroom over the past several years, we became aware of the dearth of materials focused on the content and form of the AP Chinese examination. Mindful also of the daily demands on teachers' time, and of the special requirements of teaching an AP-based curriculum, we have compiled this volume of AP Chinese practice questions for use by students both in exam preparation and for general language study. Its questions are based on the general parameters for the AP Chinese examination established by the College Board, as well as on sample questions published by the College Board, and the examination format adopted in the latest 2009 AP Chinese Language and Culture Examination.

This workbook has eight sets of practice questions. The first, third, fifth, and seventh sets were authored by Sunny X. Yu, while the second, fourth, sixth, and eighth sets were by Bih-hsya Hsieh. Following the completion of the initial draft, we collaborated in revising each set until it reached its present form. Over the process of compiling this workbook, we considered both the character of the AP Chinese examination as a test of language proficiency, as well as the considerable variety of textbooks and other materials used in different language programs across the country. As a result, we have tried to include vocabulary and grammar in common usage and of a suitable level of difficulty, while also consciously inserting some more challenging vocabulary, with the goal of augmenting students' knowledge of vocabulary as they engage in the exercises. In the area of culture, we have included some commonly shared cultural knowledge in the readings, to give the students opportunities to fully develop their powers of expression on such topics, for deployment in the exam section on cultural presentation. In the section on listening comprehension and conversation, we have tried to adhere to the principles of naturalness, practical applicability, and fidelity to realistic situations in language expression.

It is our sincere desire that this volume of practice questions achieves the goals of comprehensiveness, lively content, and appropriate level of difficulty to which it aspires, and that it closely matches the form and content of the actual AP examination. Nevertheless, we realize that shortcomings are inevitable due to our various limitations in experience, time, and knowledge, and we hope that our readers will offer corrections and suggestions for improvement. We wish to thank the many colleagues and students who have given their advice and ideas during our work on this project. We would also like to express our deep gratitude to the CLERC Publishing for their unstinting support, and in particular, to Mr. John Zhang for his leadership and Ms. Xiangyan Liu for her assistance in bringing this book to publication.

Sunny X. Yu
Piedmont High School
xsunnyyu@aol.com

Bih-hsya Hsieh
San Francisco University High School

前　　言

　　自2007年五月美国大学理事会首次举办AP中文考试以来，全美很多学校都相继开设了中文项目，一些已成立中文项目的高中也增设了AP中文课程。学生人数的增加、学生学习中文兴趣的提升，以及学生中文水平的逐年提高，更激发了中文教师从事教学工作的热情和干劲。在过去数年的实际教学中，我们意识到目前针对AP中文考试形式及内容编写的材料非常有限，我们也十分了解一线教师工作的繁忙以及AP中文教学的需求，因此我们不揣野人献曝，以大学理事会所颁布的AP中文教学大纲为范畴，以大学理事会所公布的AP部分中文考试的样题为尺度，以2009年最新AP考试形式为准绳，编写了这本AP中文模拟试题练习册，以供学生平时练习及考前准备之用。

　　本册共有八套模拟试题，其中第一、三、五、七套题由于晓华负责，第二、四、六、八套题由谢碧霞负责，初步编写完竣，再共同推敲、改写及定稿。在编写过程中，我们既考虑到AP中文考试为水平考试的性质，又顾及到目前各校中文课程使用教材不一的特点，尽可能地包括常用的、难易程度适中的词汇与语法，并有意识地穿插少量较难的词汇，以期学生在练习的同时，能够对生词理解的掌握有所助益。在文化知识方面，我们把常识性的文化知识融入于阅读之中，对于一些较重要的文化知识，学生有机会在文化演绎表达部分得以充分发挥。听力对话部分，我们尽可能注意到语言情境内容的真实自然及实用性。

　　虽然我们的初衷是希望本册模拟试题能够兼具内容丰富、程度适中、涵盖面广的特性，并与实际的AP考题题型及内容同步，但囿于个人经验、水平及时间，本书定有不足及需改正之处，尚祈诸位先进多所包涵并不吝指教。对于诸多曾经给予我们建议及宝贵意见的同行与学生，我们在此一并致谢。此外，此书得以问世，我们也由衷感谢CLERC出版社的鼎力支持及张晓江先生的鞭策与协助，以及刘湘燕小姐的编辑与校对。

谢碧霞　　　　　　　　　　　　　　　　　于晓华
San Francisco University High School　　Piedmont High School
bihhsya.hsieh@sfuhs.org　　　　　　　　xsunnyyu@aol.com

Free Online Access to Audio Recordings

A FREE downloadable audio file for the listening and speaking sections of the book is provided at http://www.nanhaibooks.com for users of this book. To download the file, please visit this site and register with your log-in CODE below:

Log-in Code:

45428733

The audio scripts for all the tests are located in the back of the book as an appendix.

For detailed information, please call (650) 259-2100 or visit us at
http://www.nanhaibooks.com

Table of Contents

目　　录

SECTION I: Multiple Choice

Part A: Listening (Rejoinders and Listening Selections)

Listening Part Directions

You will answer two types of questions: rejoinders and questions based on listening selections. For all tasks, you will have a specific amount of response time. In this part of the exam, you may NOT move back and forth among questions.

Listening Part Directions: Rejoinders (10%, 10 minutes)

You will hear several short conversations or parts of conversations followed by four choices, designated (A), (B), (C), and (D). Choose the one that continues or completes the conversation in a logical and culturally appropriate manner. You will have 5 seconds to answer each question.

1. (A) (B) (C) (D)   9. (A) (B) (C) (D)
2. (A) (B) (C) (D)   10. (A) (B) (C) (D)
3. (A) (B) (C) (D)   11. (A) (B) (C) (D)
4. (A) (B) (C) (D)   12. (A) (B) (C) (D)
5. (A) (B) (C) (D)   13. (A) (B) (C) (D)
6. (A) (B) (C) (D)   14. (A) (B) (C) (D)
7. (A) (B) (C) (D)   15. (A) (B) (C) (D)
8. (A) (B) (C) (D)

Selection 1: Announcement (Selection plays one time.)

16. The donation is for the benefit of

    A) the school

    B) the students

    C) the homeless

    D) the victims of a natural disaster

17. How will the clothes be collected?

    A) Students will mail the clothes to the main office.

    B) Students will send the clothes directly to a non-profit organization.

    C) Students will leave them in the boxes in the classrooms.

    D) Students will collect the clothes during fourth period.

18. What sizes of clothes are preferred?

    A) Any size

    B) Both large and small

    C) Extra large only

    D) Children's sizes only

19. How long will the donation period last?

    A) Until the end of the month

    B) Until the end of the semester

    C) Until enough clothes have been collected

    D) For one week

Selection 2: Conversation (Selection plays one time.)

20. The boy asks the girl to go to a

    A) volunteer event

    B) dance party

    C) birthday party

    D) movie theatre

21. Why does the girl not want to go with the boy?

    A) She has to do homework.

    B) She has to volunteer at an event.

    C) She does not enjoy dancing.

    D) She thinks the boy is too aggressive.

22. What is the outcome of the boy's invitation?

    A) The girl will go to the party with someone else.

    B) The girl accepted the boy's invitation.

    C) The girl will not go to the party with the boy.

    D) The girl would like to think about it some more.

Selection 3: Voice Message (Selection plays two times.)

23. Where did the boy stay with his uncle?

    A) San Francisco

    B) Los Angeles

    C) Beijing

    D) Shanghai

24. The boy visited his uncle during

    A) the summer

    B) spring break

    C) Christmas break

    D) Chinese New Year

25. Why is the boy worried about going to school the next day?

    A) He has a lot of homework to do.

    B) He is tired of going to school.

    C) He is experiencing jet lag.

    D) He is still very excited about his recent trip.

26. Which of the following is TRUE about the boy's return flight?

    A) It arrived on time.

    B) It arrived thirty minutes early.

    C) It was delayed by thirty minutes.

    D) It was delayed by one hour.

Selection 4: Instructions (Selection plays two times.)

27. The instructions are on how to use a

    A) fax machine

    B) cell phone

    C) laptop

    D) music player

28. What is the cost of sending a message?

    A) Free

    B) Ten cents

    C) It depends on the service plan.

    D) It depends on the time of the day.

29. What is the second step in sending a text message?

    A) Press the "Text Message" button.

    B) Input the phone number or name of the recipient.

    C) Type the text message.

    D) Input your phone number.

30. The maximum number of recipients for a message is

    A) one

    B) two

    C) three

    D) a few

31. What is the forecast for today's weather?

    A) Heavy snow

    B) Moderate rain

    C) Strong winds

    D) Cool breeze

Selection 5: Report (Selection plays two times.)

32. What will happen in the next few days?

    A) It will get warmer.

    B) It will get colder.

    C) It will continue to rain.

    D) It will begin to snow.

33. What will happen in the next few days?

    A) It will get warmer.

    B) It will get colder.

    C) It will continue to rain.

    D) It will begin to snow.

34. The forecast advises to

    A) apply sunblock when going outside

    B) carry an umbrella

    C) wear multiple layers

    D) stay indoors

35. What is the scope of the forecast?

    A) Nationwide

    B) Citywide

    C) Statewide

    D) Worldwide

Part B: Reading Selections (25%, 60 minutes)

Reading Part Directions

In this part of the exam, you may move back and forth among all the questions. You will read several selections in Chinese. Each selection is accompanied by a number of questions in English. For each question, choose the response that is best according to the selection. You will have 60 minutes to answer all questions.

Read this e-mail.

[Simplified Character Version]	[Traditional Character Version]
发件人：小红 收件人：妈妈 邮件主题：在中国旅游 发件日期：2009年7月18日	發件人：小紅 收件人：媽媽 郵件主題：在中國旅遊 發件日期：2009年7月18日
亲爱的妈妈： 　　您好！今天是我在北京的第四天。前两天，我去了天安门、故宫、长城和十三陵，昨天我逛了王府井。据说王府井是北京最有名的一条商业街，但是我最感兴趣的不是那些卖各种世界名牌的商店，也不是被称作中华老字号的商店，更不是观看街头表演，而是王府井的小吃街。在王府井商业街里有一个小胡同，里面全都是专卖各种小吃的店铺。每个店铺所卖的食品都具有非常独特的地方风味。比如，新疆的烤羊肉串、陕西的羊肉泡馍、四川的麻辣粉儿，还有上海的小笼包等等，多得吃不过来。我想，将来有机会，我一定带您来这儿一起品尝这里的美食。 　　明天我就要离开北京去昆明、广州、珠海等地了，大约一周后到香港。希望您在家安心养病，不要担心我，我会随时给您写信或打电话联络。 再见！ 　　　　　　　　　　　　女儿 小红上	親愛的媽媽： 　　您好！今天是我在北京的第四天。前兩天，我去了天安門、故宮、長城和十三陵，昨天我逛了王府井。據說王府井是北京最有名的一條商業街，但是我最感興趣的不是那些賣各種世界名牌的商店，也不是被稱作中華老字號的商店，更不是觀看街頭表演，而是王府井的小吃街。在王府井商業街裡有一個小胡同，裡面全都是專賣各種小吃的店舖。每個店舖所賣的食品都具有非常獨特的地方風味。比如，新疆的烤羊肉串、陝西的羊肉泡饃、四川的麻辣粉兒，還有上海的小籠包等等，多得吃不過來。我想，將來有機會，我一定帶您來這兒一起品嚐這裡的美食。 　　明天我就要離開北京去昆明、廣州、珠海等地了，大約一週後到香港。希望您在家安心養病，不要擔心我，我會隨時給您寫信或打電話聯絡。 再見！ 　　　　　　　　　　　　女兒 小紅上

1. What was the most memorable location of her trip?

    A) The Forbidden City

    B) The Great Wall

    C) Tiananmen Square

    D) Wangfujing Snack Street

2. Which of the following statement is TRUE?

    A) Spicy bean noodles are from Beijing.

    B) Steamed pork dumplings are from Shanghai.

    C) Lamb kabobs are from Sichuan.

    D) There are various snacks from the world at Wangfujing Snack Street.

3. What aspect of Wangfujing Street does Xiaohong like the most?

    A) Eating the snacks of Wangfujing

    B) Shopping in internationally known brand name stores

    C) Shopping in traditional Chinese stores

    D) Watching street performances

4. What part of China will Xiaohong visit next?

    A) The North

    B) The South

    C) The East

    D) The West

5. Which of the following statement about Xiaohong's mother is TRUE?

    A) She met with Xiaohong in Hong Kong the following week.

    B) She was sick at home.

    C) She continued to stay in Beijing after Xiaohong left.

    D) She was waiting for Xiaohong to come to Kunming the next day.

Read this public sign.

[Simplified Character Version]	[Traditional Character Version]
此处危险！请勿靠近！	此處危險！請勿靠近！

6. What does the warning on the sign suggest?

   A) Do not approach!

   B) Security check needed!

   C) Enter with caution!

   D) Watch both sides of the street before crossing!

7. Where would this sign most likely appear?

   A) On a high-voltage electric fence

   B) Beside a swimming pool

   C) On a children's play structure

   D) In a parking lot

Read this public sign.

[Simplified Character Version]	[Traditional Character Version]
平时注入一滴水 难时拥有太平洋	平時注入一滴水 難時擁有太平洋

8. Where is the sign most likely seen?

   A) On a school bus

   B) Near the sink of the public restrooms

   C) Near the beach

   D) In restaurants

9. The purpose of the sign is to

   A) tell people that travelling across the Pacific Ocean is dangerous

   B) encourage people to save water

   C) say that the Pacific Ocean is the best source for drinking water

   D) remind people to always have plenty of drinking water

Read this advertisement on a poster.

[Simplified Character Version]	[Traditional Character Version]
汽车拍卖会	汽車拍賣會
本市最盛大的汽车拍卖会。有三百多辆豪华型和经济型的各式汽车可供挑选。具体事宜如下：	本市最盛大的汽車拍賣會。有三百多輛豪華型和經濟型的各式汽車可供挑選。具體事宜如下：
一、汽车拍卖种类： 　1. 各式轿车 　2. 各式轻型卡车 　3. 政府没收车 　4. 银行回收车	一、汽車拍賣種類： 　1. 各式轎車 　2. 各式輕型卡車 　3. 政府沒收車 　4. 銀行回收車
二、拍卖日期：2月7日（星期六）上午九点至下午三点	二、拍賣日期：2月7日（星期六）上午九點至下午三點
三、看车日期：2月6日（星期五）上午十点至下午五点	三、看車日期：2月6日（星期五）上午十點至下午五點
四、拍卖地点及联系电话：江南市市政府东区停车场。电话：（956）300-4000	四、拍賣地點及聯繫電話：江南市市政府東區停車場。電話：（956）300-4000
五、注意事项： 　1. 风雨无阻，免费入场 　2. 自由出价，提供贷款 　3. 买方需支付10%的费用给拍卖行 　4. 此次拍卖与任何政府机构无关	五、注意事項： 　1. 風雨無阻，免費入場 　2. 自由出價，提供貸款 　3. 買方需支付10%的費用給拍賣行 　4. 此次拍賣與任何政府機構無關

10. Which of the following car categories will NOT be offered at the auction?

   A) Sports cars

   B) Light trucks

   C) Bank owned cars

   D) Government repossessed cars

11. According to the notice, which of the following statement is TRUE?

   A) Buyers must pay a 10% fee to the seller.

   B) Auction participants must pay an entrance fee.

   C) The auction will be canceled if there is rain.

   D) This auction is organized by a government agency.

12. Where is the auction going to be held?

    A) At an auto dealership

    B) In a parking lot next to city hall

    C) In the eastern part of the city

    D) In a parking lot in front of a bank

13. Which of the following is FALSE?

    A) The buyer can view the cars prior to the auction.

    B) The buyer can name their own price.

    C) The buyer must have good credit.

    D) The buyer can obtain loans.

Read this advertisement.

[Simplified Character Version]	[Traditional Character Version]
德州州立大学女留学生，找人分租一套两室一厅一浴独立单元。月租五百，两人平分。单独睡房，共用客厅及厨浴。分租人须是在校大学生，不吸烟，无宠物，男女不限。意者请下午三点钟后电（321）123-4567联系。	德州州立大學女留學生，找人分租一套兩室一廳一浴獨立單元。月租五百，兩人平分。單獨睡房，共用客廳及廚浴。分租人須是在校大學生，不吸煙，無寵物，男女不限。意者請下午三點鐘後電（321）123-4567聯繫。

14. Who put up this advertisement?

    A) An international student

    B) The apartment owner

    C) A real estate agent

    D) The college's housing service

15. What type of roommate is preferred?

    A) Female college student

    B) Male college student

    C) Non-smoking college student

    D) College student with pets

16. How much is the rent?

    A) $500 per person

    B) $250 per person

    C) $1,000 per person

    D) It depends on the size of the room.

17. What is the preferred contact time?

    A) Before 3:00 pm

    B) After 3:00 pm

    C) At 3:00 pm

    D) Around 3:00 pm

18. Where is the apartment located?

    A) California

    B) Oregon

    C) Washington

    D) Texas

Read this letter.

[Simplified Character Version]	[Traditional Character Version]
大伟，你好！	大偉，你好！
随父母从北京迁居纽约已经快一周了，我非常想念你和其他的同学们。　　这是我第一次来纽约，对这里的一切都感到新奇。纽约建立于1624年，是世界金融和贸易中心，非常繁华。我逛了举世闻名的时代广场和帝国大厦,也看了自由女神像。可惜那两座雄伟的世贸大厦已经不复存在，否则在纽约世贸大厦顶层看纽约全貌也是一件绝妙的事。9/11摧毁的世贸大厦现在已经被围了起来，据说这里准备重新盖更高更壮观的摩天大厦。如果将来你有机会来纽约，我可以做你的导游，我们可以一起登上新的世贸大楼，观赏纽约迷人的夜景。	隨父母從北京迁居紐約已經快一周了，我非常想念你和其他的同學們。　　這是我第一次來紐約，對這裡的一切都感到非常新奇。紐約建立於1624年，是世界金融和貿易中心，非常繁華。我逛了舉世聞名的時代廣場和帝國大廈,也看了自由女神像。可惜那兩座雄偉的世貿大廈已經不復存在，否則在紐約世貿大廈頂層看紐約全貌也是一件絕妙的事。9/11摧毀的世貿大廈已經被圍了起來，據說這裡準備重新蓋更高更壯觀的摩天大廈。如果將來你有機會來紐約，我可以做你的導遊，我們可以一起登上新的世貿大樓，觀賞紐約迷人的夜景。
祝好！　　　　　　　　　　小明　　　　　　　　2009年10月16日	祝好！　　　　　　　　　　小明　　　　　　　　2009年10月16日

19. Why did Xiaoming come to New York?

    A) To visit his father and mother

    B) His family moved to New York.

    C) He works in New York.

    D) To visit a friend with his parents

20. Which of the following statements is NOT TRUE?

    A) Xiaoming has been in New York before.

    B) Xiaoming visited Time Square and the Empire State Building.

    C) Xiaoming hopes to give his friend a tour.

    D) Xiaoming misses his friend very much.

21. What did he see at the site of the World Trade Center?

    A) The construction of a new building

    B) A fence surrounding the site

    C) A newly developed park

    D) A visitor's center

22. How long has Xiaoming been in New York?

    A) Less than a week

    B) One month

    C) One year

    D) A week

Read this article.

[Simplified Character Version]	[Traditional Character Version]
问路	問路

马克第一次到中国旅游，访问了中国的两个城市：北京和哈尔滨。他有一个非常有趣的发现。在北京，当他问路时，当地人都是答：向东，向西，向南或者向北，总是以东、南西、北来指示方向。但是在哈尔滨，当地的人都是以向左、向右、向前或者向后来指示方向。他对此感到非常好奇。
    他参考了北京和哈尔滨的地理位置和城市发展历史后发现，北京地处内陆华北平原，城市以紫禁城为中心，街道像一个个方块向外层层扩展。主要街道布局为东西或南北方向。而哈尔滨紧邻松花江，由于弯曲的河道，哈尔滨的街道像蜘蛛网一样由江边向两岸扩展，城市的主要街道弯弯曲曲。马克想，也许城市规划的不同就是为什么那些土生土长的北京人和哈尔滨人回答问路时方法不同的主要原因吧。
	馬克第一次到中國旅遊，訪問了中國的兩個城市：北京和哈爾濱。他有一個非常有趣的發現。在北京，當他問路時，當地人都是回答：向東，向西，向南或者向北，總是以東、南、西、北來指示方向。但是在哈爾濱，當地的人都是以向左、向右、向前或者向後來指示方向。他對此感到非常好奇。
	    他參考了北京和哈爾濱的地理位置和城市發展歷史後發現，北京地處內陸華北平原，城市以紫禁城為中心，街道像一個個方塊向外層層擴展。主要街道佈局為東西或南北方向。而哈爾濱緊鄰松花江，由於彎曲的河道，哈爾濱的街道像蜘蛛網一樣由江邊向兩岸擴展，城市的主要街道彎彎曲曲。馬克想，也許城市規劃的不同就是為什麼那些土生土長的北京人和哈爾濱人回答問路時方法不同的主要原因吧。

23. Beijing locals like to give directions using

    A) Street signs

    B) "Left, right, forward, backward"

    C) "East, west, north, south"

    D) Maps

24. Which of the following is the best description of the streets of Beijing?

    A) They are twisted like a spider's web.

    B) They are narrow.

    C) They are straight and orderly.

    D) They are twisted like a bird's nest.

25. Why do local people of Beijing and Harbin give directions in different ways?

    A) Beijing is an older city than Harbin.

    B) Harbin's population is larger.

    C) The layout of the streets of the two cities is different.

    D) Beijing is the capital of China.

Read this poster.

[Simplified Character Version]	[Traditional Character Version]
座谈会: 如何增强你的竞争力	座談會: 如何增強你的競爭力
时间：2009 年3月4日 上午9点至下午5点 地点：旧金山牛宫 讲员：麦克·费普斯（Michael Phelps）	時間：2009 年3月4日 上午9點至下午5點 地點：舊金山牛宮 講員：麥克·費普斯(Michael Phelps)
在北京举办的第28届奥运会上，麦克·费普斯是所有参赛选手中最轰动的运动员。他在本届奥运会上赢得八块金牌，这在奥运历史上是前所未有的。到目前为止，麦克总共获得了十四枚奥运金牌，破了三十七个游泳世界记录。麦克·菲普斯被誉称为世界游泳史上最优秀的游泳运动员。在座谈会上，麦克将亲自讲述他的个人成长经历，以及如何激励自己、刻苦训练，使自己具有更强竞争力的过程。	在北京舉辦的第28届奥運會上，麥克·費普斯是所有參賽選手中最轟動的運動員。他在本届奥運會上贏得八塊金牌，這在奥運歷史上是前所未有的。到目前為止，麥克總共獲得了十四枚奥運金牌，破了三十七個游泳世界紀錄。麥克·菲普斯被譽稱為世界游泳史上最優秀的游泳運動員。在座談會上，麥克將親自講述他的個人成長經歷，以及如何激勵自己、刻苦訓練，使自己具有更強競爭力的過程。

26. What is the purpose of the seminar?

    A) To display Phelps' gold medals

    B) To share Phelps' personal experience for success

    C) To celebrate Phelps' contribution to swimming

    D) To share swimming techniques

27. What does "竞争力"(競爭力) mean?

    A) Motivation

    B) Power

    C) Competitive edge

    D) Ability

28. How many Olympic gold medals has Michael Phelps won in his career so far?

    A) 8

    B) 14

    C) 28

    D) 7

29. How many world records has Michael Phelps broken by the end of 2008?

    A) 8

    B) 14

    C) 28

    D) 37

30. Where is the seminar held?

    A) Seattle

    B) San Francisco

    C) Beijing

    D) Baltimore

Read this story.

[Simplified Character Version]	[Traditional Character Version]
四月的一天，爷孙二人牵着一头小毛驴去赶集。集市上人山人海，有说书唱戏的，有打拳卖艺的，也有卖烧饼的，非常热闹。逛了半天，他们有些累了。爷爷心疼孙子，就让他骑着驴走，自己在后面跟着。没走多远，听见有人说："那孩子真不懂事儿，他自己骑在驴上，让爷爷在后面跟着走。"听了这话，孙子马上跳下来，把爷爷扶上驴，自己在后面赶着驴走。 没走多远，又有人说："这个老头儿真可笑，自己骑在驴上，倒让小孙子给他赶驴，不疼爱孩子。"听了这话，爷爷又忙跳下驴来。孙子在前面牵着，爷爷在后面赶着向前走。没走多远，看见的人又嘲笑说："你看这一老一少，真是一对大傻瓜，有驴不骑，却在地上走。"听了这话，爷爷赶忙又把孙子扶到驴上，然后自己也爬上去。祖孙俩一前一后，同时骑在驴上，压得小毛驴直冒汗。没走多远，又有人批评说："哼！这两个人简直是在虐待小驴。"听了这话，祖孙二人一块儿跳下驴来，心想，这驴到底怎么骑才好？ 爷孙俩对视了半天，爷爷说："孩子，只有一个办法了，咱们干脆抬着驴子走吧。"说完，两个人把驴子的四条腿绑起来，用一根棍子抬着走了。孙子累得要死，生气地说："这头驴好麻烦，没有它就好了。"爷爷上气不接下气地说："驴子不会说话，不能怨它。就是那些多事儿的人，闹得咱们不知所措，才抬着驴子走的。"	四月的一天，爺孫二人牽著一頭小毛驢去趕集。集市上人山人海，有說書唱戲的，有打拳賣藝的，也有賣燒餅的，非常熱鬧。逛了半天，他們有些累了。爺爺心疼孫子，就讓他騎著驢走，自己在後面跟著。沒走多遠，聽見有人說：「那孩子真不懂事兒，他自己騎在驢上，讓爺爺在後面跟著走。」聽了這話，孫子馬上跳下來，把爺爺扶上驢，自己在後面趕著驢走。 沒走多遠，又有人說：「這個老頭兒真可笑，自己騎在驢上，倒讓小孫子給他趕驢，不疼愛孩子。」聽了這話，爺爺又忙跳下驢來。孫子在前面牽著，爺爺在後面趕著向前走。沒走多遠，看見的人又嘲笑說：「你看這一老一少，真是一對大傻瓜，有驢不騎，卻在地上走。」聽了這話，爺爺趕忙又把孫子扶到驢上，然後自己也爬上去。祖孫倆一前一後，同時騎在驢上，壓得小毛驢直冒汗。沒走多遠，又有人批評說：「哼！這兩個人簡直是在虐待小驢。」聽了這話，祖孫二人一塊兒跳下驢來，心想，這驢到底怎麼騎才好？ 爺孫倆對視了半天，爺爺說：「孩子，只有一個辦法了，咱們乾脆抬著驢子走吧。」說完，兩個人把驢子的四條腿綁起來，用一根棍子抬著走了。孫子累得要死，生氣地說：「這頭驢好麻煩，沒有它就好了」。爺爺上氣不接下氣地說：「驢子不會說話，不能怨它。就是那些多事兒的人，鬧得咱們不知所措，才抬著驢子走的。」

31. Which of the following statements is TRUE?

A) The story took place during the spring.

B) A grandfather and his grandson went to visit their relatives.

C) People were selling books at the market.

D) A father and son went shopping with a donkey.

32. Why did the townspeople complain when they saw the boy riding the donkey?

    A) The boy was too heavy.

    B) The boy should let his grandfather ride the donkey.

    C) The donkey was tired.

    D) The grandfather was upset.

33. The grandfather got on the donkey because

    A) he was tired

    B) he was upset with the boy

    C) he thought that was what the townspeople wanted him to do

    D) he thought the donkey was strong enough to carry him

34. Why did both the boy and the grandfather get on the donkey?

    A) The donkey was refreshed from a rest.

    B) The townspeople wanted to take the donkey away.

    C) The townspeople complained that nobody was using the donkey.

    D) Both the boy and grandfather were tired.

35. What did the boy and grandfather do with the donkey in the end?

    A) They sold it on the market.

    B) They walked the donkey home.

    C) They carried the donkey home on a stick.

    D) They both rode the donkey home.

SECTION II: Free Response

Part A: Writing (Story Narration and E-mail Response)

Writing Part Directions

You will be asked to perform two writing tasks in Chinese. In each case, you will be asked to write for a specific purpose and to a specific person. You should write in as complete and as culturally appropriate a manner as possible, taking into account the purpose and the person described. In this part of the exam, the student may NOT move back and forth among questions.

Story Narration (15%, 15 minutes)

The four pictures present a story. Imagine you are writing the story for a friend. Narrate a complete story as suggested by the pictures. Give your story a beginning, a middle, and an end.

E-Mail Response (10%, 15 minutes)

Read this e-mail from a friend and then type a response.

[Simplified Character Version]	[Traditional Character Version]
发件人：小强 邮件主题：玩电子游戏	發件人：小強 郵件主題：玩電子遊戲
最近我非常着迷电子游戏。每天放学后一回到家，作业都还没做，就急着打电子游戏，而且每天都玩到深夜。第二天上学常常迟到，上课没精神，学习成绩也下降了。爸爸和妈妈经常跟我生气，但我还是管不住自己。你说我该怎么办？	最近我非常著迷電子遊戲。每天放學後一回到家，作業都還沒做，就急著打電子遊戲，而且每天都玩到深夜。第二天上學常常遲到，上課沒精神，學習成績也下降了。爸爸和媽媽經常跟我生氣，但我還是管不住自己。你說我該怎麼辦？

Part B: Speaking (Conversation and Cultural Presentation)

Conversation (10%, 4 minutes)

Speaking Part Directions: Conversation

You will participate in a simulated conversation. Each time it is your turn to speak, you will have 20 seconds to record. You should respond as fully and as appropriately as possible. In this part of the exam, you may NOT move back and forth among questions.

You will have a conversation with your friend Xiaofan about the SAT class she is taking.

Cultural Presentation (15%, 7 minutes)

Set 2 中文模拟试题集
CHINESE LANGUAGE AND CULTURE

SECTION I: Multiple Choice

Part A: Listening (Rejoinders and Listening Selections)

Listening Part Directions

You will answer two types of questions: rejoinders and questions based on listening selections. For all tasks, you will have a specific amount of response time. In this part of the exam, you may NOT move back and forth among questions.

Listening Part Directions: Rejoinders (10%, 10 minutes)

You will hear several short conversations or parts of conversations followed by four choices, designated (A), (B), (C), and (D). Choose the one that continues or completes the conversation in a logical and culturally appropriate manner. You will have 5 seconds to answer each question.

1. (A)   (B)   (C)   (D)
2. (A)   (B)   (C)   (D)
3. (A)   (B)   (C)   (D)
4. (A)   (B)   (C)   (D)
5. (A)   (B)   (C)   (D)
6. (A)   (B)   (C)   (D)
7. (A)   (B)   (C)   (D)
8. (A)   (B)   (C)   (D)

9. (A)   (B)   (C)   (D)
10. (A)   (B)   (C)   (D)
11. (A)   (B)   (C)   (D)
12. (A)   (B)   (C)   (D)
13. (A)   (B)   (C)   (D)
14. (A)   (B)   (C)   (D)
15. (A)   (B)   (C)   (D)

Listening Part Directions: Listening Selections (15%, 10 minutes)

You will listen to several selections in Chinese. For each selection, you will be told whether it will be played once or twice. You may take notes as you listen. Your notes will not be graded. After listening to each selection, you will see questions in English. For each question, choose the response that is best according to the selection. You will have 12 seconds to answer each question.

Selection 1: Announcement (Selection plays one time.)

16. This announcement would be broadcast

    A) at the railroad station

    B) at the airport

    C) at the subway station

    D) on the plane

17. This announcement is to remind the passengers

    A) to get ready for departure

    B) where to claim baggage

    C) to go to the counter to check in

    D) where to buy the ticket

Selection 2: Conversation (Selection plays one time.)

18. Xiaowen is dressed up because

    A) she is going to work

    B) she is going for a job interview

    C) she is going to apply for a job

    D) she is going on a date

19. What is good about the coffee shop for Xiaowen?

    A) It is close to school.

    B) It has very good coffee.

    C) Her friends like to hang out there.

    D) The coffee there is inexpensive.

20. Based on this conversation, Xiaowen's mother tried to

    A) encourage her to get some working experience

    B) prevent her from going out today

    C) take her to the coffee shop herself

    D) tell her to study hard

21. Xiaowen was worried about being late because

    A) she had spent too much time dressing up

    B) she did not want her boyfriend to wait too long

    C) she did not want the employer to have a bad impression of her

    D) she just missed the bus

22. Xiaowen would like to have a job because

    A) she wants to be independent

    B) she thinks making extra money is important

    C) she regards having working experience to be beneficial to her college application

    D) she thinks working is fun

Selection 3: Voice Message (Selection plays two times.)

23. The voice mail instructions are most likely for

    A) a childcare center

    B) a library

    C) an athletic center

    D) a school

24. If you would like to talk to the head of the organization, you are asked to press

    A) 0

    B) 1

    C) 2

    D) 3

25. If you would like to inquire about the location of a certain game, you are asked to press

    A) 0

    B) 1

    C) 4

    D) 5

26. You need to press "0", if you would like to

    A) leave a message for your child

    B) renew a book

    C) report an absence

    D) donate books to the library

Selection 4: Voice Message (Selection plays two times.)

27. According to the passage, which of the following statements is TRUE?

    A) Lili was late for school this morning.

    B) Her English class is the last class of the day.

    C) She has an English test today.

    D) She does not have an English class today.

28. Lili's homework was left on

    A) the right side of her desk

    B) the top shelf of the bookcase to the left of her desk

    C) her bed

    D) the top shelf of the bookcase to the right of her desk

29. When Lili's mother arrives at school, she is supposed to

    A) go directly to Lili's class

    B) give the homework to the teacher

    C) give the homework to the front desk person

    D) ask to see Lili

30. Why doesn't Lili want her mother to call her?

    A) She left the cell phone at home.

    B) She has classes all afternoon.

    C) She won't have time to come out to see her.

    D) It would take too much of her time.

Selection 5: Report (Selection plays two times.)

31. The survey was NOT done
    A) in the shopping center
    B) in front of schools
    C) in front of movie theaters
    D) in the parks

32. This survey was done by
    A) high school students
    B) a parents association
    C) a TV journalist
    D) an official at a public policy institute

33. What is the percentage of the students who spend more than three hours on the internet every evening?
    A) 5%
    B) 15%
    C) 18%
    D) 80%

34. Parents are opposed to their kids spending too much time on the internet because they would rather see them spend more time on
    A) communicating with parents
    B) helping parents with housework
    C) working on their homework
    D) sleeping

35. According to this survey, which of the following statements is TRUE?
    A) Students feel they indeed spend too much time on the internet.
    B) When students talk to friends on the internet, it's not necessarily chatting.
    C) In addition to internet shopping, students also utilize the resources on the internet to do research.
    D) Students spend the majority of their internet time on playing computer games and chatting

Part B: Reading Selections (25%, 60 minutes)

Reading Part Directions

In this part of the exam, you may move back and forth among all the questions. You will read several selections in Chinese. Each selection is accompanied by a number of questions in English. For each question, choose the response that is best according to the selection. You will have 60 minutes to answer all questions.

Read this e-mail.

[Simplified Character Version]	[Traditional Character Version]
发件人：白大卫 收件人：李京 邮件主题：邀请共度感恩节 发件日期：2009年11月18日	發件人：白大衛 收件人：李京 郵件主題：邀請共度感恩節 發件日期：2009年11月18日
李京： 感恩节快到了，我想请你来我家跟我们全家一起过感恩节。我妈妈每年都会烤一只大火鸡，再做几样拿手的好菜，还会烤又香又好吃的苹果饼和南瓜饼。我知道你从来没在美国度过感恩节，非常希望你能来我家看看典型的美国家庭是怎么过节的。我父母常常听到我提起你，他们很想认识你，对于你为什么远离亲人来美国上高中，都非常好奇，也想知道中国人有什么年节、怎么庆祝。你不用担心到我家来怎么走，我可以开车去接你；另外，你什么东西都不用带，带上个好胃口就行了。尽早给我发个回邮吧！ 大卫	李京： 感恩節快到了，我想請你來我家跟我們全家一起過感恩節。我媽媽每年都會烤一隻大火雞，再做幾樣拿手的好菜，還會烤又香又好吃的蘋果餅和南瓜餅。我知道你從來沒在美國度過感恩節，非常希望你能來我家看看典型的美國家庭是怎麼過節的。我父母常常聽到我提起你，他們很想認識你，對於你為什麼遠離親人來美國上高中，都非常好奇，也想知道中國人有什麼年節、怎麼慶祝。你不用擔心到我家來怎麼走，我可以開車去接你；另外，你什麼東西都不用帶，帶上個好胃口就行了。儘早給我發個回郵吧！ 大衛

1. Dawei invited Li Jing to celebrate

   A) Christmas with his family

   B) Thanksgiving with his family

   C) Easter with his family

   D) Halloween with his family

2. Which of the following statements is TRUE?

   A) Dawei's parents have met Li Jing before.

   B) Li Jing knows how to get to Dawei's house.

   C) Li Jing's parents do not live in America.

   D) Li Jing likes the food Dawei's mother makes.

3. Which of the following statements is FALSE ?

   A) Dawei's parents are not familiar with Chinese festivals.

   B) Li Jing has a good appetite.

   C) Li Jing is not supposed to take any gifts with him to Dawei's house.

   D) Dawei's parents are curious about Li Jing.

Read this public sign.

[Simplified Character Version]	[Traditional Character Version]
保持校园清洁 请勿乱丢纸屑果皮	保持校園清潔 請勿亂丟紙屑果皮

4. Where would this sign most likely appear?

   A) In a park

   B) At a school

   C) In a concert hall

   D) In a movie theater

5. What is the purpose of this sign?

   A) To educate people to recycle

   B) To encourage people to save energy

   C) To tell people to take good care of their property

   D) To ask people to keep the environment clean

Read this public sign.

[Simplified Character Version]	[Traditional Character Version]
随手关灯一小步 节约能源一大步	隨手關燈一小步 節約能源一大步

6. Where would this sign most likely appear?

    A) By a light switch

    B) By a faucet

    C) By a window

    D) On a refrigerator

7. The purpose of this sign is to

    A) remind people to save water

    B) remind people to save electricity

    C) remind people not to waste food

    D) remind people to save money

Read this letter.

[Simplified Character Version]	[Traditional Character Version]
小易：	小易：
我可以借用你的英汉词典吗？虽然我自己有一本，可是十天前被小张借走了，他现在人在南方旅行，所以拿不回来。目前我正在翻译一篇英文文章，里面有一些词语，我不知如何用中文表达，所以必须求助于英汉词典。你可以帮我这个忙吗？我会好好爱护你的词典的，三天后一定归还。　感激不尽！	我可以借用你的英漢詞典嗎？雖然我自己有一本，可是十天前被小張借走了，他現在人在南方旅行，所以拿不回來。目前我正在翻譯一篇英文文章，裡面有一些詞語，我不知如何用中文表達，所以必需求助於英漢詞典。你可以幫我這個忙嗎？我會好好愛護你的詞典的，三天後一定歸還。　感激不盡！
丽明 10月21日	麗明 10月21日

8. According to this note, what does Liming want to do?

    A) She wants Xiao Yi to give her English-Chinese dictionary to Xiao Zhang.

    B) She wants Xiao Zhang to lend her an English-Chinese dictionary.

    C) She would like Xiao Yi to lend her an English-Chinese dictionary.

    D) She would like Xiao Yi to return the English-Chinese dictionary to her.

9. According to the note, which of the following statements is TRUE?

    A) Xiao Zhang went traveling after he borrowed a dictionary from Liming.

    B) Xiao Zhang needed the dictionary for traveling.

    C) Xiao Zhang promised Liming to take good care of her dictionary.

    D) Xiao Yi would not lend the dictionary to Liming unless she agrees to return in three days.

10. What does Liming need an English-Chinese dictionary for?

    A) She is preparing for a translation exam.

    B) She is translating an English article into Chinese.

    C) She doesn't know certain English words.

    D) She is writing a Chinese article on translation from English to Chinese.

Read this advertisement on a poster.

[Simplified Character Version]	[Traditional Character Version]
美美服饰店结束营业大减价	美美服飾店結束營業大減價
女装六五折 （名牌外套除外） 男士衬衫一律七折， 长裤八折 童装一律对折 只收现金，不收信用卡。恕不代客更改 尺寸。	女裝六五折 （名牌外套除外） 男士襯衫一律七折， 長褲八折 童裝一律對折 只收現金，不收信用卡。恕不代客更改 尺寸。

11. The store is having a sale because

    A) it is a pre-season sale

    B) it is going out of business

    C) it is an end of the year sale

    D) it is an anniversary sale

12. What is not on sale?

    A) Ladies designer jackets

    B) Ladies designer dresses

    C) Children's pants

    D) Men's clothing

13. What clothes have the biggest discount?

    A) Children's clothes

    B) Ladies clothes

    C) Men's shirts

    D) Men's pants

14. Which of the following statements is TRUE?

    A) If you cannot find the right size, they can order for you.

    B) If you cannot find the right size, they can alter for you.

    C) They don't provide alteration service.

    D) They accept credit card payment.

Read this advertisement.

[Simplified Character Version]	[Traditional Character Version]
中文联谊会急征中文报编辑 编辑的工作主要包括两部分：一是从中文报刊、杂志及互联网上选择适合学生的文章；二是编选同学们的来稿。应征者的中文、美术都要有一定的水平，能熟练使用电脑，工作时间一周十至十五小时不等。有兴趣的同学请于本周五前与学生活动中心的李老师电邮联系：lqz@abc.edu	中文聯誼會急徵中文報編輯 編輯的工作主要包括兩部分：一是從中文報刊、雜誌及互聯網上選擇適合學生的文章；二是編選同學們的來稿。應徵者的中文、美術都要有一定的水平，能熟練使用電腦，工作時間一周十至十五小時不等。有興趣的同學請於本週五前與學生活動中心的李老師電郵聯繫：lqz@abc.edu

15. This advertisement is to solicit

    A) subscription to a school Chinese newspaper

    B) reporters for school activities

    C) editors for a school Chinese newspaper

    D) application for computer work

16. The students who are interested need to

    A) have a computer

    B) know Teacher Li

    C) have certain art skills

    D) be native Chinese speakers

17. Which of the following statements is FALSE?

    A) The work requires computer skills.

    B) Any applications submitted after this Friday won't be accepted.

    C) The work requires writing articles in Chinese.

    D) The work involves reading a lot of articles from various sources.

Read this letter.

[Simplified Character Version]	[Traditional Character Version]
大山表哥： 　　你好！谢谢你前几天给我寄来的生日礼物，那个光盘里的歌曲真好听，我边听边学，一下子就学会了好几首。 　　昨天我们学校有个才艺表演，你绝对想不到，内向的我居然也抱着吉他上台了，边弹边唱，表演的就是那个光盘里的两首歌。唱完了，台下的老师和同学都为我热烈鼓掌，还大叫"再来一个！再来一个！"，我兴奋得满脸通红，因为这是我第一次上台表演，唱的还是中国民谣呢。说来也许你不相信，表演之前，我甚至还紧张得全身发抖呢！ 　　我要再次谢谢你，因为是你为我精心挑选的礼物，使得我克服了本来不敢在大家面前表演的心理障碍。最后祝你 健康快乐！ 　　　　　　　　　　　　毛毛 　　　　　　　　　　2009年10月24日	大山表哥： 　　你好！謝謝你前幾天給我寄來的生日禮物，那個光碟裡的歌曲真好聽，我邊聽邊學，一下子就學會了好幾首。 　　昨天我們學校有個才藝表演，你絕對想不到，內向的我居然也抱著吉他上臺了，邊彈邊唱，表演的就是那個光碟裡的兩首歌。唱完了，台下的老師和同學都為我熱烈鼓掌，還大叫「再來一個！再來一個！」，我興奮得滿臉通紅，因為這是我第一次上臺表演，唱的還是中國民謠呢。說來也許你不相信，表演之前，我甚至還緊張得全身發抖呢！ 　　我要再次謝謝你，因為是你為我精心挑選的禮物，使得我克服了本來不敢在大家面前表演的心理障礙。最後祝你 健康快樂！ 　　　　　　　　　　　　毛毛 　　　　　　　　　　2009年10月24日

18. What birthday present did Dashan give Maomao ?

    A) A CD
    B) MP3 files
    C) A guitar
    D) Sheet music

19. Why did Maomao's face turn red?

    A) Because she forgot one line while singing.
    B) Because she played one note wrong and felt embarrassed.
    C) Because her teacher complimented her in front of everyone.
    D) Because her performance was well received.

20. Which of the following statements is TRUE?

    A) Dashan gave the present to Maomao in person.
    B) Maomao has a lot of experience performing for others.
    C) Maomao learns to sing songs very fast.
    D) Maomao chose the present herself.

21. Which of the following statements is FALSE ?

    A) Maomao knows how to play the guitar.
    B) Dashan taught Maomao how to overcome psychological handicaps.
    C) The audience urged Maomao to sing more songs.
    D) This is Maomao's first performance in public.

22. The songs that Maomao sang

    A) were the ones that she had practiced for a long time
    B) were the ones that she was familiar with from childhood
    C) are Chinese popular songs
    D) are Chinese folk songs

23. Maomao regards herself to be quite

    A) introverted
    B) outgoing
    C) cheerful
    D) passionate

Read this article.

[Simplified Character Version]	[Traditional Character Version]
中文演讲比赛	中文演講比賽
今天学校举办了题为"学中文的苦与乐"的中文演讲比赛，参加的学生汉语都说得非常流利。我因为每天课后都得参加足球队的练习，没时间准备，所以只去当听众。他们演讲的内容都十分生动有趣，听众不时爆出笑声。比方说，有个同学说她刚学汉语时，四声搞不清楚，本来要说"你真酷"，结果说成了"你真苦"。还有同学说，很多词语不会用中文表达，就直接从英文翻译成中文，像是把带狗出去散步——也就是遛狗——说成了"走狗"，或者是载人一程，到了目的地，先把人放下车，说成了"丢人"。我听了他们的演讲以后，觉得获益良多，中文水平无形中提升了不少。	今天學校舉辦了題為「學中文的苦與樂」的中文演講比賽，參加的學生漢語都說得非常流利。我因為每天課後都得參加足球隊的練習，沒時間準備，所以只去當聽眾。他們演講的內容都十分生動有趣，聽眾不時爆出笑聲。比方說，有個同學說她剛學漢語時，四聲搞不清楚，本來要說「你真酷」，結果說成了「你真苦」。還有同學說，很多詞語不會用中文表達，就直接從英文翻譯成中文，像是把帶狗出去散步——也就是遛狗——說成了「走狗」，或者是載人一程，到了目的地，先把人放下車，說成了「丟人」。我聽了他們的演講以後，覺得獲益良多，中文水平無形中提升了不少。

24. The Chinese speech contest is

　　A) for students who speak Chinese fluently

　　B) for students to tell about their own experiences in learning Chinese

　　C) for students to tell the difference among the four tones

　　D) for students to tell some Chinese jokes

25. According to this passage, the narrator

　　A) was very polite and applauded every speaker

　　B) went there to improve his level of Chinese proficiency

　　C) participated in the speech contest

　　D) understood Chinese very well

26. What do you think "丢人"means?

    A) Losing "face"

    B) Losing people

    C) Dropping someone off

    D) Throwing people

27. The example given on the mess-up of the tones in one of the speeches involves

    A) the second tone and the third tone

    B) the third tone and the fourth tone

    C) the first tone and the third tone

    D) the second tone and the fourth tone

Read this poster.

[Simplified Character Version]	[Traditional Character Version]
武术活动时间取消及更改通知	武術活動時間取消及更改通知
因王大中老师应美国加州大学邀请出国访问，王老师所授周一、三、五下午四时的武术课暂停，周二、四下午五时的课暂由李平老师代课。所有课程等王老师归国后恢复原来上课时间。至于王老师何时返校授课，将另贴海报通知。 　　　　　　　　　　　中国武术社	因王大中老師應美國加州大學邀請出國訪問，王老師所授週一、三、五下午四時的武術課暫停，週二、四下午五時的課暫由李平老師代課。所有課程等王老師歸國後恢復原來上課時間。至於王老師何時返校授課，將另貼海報通知。 　　　　　　　　　　　中國武術社

28. This poster is intended for

    A) the general public

    B) the martial arts class students

    C) the students at the University of California

    D) American students

29. Which of the following statements is TRUE?

    A) Wang Laoshi has classes every weekday.

    B) None of Wang Laoshi's students can continue classes during his absence.

    C) Wang Laoshi is going to America to visit relatives.

    D) Wang Laoshi has informed the students of his return date.

30. During Wang Laoshi's absence

    A) his Wednesday class will be canceled

    B) Li Laoshi will be subbing in his Thursday morning class

    C) Li Laoshi will be subbing in his Friday afternoon class

    D) all of his students can continue their classes

31. Upon Wang Laoshi's return, students will be notified by

    A) email

    B) text message

    C) poster announcement

    D) none of the above

Read this story.

[Simplified Character Version]	[Traditional Character Version]
二月十四日情人节，依照西洋的习俗，可以赠送玫瑰花或巧克力给喜爱的人。农历的七月七日则是中国传统习俗中的情人节，有许多关于牛郎和织女的传说。其中有一个传说是牛郎和织女本来都住在天上，后来他们堕入爱河，展开了一段美丽的爱情。从此牛郎放牛不尽力，织女也不专心织布，惹得玉皇大帝非常生气，就把他们分别放逐到银河两岸。　一年当中只有七月七日晚上，有喜鹊鸟飞来筑成一座桥，他们才能在鹊桥上相会，天明时又要各自回到银河的两岸去，日日夜夜隔着银河思念爱人。这是一个凄美的传说，也引发了许多诗人无穷的想像，写下了不少传诵古今的篇章。	二月十四日情人節，依照西洋的習俗，可以贈送玫瑰花或巧克力給喜愛的人。農曆的七月七日則是中國傳統習俗中的情人節，有許多關於牛郎和織女的傳說。其中有一個傳說是牛郎和織女本來都住在天上，後來他們墮入愛河，展開了一段美麗的愛情。從此牛郎放牛不盡力，織女也不專心織布，惹得玉皇大帝非常生氣，就把他們分別放逐到銀河兩岸。　一年當中只有七月七日晚上，有喜鵲鳥飛來築成一座橋，他們才能在鵲橋上相會，天明時又要各自回到銀河的兩岸去，日日夜夜隔著銀河思念愛人。這是一個凄美的傳說，也引發了許多詩人無窮的想像，寫下了不少傳誦古今的篇章。

32. According to this passage, which of the following statements is TRUE?

    A) Chinese give chocolate to people they like on the seventh day of the seventh month in the lunar calendar.

    B) There are a lot of writings about Valentine's Day in China.

    C) The story of 牛郎 and 织女 (織女) is well known among the school kids.

    D) The romance of 牛郎 and 织女 (織女) has inspired the Chinese poets to write about it.

33. Why were 牛郎 and 织女 (織女) separated by the Jade Emperor?

    A) The Jade Emperor was jealous of their love.

    B) They became irresponsible about their respective work duties.

    C) They did not ask for the Jade Emperor's approval.

    D) They were slandered by other people.

34. According to this story, 牛郎 and 织女 (織女)were banished to opposite banks of

    A) the Milky Way

    B) the Yellow River

    C) the Yangtzu River

    D) the Love River

35. What animals help build a bridge for 牛郎 and 织女 (織女) to meet once a year?

    A) Cows

    B) Rabbits

    C) Fish

    D) Magpies

SECTION II: Free Response

Part A: Writing (Story Narration and E-mail Response)

Writing Part Directions

You will be asked to perform two writing tasks in Chinese. In each case, you will be asked to write for a specific purpose and to a specific person. You should write in as complete and as culturally appropriate a manner as possible, taking into account the purpose and the person described. In this part of the exam, the student may NOT move back and forth among questions.

Story Narration (15%, 15 minutes)

The four pictures present a story. Imagine you are writing the story to a friend. Narrate a complete story as suggested by the pictures. Give your story a beginning, a middle, and an end.

E-Mail Response (10%, 15 minutes)

Read this e-mail from a friend and then type a response.

[Simplified Character Version]	[Traditional Character Version]
发件人：谢明 邮件主题：暑期活动	發件人：謝明 郵件主題：暑期活動
今年暑假我有两个学习的机会，一个是到一个夏令营去打工当辅导员，有六个星期，另一个是到我家附近的大学去上两门跟电脑有关的课程，要上两个月的课。我没法儿同时做两项活动，你觉得我应该选哪项活动比较好？请你给我一些具体的建议。 谢谢！	今年暑假我有兩個學習的機會，一個是到一個夏令營去打工當輔導員，有六個星期，另一個是到我家附近的大學去上兩門跟電腦有關的課程，要上兩個月的課。我沒法兒同時做兩項活動，你覺得我應該選哪項活動比較好？請你給我一些具體的建議。 謝謝！

Part B: Speaking (Conversation and Cultural Presentation)

Conversation (10%, 4 minutes)

Speaking Part Directions: Conversation

You will participate in a simulated conversation. Each time it is your turn to speak, you will have 20 seconds to record. You should respond as fully and as appropriately as possible. In this part of the exam, you may NOT move back and forth among questions.

You will have a conversation with Wang Zhong, your host parent, about dining at a local Chinese restaurant.

Cultural Presentation (15%, 7 minutes)

中文模拟试题集
CHINESE LANGUAGE AND CULTURE

Set 3

SECTION I: Multiple Choice

Part A: Listening (Rejoinders and Listening Selections)

Listening Part Directions

You will answer two types of questions: rejoinders and questions based on listening selections. For all tasks, you will have a specific amount of response time. In this part of the exam, you may NOT move back and forth among questions.

Listening Part Directions: Rejoinders (10%, 10 minutes)

You will hear several short conversations or parts of conversations followed by four choices, designated (A), (B), (C), and (D). Choose the one that continues or completes the conversation in a logical and culturally appropriate manner. You will have 5 seconds to answer each question.

1. (A) (B) (C) (D)
2. (A) (B) (C) (D)
3. (A) (B) (C) (D)
4. (A) (B) (C) (D)
5. (A) (B) (C) (D)
6. (A) (B) (C) (D)
7. (A) (B) (C) (D)
8. (A) (B) (C) (D)

9. (A) (B) (C) (D)
10. (A) (B) (C) (D)
11. (A) (B) (C) (D)
12. (A) (B) (C) (D)
13. (A) (B) (C) (D)
14. (A) (B) (C) (D)
15. (A) (B) (C) (D)

Listening Part Directions: Listening Selections (15%, 10 minutes)

You will listen to several selections in Chinese. For each selection, you will be told whether it will be played once or twice. You may take notes as you listen. Your notes will not be graded. After listening to each selection, you will see questions in English. For each question, choose the response that is best according to the selection. You will have 12 seconds to answer each question.

Selection 1: Announcement (Selection plays one time.)

16. What is the main topic of the conversation?

    A) How to look for information on the internet

    B) How to apply to colleges

    C) Attending a college seminar

    D) Meeting friends

17. What is the benefit of attending the meeting?

    A) Networking with college admissions staff

    B) Having fun with friends

    C) Obtaining answers unavailable on the internet

    D) Learning how to use the internet

18. Why can't the girl go to the seminar?

    A) Because the boy can bring her all the information

    B) Because she can get all the information online

    C) Because she has another arrangement

    D) Because she is not interested

19. How will the boy pass on the information to the girl?

    A) He will mail it to her.

    B) He will call her.

    C) He will fax it to her.

    D) He will give it in person or email it.

Selection 2: Announcement (Selection plays two times.)

20. What's the purpose of this announcement?

    A) To remind the students about Teachers' Day

    B) To inform the students that there will be a Teachers' Day celebration

    C) To tell everyone to bring a gift for their teachers

    D) To announce that there will be no lunch served on Teachers' Day

21. What will happen on Teachers' Day?

    A) Donations will be collected for teachers.

    B) The teachers will sing for the students.

    C) There will be a performance to watch.

    D) All teachers will take the day off.

22. For Teachers' Day, the students are going to

    A) dance and sing

    B) prepare a lunch for teachers

    C) receive a gift from teachers

    D) write a thank you card to their favorite teacher

Selection 3: Voice Message (Selection plays two times.)

23. Why did Xiaomei call her teacher?

    A) To complain that the museum is too far

    B) To suggest a field trip to the museum

    C) To say that her mom can drive students to the museum

    D) To say that her mom's car needs repairs

24. Why can't Xiaomei's mom drive the students back from the museum?

    A) She needs to go to work.

    B) She has a doctor's appointment.

    C) She will have to meet another parent.

    D) She needs to pick up someone at the airport.

25. What did Xiaomei suggest to resolve the problem?

    A) To take the bus

    B) To only take six students

    C) To ask other parents for help

    D) To take the subway

Selection 4: Instructions (Selection plays one time.)

26. The fire drill route is changed because

    A) the new route is shorter

    B) there is construction going on

    C) the new route is safer

    D) the gathering location was changed

27. What do the students do right after exiting from the back door?

    A) Walk straight

    B) Turn left

    C) Turn right

    D) Wait until everyone gets there

28. Where do the students gather?

    A) On the footpath behind the school

    B) Inside the community center

    C) In the backyard of the school

    D) On the lawns

29. What should the teacher do after gathering?

    A) Ask the students to sit down and stay quiet.

    B) Take roll call.

    C) Get the first aid kits ready.

    D) Go back to the classroom to make sure everyone is out.

Selection 5: Report (Selection plays two times.)

30. The report is about
    A) a job fair
    B) the college selection process
    C) an alumni reception
    D) career pathways

31. Who gave the speeches?
    A) Counselors at the college center
    B) School counselors
    C) Former graduates
    D) Career specialists

32. How often does the school organize this activity?
    A) Twice a year
    B) Once a year
    C) Once a month
    D) Not mentioned

Selection 6: Conversation (Selection plays one time.)

33. The man is going to get a visa himself because
    A) his parents think he needs to learn the process
    B) his friend told him how to obtain one
    C) he has experience from a previous trip
    D) his parents are both away on business trips

34. How many documents will the man need to present to obtain a visa?
    A) 2
    B) 3
    C) 4
    D) 5

35. What is the fee for triple entries to China?

    A) $65
    B) $90
    C) $130
    D) $165

Part B: Reading Selections (25%, 60 minutes)

Reading Part Directions

In this part of the exam, you may move back and forth among all the questions. You will read several selections in Chinese. Each selection is accompanied by a number of questions in English. For each question, choose the response that is best according to the selection. You will have 60 minutes to answer all questions.

Read this e-mail.

[Simplified Character Version]	[Traditional Character Version]
发件人：大明 收件人：小刚 邮件主题：北京旅游指南 邮件日期：2009年6月3日	發件人：大明 收件人：小剛 郵件主題：北京旅遊指南 郵件日期：2009年6月3日
小刚： 　　听说你近期要到北京去学习三个月，真是太好了！北京是世界上最著名的旅游城市之一，有数百个非常吸引人的观光景点，包括长城、故宫、天安门广场、颐和园、天坛公园、奥运会运动场馆等等。除了去这些有名的景点参观以外，我建议你到北京市区居民住的地方走走，这样你会对北京人及北京的文化有更为真切的感受。我手上有一本非常好的北京旅游指南。该指南除了介绍旅游景点，还对150个特色商店、市场、老街和北京传统的胡同分别做了介绍。该指南标明了一些北京最好的购物区，并附有街道图以及商店地址、电话、营业时间等资料。该指南还附有地铁和公交车的交通图和其它非常实用的自助旅游资讯。我现在马上就去邮局给你寄去，希望能对你有帮助。 祝你在北京愉快！ 　　　　　　　　　　　　　　大明	小剛： 　　聽說你近期要到北京去學習三個月，真是太好了！北京是世界上最著名的旅遊城市之一，有數百個非常吸引人的觀光景點，包括長城、故宮、天安門廣場、頤和園、天壇公園、奧運會運動場館等等。除了去這些有名的景點參觀以外，我建議你到北京市區居民住的地方走走，這樣你會對北京人及北京的文化有更為真切的感受。我手上有一本非常好的北京旅遊指南。該指南除了介紹旅遊景點，還對150個特色商店、市場、老街和北京傳統的胡同分別做了介紹。該指南標明了一些北京最好的購物區，並附有街道圖以及商店地址、電話、營業時間等資料。該指南還附有地鐵和公交車的交通圖和其它非常實用的自助旅遊資訊。我現在馬上就去郵局給你寄去，希望能對你有幫助。 祝你在北京愉快！ 　　　　　　　　　　　　　　大明

1. Which tourist attraction of Beijing is NOT mentioned in this email?

　　A) The Great Wall

　　B) The Summer Palace

　　C) The Forbidden City

　　D) Beihai Park

2. Which place in particular did Daming suggest Xiaogang to visit?

   A) The famous shopping centers

   B) Universities

   C) Areas where common people live

   D) Beijing's popular subways

3. What information is NOT included in the Travelers' Handbook?

   A) A map of the transportation system

   B) Stores

   C) Schools

   D) Traditional alleys

Read this advertisement.

[Simplified Character Version]	[Traditional Character Version]
美中青少年领导才能训练营	美中青少年領導才能訓練營
活动时间：2009年8月2日至8月15日 活动地点：北京、上海 活动费用：$3,600（含国际机票、食宿和国内交通，但签证自理）在4月15日前报名者可享受$100优惠 活动内容：领导才能训练课程（8课时）、中国文化学习（8课时）、参观北京和上海的名胜古迹、品尝中国美食	活動時間：2009年8月2日至8月15日 活動地點：北京、上海 活動費用：$3,600（含國際機票、食宿和國內交通，但簽證自理）在4月15日前報名者可享受$100優惠 活動內容：領導才能訓練課程（8課時）、中國文化學習（8課時）、參觀北京和上海的名勝古跡、品嚐中國美食
报名资格： 1. 14-18岁高中生 2. 初级以上中文说写能力 3. 在校平均成绩B以上 4. 交一篇300-500字的短文，简单介绍个人教育背景、语言能力及参加活动的目的 5. 家长同意书	報名資格： 1. 14-18歲高中生 2. 初級以上中文說寫能力 3. 在校平均成績B以上 4. 交一篇300-500字的短文，簡單介紹個人教育背景、語言能力及參加活動的目的 5. 家長同意書
欲知详情请与美中青年文化办事处联系 电话：(321)123-4567	欲知詳情請與美中青年文化辦事處聯繫 電話：(321)123-4567

4. What is this advertisement for?

    A) A youth leadership training program

    B) A cultural exchange program

    C) A trip abroad

    D) A scholarship competition for college students

5. Which of the following expenses IS NOT included in the fee?

    A) International air ticket

    B) Domestic transportation

    C) Food and hotel

    D) Visa application

6. Which of the following qualifications is NOT required?

    A) One must be a college student

    B) A GPA above a "B" average

    C) Parental consent

    D) Knowledge of the Chinese language

Read this public sign.

[Simplified Character Version]	[Traditional Character Version]
脚下留青	腳下留青

7. The sign is to tell people

    A) that walking maintains health

    B) to be careful while walking

    C) that there are trees down the hill

    D) not to step on the grass

8. Where would this sign most likely appear?

    A) In a hospital

    B) At a school

    C) On lawns

    D) At the base of a mountain

Read this article.

[Simplified Character Version]	[Traditional Character Version]
京杭大运河是世界上最长的一条人工开凿的运河，北起北京，南到杭州，经北京、天津两直辖市及河北、山东、江苏、浙江四省，贯通海河、黄河、淮河、长江、钱塘江五大水系。运河全长约1750公里，是苏伊士运河长度的16倍，巴拿马运河的33倍。 京杭大运河也是世界上最古老的运河之一。我们今天所说的大运河开掘于春秋时期，大约于2500年前，到了公元1293年全线通航，前后共持续了1779年。京杭大运河和万里长城并称为中国古代的两项伟大工程，闻名于全世界。	京杭大運河是世界上最長的一條人工開鑿的運河，北起北京，南到杭州，經北京、天津兩直轄市及河北、山東、江蘇、浙江四省，貫通海河、黃河、淮河、長江、錢塘江五大水系。運河全長約1750公里，是蘇伊士運河長度的16倍，巴拿馬運河的33倍。 京杭大運河也是世界上最古老的運河之一。我們今天所說的大運河開掘於春秋時期，大約於2500年前，到了公元1293年全線通航，前後共持續了1779年。京杭大運河和萬里長城並稱為中國古代的兩項偉大工程，聞名於全世界。

9. When did the construction of the Great Jing-Hang Canal begin?

    A) 1750 years ago

    B) 1293 years ago

    C) 1779 years ago

    D) 2500 years ago

10. Which river does the Great Jing-Hang Canal NOT link up with?

    A) Songhua River

    B) Yangzi River

    C) Yellow River

    D) Huai River

11. How many provinces does the Great Jing-Hang Canal pass through?

    A) Two

    B) Three

    C) Four

    D) Five

12. Where is the north end of the Great Jing-Hang Canal?

    A) Tianjin

    B) Jinan

    C) Shanghai

    D) Beijing

13. How much longer is the Great Jing-Hang Canal than the Panama Canal?

    A) 16 times longer

    B) 33 times longer

    C) 61 times longer

    D) 49 times longer

Read this notice.

[Simplified Character Version]	[Traditional Character Version]
足球赛 　　由本校学生会主办的足球赛将于2009年4月27日（星期六）下午5点在学校足球场举行，参赛队分别为我校校队和香港大学校队。令人高兴的是，中国足球协会的教练和国家队的队员将到场观看比赛，并在赛后与参赛的双方队员举行座谈。欢迎同学们届时观看。 学生会 4月24日（星期三）	足球賽 　　由本校學生會主辦的足球賽將於2009年4月27日（星期六）下午5點在學校足球場舉行，參賽隊分別為我校校隊和香港大學校隊。令人高興的是，中國足球協會的教練和國家隊的隊員將到場觀看比賽，並在賽後與參賽的雙方隊員舉行座談。歡迎同學們屆時觀看。 學生會 4月24日（星期三）

14. Who organized this soccer game?

    A) Hong Kong University

    B) Chinese Soccer Association

    C) Chinese Soccer Team

    D) The School Student Union

15. The soccer match is between which two teams?

    A) Hong Kong University soccer team and the home team

    B) Hong Kong University soccer team and the National Soccer Team

    C) The National Soccer Team and the home team

    D) None of the above

16. What will follow after the game?

    A) A celebration dinner

    B) A discussion

    C) A chance for students to meet the players

    D) Another soccer game

Read this advertisement.

[Simplified Character Version]	[Traditional Character Version]

2009 年北京人文大学
暑期中文班招生
 	
一、强化中文学习四周（6月28日到7月26日）
  1. 小班上课
  2. 阅读、口语和写作练习
  3. 提供一对一语言训练
  4. 周三晚观看文艺演出，周六游览历史文化景点
  5. 住本校学生宿舍，两人间，设备齐全，安全舒适
 	
二、语言实习文化旅游十二天（7月24日至8月6日）所去城市包括北京、西安、山东曲阜和上海
 	
三、费用 $3,980，包括学费、吃住、教材、参观和观看演出，以及所有旅行的相关费用，不含国际机票和签证费
 	
四、报名资格：大学生、研究生及年满18岁的高中生。即日起接受报名至4月20日止，名额为50人，额满为止
 	
详情请洽金山大学中文系
  电话：(456)654-4567
	2009 年北京人文大學
	暑期中文班招生
	
	一、強化中文學習四周（6月28日到7月26日）
	  1. 小班上課
	  2. 閱讀、口語和寫作練習
	  3. 提供一對一語言訓練
	  4. 週三晚觀看文藝演出，週六遊覽歷史文化景點
	  5. 住本校學生宿舍，兩人間，設備齊全，安全舒適
	
	二、語言實習文化旅遊十二天（7月24日至8月6日）所去城市包括北京、西安、山東曲阜和上海
	
	三、費用 $3,980，包括學費、吃住、教材、參觀和觀看演出，以及所有旅行的相關費用，不含國際機票和簽證費
	
	四、報名資格：大學生、研究生及年滿18歲的高中生。即日起接受報名至4月20日止，名額為50人，額滿為止
	
	詳情請洽金山大學中文系
	  電話：(456)654-4567

17. Which of the following subjects is NOT offered in this summer program?

    A) Drawing

    B) Reading

    C) Speaking

    D) Writing

18. Which of the following statement is NOT TRUE?

    A) The class size will be small.

    B) There will be two students per bedroom.

    C) College students cannot apply for the program.

    D) Students can watch a show on every Wednesday night.

19. Which of the following expense is NOT covered in the fee?

    A) Tuition

    B) Food and living

    C) Domestic transportation

    D) International airfare

Read this letter.

[Simplified Character Version]	[Traditional Character Version]
敬爱的李老师：	敬愛的李老師：
您好！您的身体还好吗？一年一度的教师节就要来临了，这让我想起您教我们中文班时的一些事。我知道您为我们班的同学做了大量的工作，付出了很多的心血，特别是您还常用自己的时间辅导我们和组织一些课外活动。同学们都说您是一位认真负责、亲切和蔼的老师。现在我虽然转学了，但是还常常想念您和中文班的同学。我现在这所学校也有许多让我尊敬的老师，不过我觉得您是最好的老师。都快一个学期了，我对这里的环境还觉得很陌生，大概还得再过一段时间才能适应。您以前对我的教诲会一直激励着我努力学习的。	您好！您的身體還好嗎？一年一度的教師節就要來臨了，這讓我想起您教我們中文班時的一些事。我知道您為我們班的同學做了大量的工作，付出了很多的心血，特別是您還常用自己的時間輔導我們和組織一些課外活動。同學們都說您是一位認真負責、親切和藹的老師。現在我雖然轉學了，但是還常常想念您和中文班的同學。我現在這所學校也有許多讓我尊敬的老師，不過我覺得您是最好的老師。都快一個學期了，我對這裡的環境還覺得很陌生，大概還得再過一段時間才能適應。您以前對我的教誨會一直激勵著我努力學習的。
祝您节日快乐！	祝您節日快樂！
您的学生 何京 2009年5月10日	您的學生 何京 2009年5月10日

20. When did He Jing write the letter?

    A) Upon transferring to a new school

    B) Before Teacher's Day

    C) On his birthday

    D) Around the New Year

21. What do the students think of Teacher Li?

    A) He is very knowledgeable and kind.

    B) He is conscientious, responsible, and amiable.

    C) He is hardworking and tough.

    D) He is sensitive and inspiring.

22. How does He Jing describe the new environment?

    A) Bizarre

    B) Pleasant

    C) Unfamiliar

    D) Similar to his previous environment

23. How long has He Jing been at his new school?

    A) Almost one week

    B) Almost one month

    C) Almost one semester

    D) Almost one year

Read this poster.

[Simplified Character Version]	[Traditional Character Version]
紧急通知	緊急通知
根据气象部门的天气预报，本市明后天将有暴风雨。学校已经收到电力局的通知，本市将有部分地区停电四十八个小时，停电时间从明天星期六早晨四时至星期一早上四时止。我校属于停电范围之内，为此学校决定，原订于星期六晚七点的家长会，改在下周六的同一时间召开，请同学们互相转告。	根據氣象部門的天氣預報，本市明後天將有暴風雨。學校已經收到電力局的通知，本市將有部分地區停電四十八個小時，停電時間從明天星期六早晨四時至星期一早上四時止。我校屬於停電範圍之內，為此學校決定，原訂於星期六晚七點的家長會，改在下週六的同一時間召開，請同學們互相轉告。
校长办公室	校長辦公室

24. This poster announces that

    A) the parents' meeting of tomorrow will be changed to next Saturday

    B) there will be a rainstorm for the next two days

    C) there will be no electricity in the school the following week

    D) the parents' meeting will be canceled

25. What does "明后天〔明後天〕" mean?

    A) Tomorrow

    B) After tomorrow

    C) Two days

    D) Tomorrow or the day after tomorrow

26. Which of the following statements is NOT TRUE?

    A) There will be a rainstorm tomorrow.

    B) There will be no parents' meeting tomorrow.

    C) There will be no electricity in the school for the next three days.

    D) The parents' meeting will be held next Saturday.

27. For how long will there be no electricity?

    A) One day

    B) Two days

    C) One weekend

    D) One week

Read this story.

[Simplified Character Version]	[Traditional Character Version]
有一个非常有趣的小故事，叫做《太阳从西边升起》。它最初刊登在一个叫《故事会》的杂志上。故事讲一个十一、二岁的小姑娘画了一幅画，参加全省少儿美术比赛。她的那幅画画得很好，但最终却因犯了个常识上的错误，把初升的太阳画到了西边而落选。老师不解地去问小姑娘，怎么会把太阳画到西边了呢？小姑娘哭着说："我就是要让太阳从西边升起……"，原来，她爸爸和妈妈吵架了，爸爸出走了，临走时说，要他重回这个家，除非太阳从西边升起。所以小姑娘就天天盼望西边出太阳了。	有一個非常有趣的小故事，叫做《太陽從西邊升起》。它最初刊登在一個叫《故事會》的雜誌上。故事講一個十一、二歲的小姑娘畫了一幅畫，參加全省少兒美術比賽。她的那幅畫畫得很好，但最終卻因犯了個常識上的錯誤，把初升的太陽畫到了西邊而落選。老師不解地去問小姑娘，怎麼會把太陽畫到西邊了呢？小姑娘哭著說：「我就是要讓太陽從西邊升起……」，原來，她爸爸和媽媽吵架了，爸爸出走了，臨走時說，要他重回這個家，除非太陽從西邊升起。所以小姑娘就天天盼望西邊出太陽了。

56

28. What mistake did the little girl make in her picture?

    A) She did not draw the picture well.

    B) She did not draw a sun in the sky.

    C) The sun is rising from the west.

    D) She did not finish.

29. Where was the story initially published?

    A) In a newspaper

    B) In a magazine

    C) At a meeting

    D) On the radio

30. What did the little girl's father say before he left the house?

    A) He will come home when the sun rises the next day.

    B) He will be back soon.

    C) He will come home only if the sun rises from the west.

    D) The sun rises from the west.

31. What kind of competition did the girl attend?

    A) Adult art competition

    B) Children's art competition

    C) City-wide art competition

    D) School-wide art competition

Read this passage.

[Simplified Character Version]	[Traditional Character Version]
梁实秋是一位中国现代著名的作家。他曾写过一篇文章来劝告人们从小就要养成良好的习惯。在那篇文章中，他写到人们的天性大致是差不多的，但是在习惯上却各有不同。习惯是慢慢养成的，在幼小的时候最容易培养，一旦养成之后，要想改变过来却不容易。比如说清晨早起是一个好习惯，这也要从小培养。很多人从小就贪睡懒觉，一遇假日便要睡到太阳高照还迟迟不起，平时也是不肯早起，上学经常迟到。这样的人长大了之后，多半不能有什么成就。好的习惯很多，他劝大家从小就要有意识地在各方面培养良好的习惯。	梁實秋是一位中國現代著名的作家。他曾寫過一篇文章來勸告人們從小就要養成良好的習慣。在那篇文章中，他寫到人們的天性大致是差不多的，但是在習慣上卻各有不同。習慣是慢慢養成的，在幼小的時候最容易培養，一旦養成之後，要想改變過來卻不容易。比如說清晨早起是一個好習慣，這也要從小培養。很多人從小就貪睡懶覺，一遇假日便要睡到太陽高照還遲遲不起，平時也是不肯早起，上學經常遲到。這樣的人長大了之後，多半不能有什麼成就。好的習慣很多，他勸大家從小就要有意識地在各方面培養良好的習慣。

32. What is the main message of the passage?

    A) Cultivate good habits early.

    B) Get up early.

    C) Do not go to school late.

    D) Do not go to sleep late.

33. Which of the following statements is TRUE?

    A) The author is a modern writer.

    B) People all have the same habits.

    C) People do not change their habits.

    D) The author suggests children sleep more on weekends or during holidays.

34. Liang Shiqiu thinks that a man who sleeps a lot

    A) will have a great future

    B) will be more intelligent

    C) will need to eat less

    D) will not be successful

35. Liang Shiqiu believes that people are born

    A) relatively the same and change over time

    B) are born different and do not change

    C) are born different and change over time

    D) are born similar to their parents

SECTION II: Free Response

Part A: Writing (Story Narration and E-mail Response)

Writing Part Directions

You will be asked to perform two writing tasks in Chinese. In each case, you will be asked to write for a specific purpose and to a specific person. You should write in as complete and as culturally appropriate a manner as possible, taking into account the purpose and the person described. In this part of the exam, the student may NOT move back and forth among questions.

Story Narration (15%, 15 minutes)

The four pictures present a story. Imagine you are writing the story to a friend. Narrate a complete story as suggested by the pictures. Give your story a beginning, a middle, and an end.

E-Mail Response (10%, 15 minutes)

Read this e-mail from a friend and then type a response.

[Simplified Character Version]	[Traditional Character Version]
发件人：康健 邮件主题：大学选择	發件人：康健 郵件主題：大學選擇
大卫： 　　告诉你一个好消息，我已经被你们学校录取了，同时我还收到了全国最好的一所公立大学的录取通知书。到底应该去哪所大学，我感到很难决定。你们学校当然是全美最好的大学之一，可是这所公立大学也很有名。在我做最后决定之前，我非常想听听你的看法和建议。请你给我介绍一下你们学校的情况，包括校园生活和当地气候等等。谢谢！	大衛： 　　告訴你一個好消息，我已經被你們學校錄取了，同時我還收到了全國最好的一所公立大學的錄取通知書。到底應該去哪所大學，我感到很難決定。你們學校當然是全美最好的大學之一，可是這所公立大學也很有名。在我做最後決定之前，我非常想聽聽你的看法和建議。請你給我介紹一下你們學校的情況，包括校園生活和當地氣候等等。謝謝！

Part B: Speaking (Conversation and Cultural Presentation)

Conversation (10%, 4 minutes)

Speaking Part Directions: Conversation

You will participate in a simulated conversation. Each time it is your turn to speak, you will have 20 seconds to record. You should respond as fully and as appropriately as possible. In this part of the exam, you may NOT move back and forth among questions.

You have been invited to have dinner with a Chinese family. You will have a conversation with a member of the family at the dinner table.

Cultural Presentation (15%, 7 minutes)

Speaking Part Directions: Cultural Presentation

You will be asked to speak in Chinese on a specific topic. Imagine you are making an oral presentation to your Chinese class. First, you will read and hear the topic for your presentation. You will have 4 minutes to prepare your presentation. Then you will have 2 minutes to record your presentation. Your presentation should be as complete as possible.

SECTION I: Multiple Choice

Part A: Listening (Rejoinders and Listening Selections)

Listening Part Directions

You will answer two types of questions: rejoinders and questions based on listening selections. For all tasks, you will have a specific amount of response time. In this part of the exam, you may NOT move back and forth among questions.

Listening Part Directions: Rejoinders (10%, 10 minutes)

You will hear several short conversations or parts of conversations followed by four choices, designated (A), (B), (C), and (D). Choose the one that continues or completes the conversation in a logical and culturally appropriate manner. You will have 5 seconds to answer each question.

1.	Ⓐ	Ⓑ	Ⓒ	Ⓓ	9.	Ⓐ	Ⓑ	Ⓒ	Ⓓ
2.	Ⓐ	Ⓑ	Ⓒ	Ⓓ	10.	Ⓐ	Ⓑ	Ⓒ	Ⓓ
3.	Ⓐ	Ⓑ	Ⓒ	Ⓓ	11.	Ⓐ	Ⓑ	Ⓒ	Ⓓ
4.	Ⓐ	Ⓑ	Ⓒ	Ⓓ	12.	Ⓐ	Ⓑ	Ⓒ	Ⓓ
5.	Ⓐ	Ⓑ	Ⓒ	Ⓓ	13.	Ⓐ	Ⓑ	Ⓒ	Ⓓ
6.	Ⓐ	Ⓑ	Ⓒ	Ⓓ	14.	Ⓐ	Ⓑ	Ⓒ	Ⓓ
7.	Ⓐ	Ⓑ	Ⓒ	Ⓓ	15.	Ⓐ	Ⓑ	Ⓒ	Ⓓ
8.	Ⓐ	Ⓑ	Ⓒ	Ⓓ					

Listening Part Directions: Listening Selections (15%, 10 minutes)

You will listen to several selections in Chinese. For each selection, you will be told whether it will be played once or twice. You may take notes as you listen. Your notes will not be graded. After listening to each selection, you will see questions in English. For each question, choose the response that is best according to the selection. You will have 12 seconds to answer each question.

Selection 1: Announcement (Selection plays one time.)

16. . The flight is delayed because

    A) there are mechanical problems

    B) it has to wait for some passengers from another flight

    C) the weather condition is not suitable for taking off

    D) there are some problems with the check-in procedure

17. The passengers are told to

    A) take the next available flight

    B) exit the aircraft

    C) go to the counter to get vouchers for meals and lodging

    D) wait in the waiting room

Selection 2: Conversation (Selection plays one time.)

18. The man and the woman came to this restaurant because

    A) the man frequently patronizes the place

    B) the restaurant received a rave review from the newspaper

    C) the woman's roommate recommends it

    D) the man's roommate suggested to them that they go there

19. It's most likely that this restaurant specializes in

    A) Sichuan cuisine

    B) Shanghai cuisine

    C) Cantonese cuisine

    D) Beijing cuisine

64

20. The woman prefers to have

    A) vegetarian dishes

    B) light dishes

    C) spicy food

    D) tofu dishes

21. The woman initially showed some doubt about the restaurant because

    A) she did not really like spicy food

    B) she was concerned that the restaurant adds MSG to their food

    C) the man's roommate did not recommend it

    D) the restaurant advertises too much on TV and the newspapers

Selection 3: Instructions (Selection plays two times.)

22. Who is giving the instructions?

    A) The nurse

    B) The pharmacist

    C) The mother

    D) The doctor

23. The recipient of the instructions was most likely concerned about having

    A) H1N1 flu

    B) a seasonal cold

    C) persistent coughs

    D) an unabated fever

24. The recipient of the instructions needs to take the bigger tablets

    A) as needed

    B) in six-hour intervals

    C) before meals

    D) twice a day, three tablets each time

25. The smaller tablets are for

    A) unabated fever

    B) persistent coughs

    C) sore throat

    D) a severe case of running nose

Selection 4: Voice Message (Selection plays two times.)

26. What made the telephone caller wonder if Xiaopeng had been busy?

    A) Xiaopeng did not pick up the phone for quite a few times.

    B) Xiaopeng's phone was busy for quite a long while.

    C) Xiaopeng's voice mailbox message indicated that he was busy.

    D) Xiaopeng did not return his phone calls.

27. Xiaopeng is a high school

    A) freshman

    B) sophomore

    C) junior

    D) senior

28. Why did the telephone caller wish to speak to Xiaopeng?

    A) Because he would like to go to a sports game with Xiaopeng.

    B) Because he would like to discuss with Xiaopeng about the graduation ceremony.

    C) Because he would like to perform with Xiaopeng at the school's talent show.

    D) Because he would like to go to a "Xiangsheng" performance.

29. The school put out the announcement

    A) in early March

    B) in mid-March

    C) at the end of April

    D) in mid-April

30. The caller mentioned Wang Laoshi, because

    A) Wang Laoshi can provide information about Xiangsheng

    B) Wang Laoshi has the tickets to the Xiangsheng performance

    C) Wang Laoshi has the costumes that they need

    D) Wang Laoshi can help them rent the costumes that they need

Selection 5: Report (Selection plays two times.)

31. The survey was conducted

    A) in person
    B) by filling out the questionnaire on paper
    C) online
    D) by telephone interviews

32. What groups of students were surveyed?

    A) The entire school
    B) The upper classmen
    C) The lower classmen
    D) 10th, 11th, and 12th grade students

33. We may conclude that most of the students who work for more than 15 hours a week do so in order to

    A) help with the family finance
    B) have more money to spend
    C) have more working experience
    D) save for college tuition

34. Among the students surveyed, how many students have had some working experience?

    A) 234 students
    B) 60% of the students
    C) 70% of the students
    D) 74% of the students

35. If the part-time job has a negative impact on school work, what would the students do?

    A) All of them would quit the job.
    B) All of them would cut down their working hours and keep the job.
    C) Some of them would try to look for less demanding work.
    D) Some of them would quit the job.

Part B: Reading Selections (25%, 60 minutes)

Reading Part Directions

In this part of the exam, you may move back and forth among all the questions. You will read several selections in Chinese. Each selection is accompanied by a number of questions in English. For each question, choose the response that is best according to the selection. You will have 60 minutes to a nswer all questions.

Read this e-mail.

[Simplified Character Version]	[Traditional Character Version]
发件人：林晓莉 收件人：全班同学 邮件主题：毕业典礼的门票 发件日期：2010年5月8日	發件人：林曉莉 收件人：全班同學 郵件主題：畢業典禮的門票 發件日期：2010年5月8日
大家好！ 不知道谁有多出来的毕业典礼门票？本来学校发给我们每人的五张票是够了，因为我们家就我爸妈、爷爷、奶奶和我哥哥参加，五张正好。可是昨天我的篮球教练跟我说，他也很想参加我的毕业典礼。我高中四年都是跟这个教练练的篮球，因为他对我的教导，我才得到了州立大学的篮球奖学金。我问学校能不能多给我一张，可他们说票都发完了。妈妈看我很为难，就说那她留在家里吧。我们一辈子才一次的高中毕业典礼，要是妈妈不能参加，我会很难过的。所以，拜托你们，谁能给我一张票？我一定请你看电影、吃饭。先谢了！ 晓莉	大家好！ 不知道誰有多出來的畢業典禮門票？本來學校發給我們每人的五張票是夠了，因為我們家就我爸媽、爺爺、奶奶和我哥哥參加，五張正好。可是昨天我的籃球教練跟我說，他也很想參加我的畢業典禮。我高中四年都是跟這個教練練的籃球，因為他對我的教導，我才得到了州立大學的籃球獎學金。我問學校能不能多給我一張，可他們說票都發完了。媽媽看我很為難，就說那她留在家裡吧。我們一輩子才一次的高中畢業典禮，要是媽媽不能參加，我會很難過的。所以，拜託你們，誰能給我一張票？我一定請你看電影、吃飯。先謝了！ 曉莉

1. How many admission tickets does Xiaoli need altogether?

    A) One

    B) Five

    C) Six

    D) Seven

2. What are the tickets for?

    A) Basketball games

    B) Movie

    C) College tour

    D) Graduation ceremony

3. To whom is the email sent?

    A) The entire school

    B) The entire class

    C) Her best friends

    D) Basketball teammates

4. What is the reason that Xiaoli's mother considers staying home?

    A) She is not interested in the event.

    B) She has seen it before.

    C) She would like to give her ticket to the basketball coach.

    D) She will be busy that day.

5. What word best describes Xiaoli's attitude toward her coach?

    A) Grateful

    B) Resentful

    C) Indifferent

    D) Mixed feeling

Read this public sign.

[Simplified Character Version]	[Traditional Character Version]
海水无情 若无救生员在场 请勿戏水	海水無情 若無救生員在場 請勿戲水

6. Where would this sign most likely appear?

    A) On the deck of a swimming pool

    B) By a river

    C) On the beach

    D) By a lake

7. What is the purpose of this sign?

    A) To warn people of the danger of water

    B) To encourage people to swim

    C) To remind people of wearing life jackets when entering the water

    D) To warn people that swimming is prohibited there

Read this public sign.

[Simplified Character Version]	[Traditional Character Version]
演出时间，请关闭所有电子用品 如手机、传呼机等，并严禁拍照	演出時間，請關閉所有電子用品 如手機、傳呼機等，並嚴禁拍照

8. This sign is most likely to be displayed

    A) in the library

    B) on an airplane

    C) in a concert hall

    D) in a gym

9. According to this sign, which of the following statements is FALSE?

    A) Pagers are not allowed to be on.

    B) All the electronics should be turned off, except for cameras.

    C) Cell phones are not allowed to be on.

    D) Taking pictures is forbidden.

Read this note.

[Simplified Character Version]	[Traditional Character Version]
文文： 　　刚刚小平打电话来，说你们明天洗车募款的活动因为学校有意见，必须取消。他要你先去跟王老师联络一下，看看学校为什么反对这项活动，能不能让学校改变他们的决定。他会先发短信给那些已报名参加活动的同学，告诉他们活动已经取消，免得他们明天白跑一趟，等学校答复了，再做安排，而后另行通知。他要你尽速跟王老师联系后，给他打个电话，或发个电邮。 　　　　　　　　　　新华 　　　　　　　3月4日中午12时	文文： 　　剛剛小平打電話來，說你們明天洗車募款的活動因為學校有意見，必須取消。他要你先去跟王老師聯絡一下，看看學校為什麼反對這項活動，能不能讓學校改變他們的決定。他會先發短信給那些已報名參加活動的同學，告訴他們活動已經取消，免得他們明天白跑一趟，等學校答覆了，再做安排，而後另行通知。他要你儘速跟王老師聯繫後，給他打個電話，或發個電郵。 　　　　　　　　　　新華 　　　　　　　3月4日中午12時

10. Because of the school's opposition, the fundraising event has to

A) be postponed until they can convince the school to change their position

B) be cancelled for the time being

C) be postponed until tomorrow

D) be postponed until they talk to Teacher Wang

11. Which of the following statements is TRUE?

A) Xiaoping knows the reasons why the school is opposed to their ideas.

B) Xiaoping still hopes that the school would change their position.

C) Xiaoping is expecting Wenwen to send him a text message.

D) Xiaoping would like Teacher Wang to have some influence on the school's decision- making process.

12. Which of the following statements is FALSE?

A) All of the students who signed up for the event will be informed of the change of plan by Xiaoping.

B) Some of the students who signed up for the event will be informed of the change of plan via email.

C) Xiaoping would like Wenwen to contact Teacher Wang as soon as possible.

D) All of the students who signed up for the event will be informed of the change of plan so that they won't have to show up for nothing.

Read this advertisement.

[Simplified Character Version]	[Traditional Character Version]
大众书店	大眾書店
庆祝本店成立三十周年 所有图书、文具一律大减价	慶祝本店成立三十週年 所有圖書、文具一律大減價
图书八折 文具七五折	圖書八折 文具七五折
营业时间：每日上午10时30分至晚上9时， 　　　　周一休息 减价活动日期：本月初四日及月末三日	營業時間：每日上午十時三十分至晚上九時， 　　　　週一休息 減價活動日期：本月初四日及月末三日

13. The sale at the bookstore is

    A) a 30-year anniversary sale

    B) to celebrate the bookstore's being established for 30 weeks

    C) a closeout sale

    D) a grand opening sale

14. When is the sale held?

    A) Every day of the week except Monday

    B) The last three days of the month

    C) The fourth of the month and the last three days of the month

    D) The first four days and the last three days of the month

15. If you would like to buy a dictionary, the discount is

    A) 80% off

    B) 75% off

    C) 20% off

    D) 25% off

16. If the original price of a calculator is $100, you can get it on the sale days for

    A) $70

    B) $75

    C) $80

    D) $85

Read this announcement.

[Simplified Character Version]	[Traditional Character Version]
亲爱的同学们： 　　学生会将在四月的第二周于学生活动中心大礼堂举办音乐周活动。活动内容包括演唱中外流行歌曲、演奏国乐或西洋古典音乐，每人以参加两项为限。如果你想演奏国乐或西洋古典音乐，除了钢琴，请自备乐器。如果你对此活动感兴趣，请于3月22日前带学生证到学生会办公室报名或电邮学生会，电邮中请写明姓名、年级、手机号码与学生证号码，以及想要参加的项目。学生会办公室在学生活动中心二层电邮是abc@xyz.edu。 欢迎大家参加。谢谢！ 　　　　　　　　　　　　学生会 　　　　　　　　　　2010年3月1日	親愛的同學們： 　　學生會將在四月的第二週於學生活動中心大禮堂舉辦音樂週活動。活動內容包括演唱中外流行歌曲、演奏國樂或西洋古典音樂，每人以參加兩項為限。如果你想演奏國樂或西洋古典音樂，除了鋼琴，請自備樂器。如果你對此活動感興趣，請於三月二十二日前帶學生證到學生會辦公室報名或電郵學生會，電郵中請寫明姓名、年級、手機號碼與學生證號碼，以及想要參加的項目。學生會辦公室在學生活動中心二層，電郵是abc@xyz.edu。 歡迎大家參加。謝謝！ 　　　　　　　　　　　　學生會 　　　　　　　　　　2010年3月1日

17. Which of the following statements is TRUE?

    A) The music activity will last two weeks.

    B) The music activity will be held in the theater.

    C) Students need not register in person.

    D) Students can participate in as many events as they wish.

18. Which of the following music is not mentioned in this announcement?

    A) Chinese popular songs

    B) Traditional Chinese music

    C) Classical music

    D) Opera

19. Which of the following statements is FALSE?

    A) Regardless of what type of music you would like to perform, you need to bring your own instrument.

    B) When registering for the event in person, students need to take the student ID with them.

    C) The student activity center has more than one storey.

    D) It's still three weeks away from the deadline to register for the event.

20. What information is needed to register for the event?

    A) The exact music piece

    B) The cell phone number

    C) The length of the music piece

    D) The composer of the music

Read this letter.

[Simplified Character Version]	[Traditional Character Version]
小宁：	小寧：
你好，好久没给你写信了。前些时候，我老是生病，整天流鼻水、咳嗽，甚至还发高烧，全身都疼，胃口也相当差。妈妈带我去了医院，医生说，我一天到晚坐在教室里上课，回家不是打电脑，就是看电视，生活习惯非常不好。再这么下去，身体肯定会越来越糟，所以现在我每天早上都到附近的公园去跑步。早晨的公园人还真多呢，有骑车的，有遛狗的，有打太极拳的，还有人跟我一样，戴着耳机，边跑边听音乐。跑了两、三个星期以后，现在身体好多了。你平常都做些什么运动呢？	你好，好久沒給你寫信了。前些時候，我老是生病，整天流鼻水、咳嗽，甚至還發高燒，全身都疼，胃口也相當差。媽媽帶我去了醫院，醫生說，我一天到晚坐在教室裡上課，回家不是打電腦，就是看電視，生活習慣非常不好。再這麼下去，身體肯定會越來越糟，所以現在我每天早上都到附近的公園去跑步。早晨的公園人還真多呢，有騎車的，有遛狗的，有打太極拳的，還有人跟我一樣，戴著耳機，邊跑邊聽音樂。跑了兩、三個星期以後，現在身體好多了。你平常都做些什麼運動呢？
祝好！	祝好！
小华 　　　　　　　　2010年2月20日	小華 　　　　　　　　2010年2月20日

21. Which of the following statements can best describe Xiaohua's health?

    A) She has been sick for quite a while.

    B) She has a severe case of allergy.

    C) Her health has improved.

    D) She often has high fevers.

22. Which of the following statements is TRUE?

    A) Xiaohua doesn't like computers.

    B) Xiaohua enjoys watching television.

    C) Xiaohua's appetite was decent.

    D) Xiaohua jogs with her mother.

23. The doctor attributes her health problem to

    A) her life style

    B) her school work load

    C) her not drinking enough water

    D) her diet

24. Based on this letter, which of the following statements is FALSE?

    A) Xiaohua listens to music while jogging.

    B) There are people walking dogs in the morning.

    C) Xiaohua is interested in Tai-chi.

    D) The park is close to where she lives.

Read this article.

[Simplified Character Version]	[Traditional Character Version]
中文与标点符号	中文與標點符號
中国以前的书籍都是没有标点符号的，读书人一般要拿着红笔，一边读，一边打圈圈来把文字隔开。这有个专门的词汇，叫做"断句"。一直要到二十世纪初期，受到西洋语文的影响，出版的书籍才有了标点符号。标点符号的使用，除了方便读书的人阅读之外，也能帮助正确地解读文义，避免产生误解。 　　历史上有好几个故事，说的都是标点符号标在不同处，文字就有不同的解读。比如，有这么一个故事：想要客人离去的主人写下"下雨天留客天留我不留"，本意是说："下雨，天留客。天留，我不留！"可是脸皮厚的客人解读成："下雨天，留客天。留我不？留！"，主人看了也只好摇摇头，无可奈何地笑了。	中國以前的書籍都是沒有標點符號的，讀書人一般要拿著紅筆，一邊讀，一邊打圈圈來把文字隔開。這有個專門的詞彙，叫做「斷句」。一直要到二十世紀初期，受到西洋語文的影響，出版的書籍才有了標點符號。標點符號的使用，除了方便讀書的人閱讀之外，也能幫助正確地解讀文義，避免產生誤解。 　　歷史上有好幾個故事，說的都是標點符號標在不同處，文字就有不同的解讀。比如，有這麼一個故事：想要客人離去的主人寫下「下雨天留客天留我不留」，本意是說：「下雨，天留客。天留，我不留！」可是臉皮厚的客人解讀成：「下雨天，留客天。留我不？留！」，主人看了也只好搖搖頭，無可奈何地笑了。

25. Based on this article, one of the unique features for the Chinese books published long ago is that

    A) there were only commas and periods

    B) there were only periods

    C) there were no punctuation marks

    D) the punctuations were printed in red

26. What is not mentioned as an advantage of using punctuation marks?

    A) To enable the readers to read

    B) To help correctly interpret the meaning of the text

    C) To help make the writing style better

    D) To avoid misunderstanding

27. Why did the host mentioned in this article shake his head in the end?

    A) He did not understand what his guest meant.

    B) He did not approve of what his guest intended to do.

    C) He was very upset with his guest.

    D) He understood what his guest meant, but there was nothing he could do.

Read this poster.

[Simplified Character Version]	[Traditional Character Version]
熊猫展览馆	熊貓展覽館
开放时间：周一至周五上午8时30分至下午5时30分 周六、日延长两个小时	開放時間：週一至週五上午八時三十分至下午五時三十分 週六、日延長兩個小時
参观方式：凭号码牌入场，每梯次观赏十分钟	參觀方式：憑號碼牌入場，每梯次觀賞十分鐘
票价：全票60元 优待票减半（老人六十五岁以上，须出示身份证；学生须出示学生证）六岁以下儿童免费	票價：全票六十元 優待票減半（老人六十五歲以上，須出示身份證；學生須出示學生證）六歲以下兒童免費
交通：地铁蓝线、黄线均可，至动物园站下车	交通：地鐵藍線、黃線均可，至動物園站下車

28. How does the staff at the zoo decide whom to let in for the exhibit?

    A) First come, first served

    B) Seniors first

    C) Every visitor will be given a number.

    D) Students first

29. How long can the visitors stay in the special exhibit section of the zoo?

  A) Ten minutes

  B) Sixty minutes

  C) Half an hour

  D) As long as the visitors wish

30. Based on the poster, which of the following statements is FALSE?

  A) The zoo is very close to the subway station.

  B) A sixty-five-year-old man with an ID only needs to pay ￥30 for admission.

  C) Kids under six are admitted free of charge.

  D) Visitors can take the green line subway to the zoo.

31. Over the weekends, how long is the exhibit hall open?

  A) 2 hours

  B) 7 hours

  C) 9 hours

  D) 11 hours

Read this story.

[Simplified Character Version]	[Traditional Character Version]
春秋时期，有个著名的琴师叫俞伯牙，他精通音律，琴艺高超。有一天晚上，月明风清，伯牙在荒山野地鼓琴，琴声悠扬，飘扬于宇宙之间。他的心想像着高山，乐音从指尖流泻而出，忽然听到有人赞美道："好！好！巍巍峨峨，仿佛高耸入云的泰山一般！"他的心想像着流水，那个人又说："好！好！仿佛滚滚无尽的流水一般！"伯牙一看，原来知晓他乐音意境的人是个路过的樵夫，叫钟子期。他为钟子期弹奏乐曲，无论他内心想表达什么，钟子期都能一一意会，从此二人成了非常要好的朋友。钟子期死后，伯牙失去知音，伤心欲绝，觉得此生再无人可理解他琴音中的意境，弹琴已无意义，竟然把琴摔坏，从此不再鼓琴。	春秋時期，有個著名的琴師叫俞伯牙，他精通音律，琴藝高超。有一天晚上，月明風清，伯牙在荒山野地鼓琴，琴聲悠揚，飄揚於宇宙之間。他的心想像著高山，樂音從指尖流瀉而出，忽然聽到有人讚美道：「好！好！巍巍峨峨，彷彿高聳入雲的泰山一般！」他的心想像著流水，那個人又說：「好！好！彷彿滾滾無盡的流水一般！」伯牙一看，原來知曉他樂音意境的人是個路過的樵夫，叫鍾子期。他為鍾子期彈奏樂曲，無論他內心想表達什麼，鍾子期都能一一意會，從此二人成了非常要好的朋友。鍾子期死後，伯牙失去知音，傷心欲絕，覺得此生再無人可理解他琴音中的意境，彈琴已無義，竟然把琴摔壞，從此不再鼓琴。

32. The musical instrument mentioned in this story is a

    A) piano

    B) lute

    C) drum

    D) Chinese flute

33. Based on the story, the musician liked to play music

    A) in the wilderness

    B) in a secluded studio

    C) with his best friend

    D) for the imperial court

34. We may conclude that the musician in the story drew inspiration from

    A) the moon and the stars

    B) the flowers and trees

    C) the mountains and the rivers

    D) the wind and the clouds

35. Why did the musician stop playing music after his friend passed away?

    A) Because his musical instrument was ruined.

    B) Because nobody could understand his music anymore.

    C) Because nobody could play with him well anymore.

    D) Because his friend told him that he would be heartbroken to play music.

SECTION II: Free Response

Part A: Writing (Story Narration and E-mail Response)

Writing Part Directions

You will be asked to perform two writing tasks in Chinese. In each case, you will be asked to write for a specific purpose and to a specific person. You should write in as complete and as culturally appropriate a manner as possible, taking into account the purpose and the person described. In this part of the exam, the student may NOT move back and forth among questions.

Story Narration (15%, 15 minutes)

The four pictures present a story. Imagine you are writing the story for a friend. Narrate a complete story as suggested by the pictures. Give your story a beginning, a middle, and an end.

E-Mail Response (10%, 15 minutes)

Read this e-mail from a friend and then type a rasponse.

[Simplified Character Version]	[Traditional Character Version]
发件人：陈健 邮件主题：住宿问题	發件人：陳健 郵件主題：住宿問題
好消息！我前阵子申请了一个到中国去学习汉语和文化的项目，昨天刚收到了录取通知。学校告诉我，我可以选择住在学校宿舍，是双人房，或者是跟一个中国家庭居住，那个家庭有一个跟我年纪差不多的孩子。你以前到中国留过学，你觉得我应该怎么选择？应该从哪些方面考虑？谢谢。	好消息！我前陣子申請了一個到中國去學習漢語和文化的項目，昨天剛收到了錄取通知。學校告訴我，我可以選擇住在學校宿舍，是雙人房，或者是跟一個中國家庭居住，那個家庭有一個跟我年紀差不多的孩子。你以前到中國留過學，你覺得我應該怎麼選擇？應該從哪些方面考慮？謝謝。

Part B: Speaking (Conversation and Cultural Presentation)

Conversation (10%, 4 minutes)

Speaking Part Directions: Conversation

You will participate in a simulated conversation. Each time it is your turn to speak, you will have 20 seconds to record. You should respond as fully and as appropriately as possible. In this part of the exam, you may NOT move back and forth among questions.

You will have a conversation with Lin Fang, a new friend in Beijing, about the 2008 Olympics.

Cultural Presentation(15%, 7 minutes)

Speaking Part Directions: Cultural Presentation

You will be asked to speak in Chinese on a specific topic. Imagine you are making an oral presentation to your Chinese class. First, you will read and hear the topic for your presentation. You will have 4 minutes to prepare your presentation. Then you will have 2 minutes to record your presentation. Your presentation should be as complete as possible.

SECTION I: Multiple Choice

Part A: Listening (Rejoinders and Listening Selections)

Listening Part Directions

You will answer two types of questions: rejoinders and questions based on listening selections. For all tasks, you will have a specific amount of response time. In this part of the exam, you may NOT move back and forth among questions.

Listening Part Directions: Rejoinders (10%, 10 minutes)

You will hear several short conversations or parts of conversations followed by four choices, designated (A), (B), (C), and (D). Choose the one that continues or completes the conversation in a logical and culturally appropriate manner. You will have 5 seconds to answer each question.

1.	(A)	(B)	(C)	(D)	9.	(A)	(B)	(C)	(D)
2.	(A)	(B)	(C)	(D)	10.	(A)	(B)	(C)	(D)
3.	(A)	(B)	(C)	(D)	11.	(A)	(B)	(C)	(D)
4.	(A)	(B)	(C)	(D)	12.	(A)	(B)	(C)	(D)
5.	(A)	(B)	(C)	(D)	13.	(A)	(B)	(C)	(D)
6.	(A)	(B)	(C)	(D)	14.	(A)	(B)	(C)	(D)
7.	(A)	(B)	(C)	(D)	15.	(A)	(B)	(C)	(D)
8.	(A)	(B)	(C)	(D)					

Listening Part Directions: Listening Selections (15%, 10 minutes)

You will listen to several selections in Chinese. For each selection, you will be told whether it will be played once or twice. You may take notes as you listen. Your notes will not be graded. After listening to each selection, you will see questions in English. For each question, choose the response that is best according to the selection. You will have 12 seconds to answer each question.

Selection 1: Announcement (Selection plays one time.)

16. The main purpose of the announcement is to

    A) tell the passengers that the restroom is temporarily closed

    B) ask the flight attendants to help the passengers

    C) tell the passengers to be seated

    D) thank the passengers for flying with the airlines

17. What are the flight attendants supposed to do after hearing the announcement?

    A) To be seated and fasten their seatbelts

    B) To make sure all passengers are seated

    C) To continue preparing the meal

    D) To make sure all children are with their parents

18. The announcement is made because

    A) too many passengers are lining up to use the restroom

    B) there are children running around

    C) the airplane is experiencing turbulence

    D) the safety lights are malfunctioning

Selection 2: Voice Message (Selection plays two times.)

19. Ziwei can't go to the group meeting because

    A) her mom is sick

    B) she has a doctor's appointment

    C) her grandfather was hospitalized

    D) she and her grandfather went to buy a car and came home too late

20. What does Ziwei prefer?

    A) To postpone the meeting until Monday

    B) To meet on Sunday instead of Saturday

    C) To ask the group to complete her task

    D) To discuss the work with the group over the phone

21. When will she be doing the group presentation?

    A) Saturday

    B) Sunday

    C) Monday

    D) In a week

Selection 3: Conversation (Selection plays one time.)

22. The girl is hesitant to go because

    A) she has too much school work

    B) her foot injury has not healed yet

    C) the boy is not planning to go

    D) she has not practiced since she was little

23. What holds the boy back from going?

    A) He does not think he is talented enough.

    B) He is too busy with other activities.

    C) His school work load will be too heavy.

    D) His parents want him to focus more on his academic performance.

24. Meiyun encourages the boy to go because

    A) she thinks he should continue with gymnastics

    B) she does not think he is that busy with school work

    C) she wants him to try out with her

    D) she wants him to cheer her on during the tryouts

25. What is the outcome of the conversation?

    A) Only the boy will try out for the team.

    B) Meiyun will further consider if she will go to try out.

    C) The boy decides not to try out.

    D) They will both try out.

Selection 4: Instructions (Selection plays two times.)

26. To qualify for the $50 rebate, the computer must be bought

    A) before June 28, 2009

    B) between June 28 and Oct.11, 2009

    C) between Oct. 11 and June 28, 2009

    D) within 45 days starting from June 28, 2009

27. The rebate form must be mailed and postmarked

    A) 4 to 5 days after the purchase

    B) 14 days after the purchase

    C) 45 days after the purchase

    D) within 45 days after the purchase

28. What documents are needed for the rebate?

    A) Purchase receipt

    B) Receipt, rebate form, product serial number, and package delivery number

    C) Receipt, rebate form, and contact information

    D) Rebate form and product number

29. How soon should customers expect to receive the rebate?

    A) Within a month

    B) Within 60 days

    C) Between 3 to 4 days

    D) Not mentioned

30. The rebate promotion is limited to people

    A) who live outside of the US

    B) who are over 18 years of age

    C) who live within the US

    D) who are American citizens

Selection 5: Report (Selection plays one time.)

31. Which city is the weather report for?

    A) Beijing

    B) Hangzhou

    C) Xi'an

    D) Shanghai

32. What does the weather report predict?

    A) Hailstorm

    B) Thunderstorm

    C) Heavy rain

    D) Strong winds

33. When will the predicted weather occur?

    A) 1:00 pm

    B) 3:00 pm

    C) Within 1 to 3 hours

    D) Between 1:00 pm and 3:00 pm

34. From where will the thunderstorm come ?

    A) East to West

    B) South to North

    C) West to East

    D) North to South

35. What does the report NOT suggest people do?

    A) Stay indoors

    B) Stay in open areas

    C) Watch the weather closely

    D) Call for help in case of emergency

Part B: Reading Selections (25%, 60 minutes)

Reading Part Directions

In this part of the exam, you may move back and forth among all the questions. You will read several selections in Chinese. Each selection is accompanied by a number of questions in English. For each question, choose the response that is best according to the selection. You will have 60 minutes to answer all questions.

Read this note.

[Simplified Character Version]	[Traditional Character Version]
小马：	小馬：
我这个周末要去参加一个校外野营活动。活动结束后，星期二早上我们直接坐车去学校，我就没有时间回家取我上学用的东西了。我想麻烦你去我家一趟，把几样东西帮我带到学校：我的帽子、笔记本、化学课本和电脑。我的帽子在一进门的那个衣架上挂着，笔记本在桌子上，化学课本在书架上，电脑在我的书包里。我父母都上夜班，所以你去我家时，他们可能都还没回家呢。但是我已经告诉我妈妈你可能会去，所以她会把我们家的后门开着。谢谢你！学校见！	我這個週末要去參加一個校外野營活動。活動結束後，星期二早上我們直接坐車去學校，我就沒有時間回家取我上學用的東西了。我想麻煩你去我家一趟，把幾樣東西帮我帶到學校：我的帽子、筆記本、化學課本和電腦。我的帽子在一進門的那個衣架上掛著，筆記本在桌子上，化學課本在書架上，電腦在我的書包裡。我父母都上夜班，所以你去我家時，他們可能都還沒回家呢。但是我已經告訴我媽媽你可能會去，所以她會把我們家的後門開著。謝謝你！學校見！
王刚 　　　　　　　　3月9日	王刚 　　　　　　　　3月9日

1. Wang Gang asked Xiaoma to help bring some stuff to school because

   A) Xiaoma lives near his house

   B) he forgot to take the things with him

   C) he has to go to school directly from the camping trip

   D) his parents are not home

2. Which item was not mentioned on the note?

   A) Computer

   B) Hat

   C) Chemistry textbook

   D) Calculator

3. Where did Wang Gang leave his hat?

   A) On a chair in the living room

   B) In his bedroom

   C) On a rack by the front door

   D) In his backpack

4. Wang Gang's parents were not home because

   A) they both left home very early that morning

   B) they are on the way to pick up Wang Gang

   C) they are on vacation

   D) they work night shifts

5. How can Xiaoma get into Wang Gang's house to pick up the stuff?

   A) From the side window

   B) The front door is usually unlocked.

   C) Xiaoma has the key to Wang Gang's house.

   D) Wang Gang's parents will leave the backdoor open for Xiaoma.

Read this e-mail.

[Simplified Character Version]	[Traditional Character Version]
发件人：小红 收件人：小包 邮件主题：学习中文的建议 邮件日期：2009年5月6日	發件人：小紅 收件人：小包 郵件主題：學習中文的建議 郵件日期：2009年5月6日
小包： 　　很高兴听到你选择中文作为你的高中外语课。你来信问我学习中文的体会，虽然我可以给你一些建议，但是我觉得现在还为时过早，因为你现在还没有开始学习，过早地提出来，你可能并不理解，我以后会慢慢告诉你。但有一点非常重要，那就是中文并不容易学，如果你决定学了，就要坚持学下去，千万不要半途而废。如果你基础没打好，你就会越学越没兴趣，到了大学有可能得改学其他语言。这不仅浪费了你的时间、精力和金钱，更重要的是如果你的成绩不理想，有可能会影响你的学习情绪，你会有挫折感。当然，如果你的成绩很好，又有足够的时间和兴趣，且经济条件允许的话，你可以选择第三其至第四外语。以上是我的一点建议，仅供你参考。 姐姐	小包： 　　很高興聽到你選擇中文作為你的高中外語課。你來信問我學習中文的體會，雖然我可以給你一些建議，但是我覺得現在還為時過早，因為你現在還沒有開始學習，過早地提出來，你可能並不理解，我以後會慢慢告訴你。但有一點非常重要，那就是中文並不容易學，如果你決定學了，就要堅持學下去，千萬不要半途而廢。如果你基礎沒打好，你就會越學越沒興趣，到了大學有可能得改學其他語言。這不僅浪費了你的時間、精力和金錢，更重要的是如果你的成績不理想，有可能會影響你的學習情緒，你會有挫折感。當然，如果你的成績很好，又有足夠的時間和興趣，且經濟條件允許的話，你可以選擇第三其至第四外語。以上是我的一點建議，僅供你參考。 姐姐

6. Why is the sister hesitant to give suggestions to her brother?

A) It is too early for her to give suggestions.

B) She doesn't know Chinese.

C) She is concerned that her brother will not continue Chinese.

D) She wants him to take another language besides Chinese.

7. What is the one suggestion that the sister gives to her brother?

A) Do not waste time, money, and energy studying Chinese.

B) Select another foreign language.

C) Chinese is too hard to learn.

D) Establish a good foundation to build upon.

8. When does the sister think her brother can study additional foreign languages?

A) When her brother has the time and money

B) When her brother is interested in other foreign languages

C) When her brother's Chinese is good

D) All of the above

9. What is the overall message of the passage?

A) Complete all the tasks that you have started

B) Do not take foreign languages

C) Chinese is a hard language

D) Accomplish things that you enjoy

Read this advertisement.

[Simplified Character Version]	[Traditional Character Version]
饮食和减肥讲座	飲食和減肥講座
减轻体重并非只是减少食物中的热量摄取，您将了解到有益于您身心健康的减肥方法，您将从日常饮食及锻炼中找到减肥的真谛。如果您感兴趣，请报名参加此次讲座。	減輕體重並非只是減少食物中的熱量攝取，您將瞭解到有益於您身心健康的減肥方法，您將從日常飲食及鍛煉中找到減肥的真諦。如果您感興趣，請報名參加此次講座。
讲座地点：中医大学礼堂 讲座时间：2009年9月20日下午一时至三时 费用：中医协会会员免费，非中医协会会员 　　　　¥15 报名办法：请电洽（620）5637-2509 主办单位：中国中医药协会	講座地點：中醫大學禮堂 講座時間：2009年9月20日下午一時至三時 費用：中醫協會會員免費，非中醫協會會員 　　　　¥15 報名辦法：請電洽（620）5637-2509 主辦單位：中國中醫藥協會

10. What is the primary purpose of the seminar?

   A) To introduce certain foods and their nutrition facts

   B) To learn how to lose weight

   C) To teach physical exercise techniques

   D) To promote diet products

11. What is the fee to attend the seminar?

   A) Members of Chinese Medicine Association ￥15

   B) Non-members free

   C) All participants ￥15

   D) Free for members of Chinese Medicine Association

12. Where is the seminar held?

   A) At the Chinese Medicine Association

   B) At the Chinese Medicine University

   C) At the Chinese People's University

   D) None of the above

13. What methods for losing weight are suggested?

   A) Eat less

   B) Eat healthy foods and exercise

   C) Buy diet products

   D) Sleep less

Read this public sign.

[Simplified Character Version]	[Traditional Character Version]
如有火警，请走楼梯！	如有火警，請走樓梯！

14. What is the message of this sign?

   A) Use the stairs in case of fire

   B) Show where the fire exits are located

   C) Do not smoke in the building

   D) Show where the fire extinguisher is located

15. Where would this sign most likely appear?

   A) At a building entrance

   B) By an elevator

   C) Near the fire extinguisher

   D) Outside of a building

Read this public sign.

[Simplified Character Version]	[Traditional Character Version]
来也匆匆，去也冲冲	來也匆匆，去也沖沖

16. Where would this sign most likely appear?

   A) Library

   B) Public restroom

   C) Emergency room

   D) Classroom

17. The purpose of the sign is to remind people

   A) to flush the toilet after using it

   B) not to waste time

   C) to move quickly from place to place

   D) not to stop here

Read this letter.

[Simplified Character Version]

表哥：

　　你好！我已通过了全国高中生统一考试，并且被省师范大学录取了。我就要步入大学的校园，成为一名大学生了！我现在的心情既激动又紧张，能进入大学的校园，学习更多的知识，参加学校的社团组织，结识更多的朋友，这一切对我来说都好新鲜。

　　在开学之前，我会有一个很长的假期，我打算去一个农村小学做义工，当一名英语代课教师。我一直对英语很有兴趣，高中期间我的英语成绩也比别的科好，去那里教孩子们英文课，对我来说是个练习英语的好机会。这些天，我为此购买了好多英文故事书和英文歌曲唱片，同时我还在抓紧我的英文口语练习，希望能做好这个工作。

　　表哥，你已经在大学里学习两年了，一定有很多宝贵的大学生活经验和我分享。另外，我们入学之后马上就要选择专业，还要选课，你能给我一些建议吗？谢谢！

祝你学业顺利！

表妹　小英
2009年7月28日

[Traditional Character Version]

表哥：

　　你好，我已通過了全國高中生統一考試，并且被省師範大學錄取了。我就要步入大學的校園，成為一名大學生了！我現在的心情既激動又緊張，能進入大學的校園，學習更多的知識，參加學校的社團組織，結識更多的朋友，這一切對我來說都好新鮮。

　　在開學之前，我會有一個很長的假期，我打算去一個農村小學做義工，當一名英語代課教師。我一直對英語很有興趣，高中期間我的英語成績也比別的科好，去那裡教孩子們英文課，對我來說是個練習英語的好機會。這些天，我為此購买了好多英文故事書和英文歌曲唱片，同時我還在抓緊我的英文口語練習，希望能做好這個工作。

　　表哥，你已經在大學裡學習兩年了，一定有很多寶貴的大學生活經驗和我分享。另外，我們入學之後馬上就要選擇專業，還要選課，你能給我一些建議嗎？謝謝！

祝你學業順利！

表妹　小英
2009年7月28日

18. What is the most likely age of Xiaoying?

　　A) 16

　　B) 18

　　C) 22

　　D) 26

19. Why did Xiaoying write the letter?

　　A) To ask her cousin to share his college experience

　　B) To invite her cousin to travel with her

　　C) To ask him for money

　　D) To discuss her doubts about becoming an English teacher

20. What is Xiaoying going to do over the summer?
    A) Travel around China
    B) Take classes
    C) Teach English
    D) Work at a supermarket

21. In preparation for her summer activities, Xiaoying has
    A) purchased a camera for her travels
    B) purchased a laptop
    C) purchased English language textbooks
    D) purchased music albums of English songs

22. What type of college is Xiaoying going to?
    A) Technology institute
    B) Teacher's university
    C) Vocational school
    D) Foreign language school

Read this poster.

[Simplified Character Version]	[Traditional Character Version]
华南大学计算机学院招聘信息	華南大學計算機學院招聘信息
因09级新生入学，学院办公室工作量突增，故拟招聘一名勤工助学学生。	因09級新生入學，學院辦公室工作量突增，故擬招聘一名勤工助學學生。
工作职责： 1. 协助学院办公室老师的日常工作 2. 负责维护学院网站 工作时间：周一至周四上午8点到10点 　　　　　　周五上午9点至12点 薪酬：面谈 招聘条件： 1. 本院08级学生 2. 具备团队精神，有责任心，工作认真严谨 3. 熟练掌握计算机基本操作	工作職責： 1. 協助學院辦公室老師的日常工作 2. 負責維護學院網站 工作時間：週一至週四上午8點到10點 　　　　　　週五上午9點至12點 薪酬：面談 招聘條件： 1. 本院08級學生 2. 具備團隊精神，有責任心，工作認真嚴謹 3. 熟練掌握計算機基本操作
有意者请与学院办公室严老师联系 电话：755-2603-3506 　　　　　　　　　　计算机学院 　　　　　　　　　　2009年8月20日	有意者請與學院辦公室嚴老師聯繫 電話：755-2603-3506 　　　　　　　　　　計算機學院 　　　　　　　　　　2009年8月20日

23. The college is hiring a student for work-study because

    A) they have received new computers that need to be installed

    B) the school has obtained increased funding

    C) the work load will increase due to new incoming students

    D) there will be students that will graduate soon

24. How many hours per week does the job entail?

    A) 8

    B) 11

    C) 12

    D) 13

25. What is the pay for the job?

    A) Minimum wage

    B) Low pay because it is a part time position

    C) The pay will be discussed during the interview.

    D) The poster does not say.

26. What is a requirement for the position?

    A) Anyone interested can apply.

    B) Applicants must be sophomores.

    C) Applicants must be athletic.

    D) Applicants must be computer science majors.

27. What does the work involve?

    A) Repairing the computers

    B) Promoting the computer science department

    C) Helping the faculty with daily tasks

    D) Developing software for the department

Read this article.

[Simplified Character Version]	[Traditional Character Version]
指南针是中国古代的四大发明之一。在指南针发明以前，人们在茫茫的大海上航行，只能靠太阳和星星的位置辨认方向。是中国人发明了指南针，帮助人们解决了这个难题。 　　早在战国时期，中国人就发现了磁石指示南北的特性，并根据这种特性制成了指示方向的仪器——司南。司南由一把光滑的磁勺和刻着方位的铜盘组成，勺把指示的方向是南方，勺头指示的方向是北方。到了宋代，人们把经过人工磁化的指南针和方位盘结合起来，制成了罗盘。有了罗盘，无论在什么情况下，人们都能准确地辨认方向了。 　　指南针后来辗转传入了欧洲，并在航海大发现中发挥出不可替代的作用，例如：明朝初期郑和带领船队七下西洋，十五世纪哥伦布发现新大陆等。但是非常有趣的是，最早解答"指南针为何能够指南"问题的并不是中国人，而是英国的科学家。	指南針是中國古代的四大發明之一。在指南針發明以前，人們在茫茫的大海上航行，只能靠太陽和星星的位置辨認方向。是中國人發明了指南針，幫助人們解決了這個難題。 　　早在戰國時期，中國人就發現了磁石指示南北的特性，並根據這種特性製成了指示方向的儀器——司南。司南由一把光滑的磁勺和刻著方位的銅盤組成，勺把指示的方向是南方，勺頭指示的方向是北方。到了宋代，人們把經過人工磁化的指南針和方位盤結合起來，製成了羅盤。有了羅盤，無論在什麼情況下，人們都能準確地辨認方向了。 　　指南針後來輾轉傳入了歐洲，並在航海大發現中發揮出不可替代的作用，例如：明朝初期鄭和帶領船隊七下西洋，十五世紀哥倫布發現新大陸等。但是非常有趣的是，最早解答「指南針為何能夠指南」問題的並不是中國人，而是英國的科學家。

28. What did people use to find their direction at sea before the compass was invented?

    A) The clouds

    B) The ocean waves

    C) Geographic features of the coastlines

    D) The position of the sun and the stars

29. What was the prototype of the compass?

    A) A non magnetic needle

    B) A nickel plate

    C) A magnetic spoon and a copper plate

    D) All of the above

30. The copper plate was invented during which dynasty?

    A) Ming Dynasty

    B) The Warring States Period

    C) Shang Dynasty

    D) Song Dynasty

31. Who was the first to discover how a compass works?

A) A Chinese scientist

B) Zheng He

C) Christopher Columbus

D) An English scientist

Read this story.

[Simplified Character Version]	[Traditional Character Version]
太行和王屋两座大山，方圆七百里。山的北面住着一位老人，叫愚公，年近九十。他家的房子正对着这两座大山，由于大山的阻隔，出入十分困难。有一天他召集全家人商议说："我想和你们一起，尽一切力量去把山移走，开出一条大路，直通山的另一边。"全家人纷纷表示赞同。 　　于是，愚公就率领着三个能挑担子的子孙，凿石头、挖土块，再用箩筐把石土运到离家很远的地方，一年到头他们才能往返一次。愚公家搬山的事，惊动了邻居。邻居家的一位老奶奶，有个小孙女，才刚七、八岁，也蹦蹦跳跳跑去帮忙。 　　黄河边上住着一个老头，人称智叟，是个很聪明的老人。他以嘲笑的语气劝阻愚公说："你怎么傻到这种地步呀！就凭你这把年纪，这点儿力气，要拔掉山上的一根树都不容易办到，又怎么能搬掉这么多的山石土块呢？"愚公长叹了一口气，说："我看你太顽固了，简直不明事理。虽然我会死，可是我还有儿子呢！儿子又生孙子，孙子又生儿子，儿子又生儿子，儿子又生孙子，这样子子孙孙都不会断绝的呀！而这两座山再也不会增高了，还怕挖不平吗？"智叟听了，无言以对。 　　山神听到了愚公的这些话，就去禀告了天帝。天帝为愚公移山的诚意所感动，就派了夸娥氏的两个儿子去背走了那两座大山。	太行和王屋兩座大山，方圓七百里。山的北面住著一位老人，叫愚公，年近九十。他家的房子正對著這兩座大山，由於大山的阻隔，出入十分困難。有一天他召集全家人商議說：「我想和你們一起，盡一切力量去把山移走，開出一條大路，直通山的另一邊。」全家人紛紛表示贊同。 　　於是，愚公就率領著三個能挑擔子的子孫，鑿石頭、挖土塊，再用籮筐把石土運到離家很遠的地方，一年到頭他們才能往返一次。愚公家搬山的事，驚動了鄰居。鄰居家的一位老奶奶，有個小孫女，才剛七、八歲，也蹦蹦跳跳跑去幫忙。 　　黃河邊上住著一個老頭，人稱智叟，是個很聰明的老人。他以嘲笑的語氣勸阻愚公說：「你怎麼傻到這種地步呀！就憑你這把年紀，這點兒力氣，要拔掉山上的一根樹都不容易辦到，又怎麼能搬掉這麼多的山石土塊呢？」愚公長歎了一口氣，說：「我看你太頑固了，簡直不明事理。雖然我會死，可是我還有兒子呢！兒子又生孫子，孫子又生兒子，兒子又生兒子，兒子又生孫子，這樣子子孫孫都不會斷絕的呀！而這兩座山再也不會增高了，還怕挖不平嗎？」智叟聽了，無言以對。 　　山神聽到了愚公的這些話，就去稟告了天帝。天帝為愚公移山的誠意所感動，就派了夸娥氏的兩個兒子去背走了那兩座大山。

32. Why does Yu Gong want to move the mountain?

   A) It blocked the path out of the village.

   B) It was blocking the river that provided water to the village.

   C) He wanted to prove his physical strength.

   D) He wanted to see beyond the mountain.

33. The older man was called 智叟 because

   A) he was arrogant

   B) he was wise

   C) he was an unhappy

   D) he was stubborn

34. What happened at the end of the story?

   A) The mountain gods sent someone to move the mountain.

   B) Yu Gong was able to move the mountain by himself.

   C) Everyone from the village helped Yu Gong move the mountain.

   D) Yu Gong could not move the mountain.

35. Yu Gong believed he could move the mountain because

   A) his neighbors would help him remove it

   B) he was praying for help from the gods

   C) the size of the mountain could only decrease if he continued to carve out the mountain

   D) a miracle would happen if he kept carving out the mountain

SECTION II: Free Response

Part A: Writing (Story Narration and E-mail Response)

Writing Part Directions

You will be asked to perform two writing tasks in Chinese. In each case, you will be asked to write for a specific purpose and to a specific person. You should write in as complete and as culturally appropriate a manner as possible, taking into account the purpose and the person described. In this part of the exam, the student may NOT move back and forth among questions.

Story Narration (15%, 15 minutes)

The four pictures present a story. Imagine you are writing the story to a friend. Narrate a complete story as suggested by the pictures. Give your story a beginning, a middle, and an end.

E-Mail Response (10%, 15 minutes)

Read this e-mail from a friend and then type a response.

[Simplified Character Version]	[Traditional Character Version]
发件人：大伟 邮件主题：参加生日聚会	發件人：大偉 郵件主題：參加生日聚會
东东： 我昨天同时收到大中和小胖儿的生日聚会邀请，时间都是下个星期日的下午两点。你知道大中是我在班上最要好的朋友，可是我和小胖儿从小一块儿长大，又一起在球队多年，我真的不忍心拒绝他们任何一个人的邀请。我感到非常为难，你觉得我参加谁的比较好？我应该怎样做才不会伤害另一个人呢？请指教，谢谢！	東東： 我昨天同時收到大中和小胖兒的生日聚會邀请，時間都是下個星期日的下午兩點。你知道大中是我在班上最要好的朋友，可是我和小胖兒從小一塊長大，又一起在球隊多年，我真的不忍心拒絕他們任何一個人的邀请。我感到非常為難，你覺得我參加誰的比較好？我應該怎樣做才不會傷害另一個人呢？請指教，謝謝！

Part B: Speaking (Conversation and Cultural Presentation)

Conversation (10%, 4 minutes)

Speaking Part Directions: Conversation

You will participate in a simulated conversation. Each time it is your turn to speak, you will have 20 seconds to record. You should respond as fully and as appropriately as possible. In this part of the exam, you may NOT move back and forth among questions.

You will have a conversation with Li Long, a Chinese student you met on the Great Wall, about your experiences in China.

Cultural Presentation(15%, 7 minutes)

Speaking Part Directions: Cultural Presentation

You will be asked to speak in Chinese on a specific topic. Imagine you are making an oral presentation to your Chinese class. First, you will read and hear the topic for your presentation. You will have 4 minutes to prepare your presentation. Then you will have 2 minutes to record your presentation. Your presentation should be as complete as possible.

SECTION I: Multiple Choice

Part A: Listening (Rejoinders and Listening Selections)

Listening Part Directions

You will answer two types of questions: rejoinders and questions based on listening selections. For all tasks, you will have a specific amount of response time. In this part of the exam, you may NOT move back and forth among questions.

Listening Part Directions: Rejoinders (10%, 10 minutes)

You will hear several short conversations or parts of conversations followed by four choices, designated (A), (B), (C), and (D). Choose the one that continues or completes the conversation in a logical and culturally appropriate manner. You will have 5 seconds to answer each question.

1. (A) (B) (C) (D)   9. (A) (B) (C) (D)
2. (A) (B) (C) (D)   10. (A) (B) (C) (D)
3. (A) (B) (C) (D)   11. (A) (B) (C) (D)
4. (A) (B) (C) (D)   12. (A) (B) (C) (D)
5. (A) (B) (C) (D)   13. (A) (B) (C) (D)
6. (A) (B) (C) (D)   14. (A) (B) (C) (D)
7. (A) (B) (C) (D)   15. (A) (B) (C) (D)
8. (A) (B) (C) (D)

You will listen to several selections in Chinese. For each selection, you will be told whether it will be played once or twice. You may take notes as you listen. Your notes will not be graded. After listening to each selection, you will see questions in English. For each question, choose the response that is best according to the selection. You will have 12 seconds to answer each question.

Selection 1: Announcement (Selection plays one time.)

16. This announcement is most likely broadcast

    A) at the train station

    B) right after the departure of the train

    C) right before approaching the final destination

    D) at the subway station

17. This announcement is to inform the passengers

    A) to be aware of thieves

    B) where to transfer to the connecting trains

    C) where to go to claim baggage

    D) where to go to file a complaint about the service

Selection 2: Conversation (Selection plays one time.)

18. The dance party Mingming is attending is

    A) the Homecoming party

    B) the senior prom

    C) Xiaoli's birthday party

    D) a party the man is hosting

19. Mingming is concerned about

    A) too much homework to do

    B) what attire to wear

    C) a coffee stain on her dress

    D) not having enough money to shop for clothes

20. The party is going to be held

    A) on Friday

    B) on Saturday

    C) tomorrow

    D) the day after tomorrow

21. The dress that Mingming wore to a friend's party last time was

    A) white with little blue flowers

    B) blue with little white flowers

    C) blue with white stripes

    D) white with little blue polka dots

22. What is Mingming most likely to wear to the dance party?

    A) Her sister's dress

    B) One of her own dresses

    C) Her friend's dress

    D) A brand new dress

Selection 3: Instructions (Selection plays two times.)

23. Who cannot apply for a library card?

    A) People who work in the city but do not reside there

    B) People who go to school in the city but do not reside there

    C) People who do not have a driver's license

    D) People who do not have a passport

24. Which type of identification is not mentioned in the instructions?

    A) Student ID

    B) Birth certificate

    C) Passport

    D) Driver's license

25. Besides IDs, what else does one need to apply for a library card?

    A) One two-inch color photo

    B) Two one-inch color photos

    C) One two-inch black-and-white photo

    D) Two one-inch black-and-white photos

26. Which of the following statements is FALSE?

    A) Everyone has to apply in person.

    B) Students have to apply in person.

    C) No mail application is accepted.

    D) You can check out books on the same day you apply for a library card.

Selection 4: Voice Message (Selection plays two times.)

27. The woman left this message

    A) to warn her father that they may lose the game this weekend

    B) to ask her father to cancel her violin lesson

    C) to ask her father for a ride home

    D) to arrange for a ride after the game

28. We may best describe the team's attitude as

    A) enthusiastic

    B) pessimistic

    C) cheerful

    D) realistic

29. Which of the following statements is TRUE?

    A) The coach doesn't have any hope for a good result this weekend.

    B) The coach would like them to practice an extra hour every day until the game.

    C) Not everyone can stay.

    D) The team thinks the opponents of the upcoming game are weak.

30. What sport does the speaker engage herself in?

    A) Volleyball

    B) Basketball

    C) Badminton

    D) Golf

Selection 5: Report (Selection plays two times.)

31. The survey was conducted by

    A) a certain class

    B) the school

    C) the student union

    D) the PTA

32. The result of the survey is

    A) unreliable because there were not enough data

    B) reliable because over 80% of the questionnaires were turned in

    C) unreliable because the data were not analyzed

    D) to help the school decide whether to penalize the students for being late

33. Which of the following vehicles is not mentioned in the report?

    A) School bus

    B) One's own car

    C) Train

    D) Public bus

34. What kind of student tends to be late for school?

    A) Those who walk

    B) Those who rely on their parents to drive them

    C) Those who ride their bicycles

    D) Those who car pool with other families

35. What is the percentage of the students surveyed who don't need parents to drive them to school or take them home at all?

    A) 15%

    B) 25%

    C) 45%

    D) 60%

Part B: Reading Selections (25%, 60 minutes)

Reading Part Directions

In this part of the exam, you may move back and forth among all the questions. You will read several selections in Chinese. Each selection is accompanied by a number of questions in English. For each question, choose the response that is best according to the selection. You will have 60 minutes to answer all questions.

Read this e-mail.

[Simplified Character Version]	[Traditional Character Version]
发件人：星星高中校长办公室 收件人：全校家长 邮件主题：开学前注意事项 发件日期：2009年8月1日 附件：1. 免费午餐申请表格 　　　2. 紧急联络表格	發件人：星星高中校長辦公室 收件人：全校家長 郵件主題：開學前注意事項 發件日期：2009年8月1日 附件：1. 免費午餐申請表格 　　　2. 緊急聯絡表格
各位家长： 　　学校定于9月1日开学，开学之前，有些重要事项希望家长注意。附件中有两份表格：一是免费午餐申请表格，如果您的孩子符合学校提供免费午餐的条件，您可以填表申请；另一份是紧急联络表格，请您在表格上填写三个亲朋好友的名字、住址和联络方式，除了电邮和手机号码之外，最重要的是他们的电话号码及您的签名。两份表格必须在开学后两个星期内交给校长秘书王小姐。如果您不用申请免费午餐，则只需缴交紧急联络表格。谢谢您的支持与合作！ 祝您暑期愉快！ 　　　　　　　　　星星高中校长办公室	各位家長： 　　學校訂於九月一日開學，開學之前，有些重要事項希望家長注意。附件中有兩份表格：一是免費午餐申請表格，如果您的孩子符合學校提供免費午餐的條件，您可以填表申請；另一份是緊急聯絡表格，請您在表格上填寫三個親朋好友的名字、住址和聯絡方式，除了電郵和手機號碼之外，最重要的是他們的電話號碼及您的簽名。兩份表格必須在開學後兩個星期內交給校長秘書王小姐。如果您不用申請免費午餐，則只需繳交緊急聯絡表格。謝謝您的支持與合作！ 祝您暑期愉快！ 　　　　　　　　　星星高中校長辦公室

1. How long do the parents have to fill out and turn in the forms after the email is sent?

    A) One month

    B) Two weeks

    C) One month and two weeks

    D) Two months

2. Where can the parents get the forms?

    A) From Miss Wang of the principal's office

    B) From the students, as the forms have been sent home with the students

    C) From the principal

    D) From the email attachment

3. One of the two forms is

    A) for lunch card purchase

    B) for free lunch application

    C) for picnic signup

    D) for homework buddy signup

4. Of the two forms, the parents are informed that

    A) both have to be turned in

    B) only one must be turned in

    C) neither one has to be turned in

    D) neither one requires a parent's signature

5. Which of the following statements is FALSE?

    A) The emergency card requires parents' contact information.

    B) The emergency card asks for the emergency contacts' telephone numbers.

    C) The emergency card asks for the emergency contacts' email addresses.

    D) The emergency card requires the emergency contacts' cell phone numbers.

Read this public sign.

[Simplified Character Version]	[Traditional Character Version]
如厕后请冲水， 给自己养成好习惯， 为别人留下好环境。	如廁後請沖水， 給自己養成好習慣， 為別人留下好環境。

6. Where would this sign most likely appear?

   A) In the classroom

   B) In front of a drinking fountain

   C) In the restroom

   D) On the deck of a swimming pool

7. The purpose of this sign is to

   A) keep the swimming pool clean

   B) have a nice environment for the students to study

   C) be sure that students do not waste water

   D) assure that the toilet is properly flushed after use

Read this public sign.

[Simplified Character Version]	[Traditional Character Version]
施工重地行人止步	施工重地行人止步

8. Where would this sign most likely appear?

   A) Inside a library

   B) On a construction site

   C) In front of a factory

   D) On a crosswalk

9. What does the sign mean?

   A) No trespassing

   B) No smoking

   C) Be aware of pedestrians

   D) No parking

Read this note.

[Simplified Character Version]	[Traditional Character Version]
小梅姐姐：	小梅姐姐：
刚才妈妈说阿姨明天要从旧金山开车来看我们，小表姐也会一道来。阿姨对去年我们一起去吃的那家烤鸭店还念念不忘，妈妈说既然她那么喜欢，那明天晚上就再到那儿去给阿姨和小表姐接风吧。可是那家店客人很多，总是大排长龙，不预先订位，恐怕到时候得等上一、两个小时。妈妈急着去开会，要我打电话去订，可是他们现在没人接电话。我得上课去了，只好麻烦你了。妈妈说爸爸公司明天晚上有个饭局，就只有我们和阿姨她们。桌子要订六点半的，座位不要太靠近厨房或厕所。谢谢你了，晚上见。	剛才媽媽說阿姨明天要從舊金山開車來看我們，小表姐也會一道來。阿姨對去年我們一起去吃的那家烤鴨店還念念不忘，媽媽說既然她那麼喜歡，那明天晚上就再到那兒去給阿姨和小表姐接風吧。可是那家店客人很多，總是大排長龍，不預先訂位，恐怕到時候得等上一、兩個小時。媽媽急著去開會，要我打電話去訂，可是他們現在沒人接電話。我得上課去了，只好麻煩你了。媽媽說爸爸公司明天晚上有個飯局，就只有我們和阿姨她們。桌子要訂六點半的，座位不要太靠近廚房或廁所。謝謝你了，晚上見。
小兰 11月15日上午10时	小蘭 11月15日上午10時

10. Who is coming to visit?

　　A) Father's sister and her daughter

　　B) Father's brother and his daughter

　　C) Mother's sister and her daughter

　　D) Mother's brother and his daughter

11. What kind of food are the family and their guests having tomorrow evening?

　　A) Roast duck

　　B) Hot pot

　　C) Steak

　　D) Salmon

12. From the note, we can infer that

   A) the family and their guests see each other very often

   B) the family and their guests do not live far from each other

   C) the guests came to see them last year

   D) the guest's daughter is older than Xiaolan but younger than Xiaomei

13. Xiaolan would like Xiaomei to make reservations because

   A) Xiaomei is older and knows how to handle it better

   B) Xiaolan has to go to a meeting right now

   C) without reservations, they may have to sit by the restroom

   D) Xiaolan does not have the time to make them now

14. Their mother would be happy if the reservation is

   A) for six people at six o'clock

   B) for six people at six-thirty and the table is far from the kitchen door

   C) for five people at six-thirty and the table is right in the center of the dining area

   D) for five people at six-thirty and as long as they don't have to wait, it doesn't matter where they would be sitting

15. Which of the following statements is TRUE?

   A) The family lives in San Francisco.

   B) Father works at a company.

   C) Mother does not have a job.

   D) Mother is not informed of Father's schedule.

Read this advertisement.

[Simplified Character Version]	[Traditional Character Version]
自助餐	自助餐
新春期间（正月初一至初六）	新春期間（正月初一至初六）
特价优惠顾客	特價優惠顧客
成人一律八五折	成人一律八五折
儿童半价（五岁至十二岁，一米二以下）	兒童半價（五歲至十二歲，一米二以下）
五岁以下儿童免费	五歲以下兒童免費

16. What is this advertisement for?

    A) For a New Year special offer

    B) For a Chinese New Year special offer

    C) For a winter vacation special offer

    D) For a summer vacation special offer

17. What type of food does this restaurant serve?

    A) Buffet

    B) Fast food

    C) A-la-carte

    D) Barbeque

18. How much discount does the promotion offer for adults?

    A) 85% off the regular price

    B) 50% off the regular price

    C) 25% off the regular price

    D) 15% off the regular price

Read this advertisement.

[Simplified Character Version]	[Traditional Character Version]
中年女性，应聘做全职家教、保姆及清洁工作 　　本人曾在国内从事中学教育工作多年，在美国有做数理家教、幼儿保姆及清洁的相关工作经验。认真负责，极具爱心及耐性，有驾照，美国合法居留身份，能用英语进行日常会话。如有需要，亦可提供雇主电话以供参考。 有意者请于每晚十时后打电话至 （415）886-2773找顾女士	中年女性，應聘做全職家教、保姆及清潔工作 　　本人曾在國內從事中學教育工作多年，在美國有做數理家教、幼兒保姆及清潔的相關工作經驗。認真負責，極具愛心及耐性，有駕照，美國合法居留身份，能用英語進行日常會話 。如有需要，亦可提供僱主電話以供參考。 有意者請於每晚十時後打電話至 （415）886-2773找顧女士

19. What kind of work did the woman not express an interest in doing?

    A) Being a nanny

    B) Gardening

    C) Tutoring

    D) House cleaning

20. Which of the following statements is FALSE?

    A) The woman has taught at secondary schools in America.

    B) The woman has a driver's license.

    C) The woman is only interested in a full time job.

    D) The woman speaks adequate English.

21. Which of the following qualities did the woman not list in the advertisement?

    A) Responsible

    B) Patient

    C) Hardworking

    D) Honest

Read this letter.

[Simplified Character Version]	[Traditional Character Version]
李老师：	李老師：
学期即将结束，我要代表我们"我爱中文"社团向您道谢。这一年来，您每周四下午都来指导我们活动，对许多同学来说，一周中最有意思的就是我们社团活动的那两个小时。您不但提供我们课外练习中文的机会，也传授了我们很多中国传统文化习俗的知识，还带领我们吟唱中国古诗、制作剪纸、编中国结。逢年过节，我们在布置得极有节日气氛的教室里，品尝年糕、元宵、粽子等等，真让人回味无穷。通过这样的活动，我们无形中更热爱学习汉语，也深深体会到中国文化的精深博大。老师，我们衷心感谢您长期对我们费心的启发与教导。	學期即將結束，我要代表我們「我愛中文」社團向您道謝。這一年來，您每週四下午都來指導我們活動，對許多同學來說，一週中最有意思的就是我們社團活動的那兩個小時。您不但提供我們課外練習中文的機會，也傳授了我們很多中國傳統文化習俗的知識，還帶領我們吟唱中國古詩、製作剪紙、編中國結。逢年過節，我們在佈置得極有節日氣氛的教室裡，品嚐年糕、元宵、粽子等等，真讓人回味無窮。通過這樣的活動，我們無形中更熱愛學習漢語，也深深體會到中國文化的精深博大。老師，我們衷心感謝您長期對我們費心的啟發與教導。
敬祝 教安 ！	敬祝 教安 ！
学生　陈亦文敬上 　　　　　2010年5月30日	學生　陳亦文敬上 　　　　　2010年5月30日

22. The student wrote this letter to Li Laoshi

    A) to express her gratitude for teaching her Chinese language this past year

    B) to express her gratitude for sponsoring the Chinese club

    C) to ask her to be the sponsor for the Chinese club next year

    D) to ask her to come to an "I Love Chinese Language Club" end-of-the-year celebration

23. From the food mentioned in the letter, what holidays we may infer have been observed in the past year?

    A) Chinese New Year, the Dragon Boat Festival, and the Mid-Autumn Festival

    B) Chinese New Year, the Lantern Festival, and the Mid-Autumn Festival

    C) Chinese New Year, the Lantern Festival, and the Dragon Boat Festival

    D) The Lantern Festival, the Dragon Boat Festival, and the Mid-Autumn Festival

24. Which of the following activities is not mentioned in the letter?

    A) Chinese poetry chanting

    B) Chinese calligraphy

    C) Chinese paper cutting

    D) Chinese knot making

Read this article.

[Simplified Character Version]	[Traditional Character Version]
公园该不该收门票	公園該不該收門票
我最近参加了一场讨论会，主题是公园该不该收门票。赞成收门票的学生认为，有了门票收入，公园有专人管理，可以维持一定的整洁和安全，再说花木也会有人按时修剪、照顾，只要门票不要订得太高，一般老百姓都负担得起。不赞成收门票的学生认为，公园是公共场所，应该是免费的，再说为了收门票，就要建围墙、修大门，难免会影响市容。讨论非常热烈，但最后并没有结论。不过，散场时有人做了一项调查，结果是赞成收门票的只有百分之十，不赞成的占了百分之七十，有百分之二十的学生没有意见。	我最近参加了一場討論會，主題是公園該不該收門票。贊成收門票的學生認為，有了門票收入，公園有專人管理，可以維持一定的整潔和安全，再說花木也會有人按時修剪、照顧，只要門票不要訂得太高，一般老百姓都負擔得起。不贊成收門票的學生認為，公園是公共場所，應該是免費的，再說為了收門票，就要建圍牆、修大門，難免會影響市容。討論非常熱烈，但最後並沒有結論。不過，散場時有人做了一項調查，結果是贊成收門票的只有百分之十，不贊成的佔了百分之七十，有百分之二十的學生沒有意見。

25. What was the forum about?

    A) How to keep the park clean

    B) Whether admission to the park should be free

    C) Where to build a fence in the park

    D) How to afford to hire gardeners to take care of the park regularly

26. Who attended this forum?

    A) Students

    B) The general public

    C) Students and teachers

    D) Students and parents

27. Some people believe that having revenues could enable the authority to

    A) build a fence and a secure main gate

    B) plant more trees and flowers in the park

    C) keep the park cleaner and safer

    D) promote the image of the city

28. What is the writer's attitude toward the issue being discussed in the forum?

    A) He agreed with the majority of the participants.

    B) He agreed with the minority of the participants.

    C) He did not agree with anyone.

    D) He did not express his personal view.

Read this poster.

[Simplified Character Version]	[Traditional Character Version]
拥抱阳光 走向自然 欢迎踊跃参加野营活动	擁抱陽光 走向自然 歡迎踴躍參加野營活動
举办单位：学生会 地点：市郊快乐谷 活动日期：4月23日至25日（三天两夜） 费用：七十五元（需要申请补助者， 　　　可至课外活动组办公室办理） 人数：六十名 报名地点：活动中心二楼206室学生会 报名时间：即日起，额满为止	舉辦單位：學生會 地點：市郊快樂谷 活動日期：4月23日至25日（三天兩夜） 費用：七十五元（需要申請補助者， 　　　可至課外活動組辦公室辦理） 人數：六十名 報名地點：活動中心二樓 206室學生會 報名時間：即日起，額滿為止

29. This activity is for

    A) fundraising

    B) community service

    C) camping

    D) enrichment

30. When can the interested students apply for this activity?

    A) Immediately

    B) April 23

    C) April 25

    D) No information is provided

31. The role that the office for the extracurricular activities plays in this activity is to

    A) provide logistical support

    B) plan and sponsor the activity

    C) offer financial assistance to those who need it

    D) assure safety of the activity

Read this story.

[Simplified Character Version]	[Traditional Character Version]
宋朝有个叫陈尧咨的人，擅长射箭，在当时举世无双，因此他对自己的射箭本领很是自负。　有一天，陈尧咨在自家的菜园子里练习射箭，有一位卖油的老头儿正巧挑着担子经过。他停了下来，放下担子，斜着眼睛看陈尧咨射箭，久久都不离开。陈尧咨的射箭本领果然名不虚传，射出的箭十有八九都射中靶心。卖油的老头儿，仍是斜眼瞅着，只稍微点了一下头。 　　陈尧咨见老头儿似乎不把他射箭的本事放在眼里，心里有点恼火，就放下弓箭走过去问老头儿说："你也懂得射箭吗？难道你认为我的射技不够精湛吗？"老头儿回答说："我觉得这也没什么特别了不起的，只不过你的手法娴熟罢了。"陈尧咨非常恼怒，质问道："你怎么敢如此轻视我的绝技！" 　　老头儿不慌不忙地说："我怎么敢呢！我不过是从我多年倒油的经验中懂得这个道理的。"说完以后，就把一个葫芦放在地上，又用一枚圆形方孔的铜钱盖在葫芦嘴上，然后用一个油勺从油桶里舀了一满勺的油，往盖着铜钱的葫芦嘴里倒。只见那油慢慢地流进了葫芦嘴。等油倒完了，铜钱竟然连一滴油都没有沾上。卖油的老头儿笑了笑，说道："我这也没有什么了不起的，纯粹是手熟而已。"陈尧咨听了之后，笑着把卖油的老头子打发走了。	宋朝有個叫陳堯咨的人，擅長射箭，在當時舉世無雙，因此他對自己的射箭本領很是自負。有一天，陳堯咨在自家的菜園子裡練習射箭，有一位賣油的老頭兒正巧挑著擔子經過。他停了下來，放下擔子，斜著眼睛看陳堯咨射箭，久久都不離開。　陳堯咨的射箭本領果然名不虛傳，射出的箭十有八九都射中靶心。賣油的老頭兒，仍是斜眼瞅著，只稍微點了一下頭。 　　陳堯咨見老頭兒似乎不把他射箭的本事放在眼裡，心裡有點惱火，就放下弓箭走過去問老頭兒說：「你也懂得射箭嗎？難道你認為我的射技不夠精湛嗎？」老頭兒回答說：「我覺得這也沒什麼特別了不起的，只不過你的手法嫻熟罷了。」陳堯咨非常惱怒，質問道：「你怎麼敢如此輕視我的絕技！」 　　老頭兒不慌不忙地說：「我怎麼敢呢！我不過是從我多年倒油的經驗中懂得這個道理的。」說完以後，就把一個葫蘆放在地上，又用一個圓形方孔的銅錢蓋在葫蘆嘴上，然後用一個油勺從油桶裡舀了一滿勺的油，往蓋著銅錢的葫蘆嘴裡倒。只見那油慢慢地流進了葫蘆嘴。等油倒完了，銅錢竟然連一滴油都沒有沾上。賣油的老頭兒笑了笑，說道：「我這也沒有什麼了不起的，純粹是手熟而已。」　陳堯咨聽了之後，笑著把賣油的老頭子打發走了。

32. What adjective best describes the archer's attitude toward his own archery skills?

　　A) Modest

　　B) Proud

　　C) Insecure

　　D) Ambitious

33. Which of the following statements is TRUE?

    A) The archer performed his skills for a large audience.

    B) The old man was a great archery master himself.

    C) The archer challenged the old man to prove his skills.

    D) The old man did not think the archer's skills were a big deal.

34. How did the archer react to the old man watching him perform archery?

    A) He did not pay attention to the old guy.

    B) He thought the old man showed contempt toward his skills.

    C) He wished he had not been disturbed by the old guy.

    D) He was afraid that the old man was better than he in archery.

35. The moral of the story is that

    A) in order to excel in anything, we need to practice over and over again

    B) one should always respect other people

    C) even among the oil vendors, there are great masters

    D) one should not show off one's own skills

SECTION II: Free Response

Part A: Writing (Story Narration and E-mail Response)

Writing Part Directions

You will be asked to perform two writing tasks in Chinese. In each case, you will be asked to write for a specific purpose and to a specific person. You should write in as complete and as culturally appropriate a manner as possible, taking into account the purpose and the person described. In this part of the exam, the student may NOT move back and forth among questions.

Story Narration (15%, 15 minutes)

The four pictures present a story. Imagine you are writing the story to a friend. Narrate a complete story as suggested by the pictures. Give your story a beginning, a middle, and an end.

E-Mail Response (10%, 15 minutes)

Read this e-mail from a friend and then type a response.

[Simplified Character Version]	[Traditional Character Version]
发件人：林文 邮件主题：打工看孩子	發件人：林文 郵件主題：打工看孩子
我们家隔壁搬来了一户人家，有两个四岁和六岁的男孩。他们的父母晚上常常不在家，让我一个星期去三个晚上帮他们看小孩，七点到十一点。我很想挣这个钱，可又担心会影响学习。请你告诉我你的经验以及对于一边学习一边打工的看法。谢谢。	我們家隔壁搬來了一戶人家，有兩個四歲和六歲的男孩。他們的父母晚上常常不在家，讓我一個星期去三個晚上幫他們看小孩，七點到十一點。我很想掙這個錢，可又擔心會影響學習。請你告訴我你的經驗以及對於一邊學習一邊打工的看法。謝謝。

Part B: Speaking (Conversation and Cultural Presentation)

Conversation (10%, 4 minutes)

Speaking Part Directions: Conversation

You will participate in a simulated conversation. Each time it is your turn to speak, you will have 20 seconds to record. You should respond as fully and as appropriately as possible. In this part of the exam, you may NOT move back and forth among questions.

You will have a conversation with Chen Chong, the community service director, about your applying for volunteering to teach English to Chinese elementary school students.

Cultural Presentation (15%, 7 minutes)

Speaking Part Directions: Cultural Presentation

You will be asked to speak in Chinese on a specific topic. Imagine you are making an oral presentation to your Chinese class. First, you will read and hear the topic for your presentation. You will have 4 minutes to prepare your presentation. Then you will have 2 minutes to record your presentation. Your presentation should be as complete as possible.

SECTION I: Multiple Choice

Part A: Listening (Rejoinders and Listening Selections)

Listening Part Directions

You will answer two types of questions: rejoinders and questions based on listening selections. For all tasks, you will have a specific amount of response time. In this part of the exam, you may NOT move back and forth among questions.

Listening Part Directions: Rejoinders (10%, 10 minutes)

You will hear several short conversations or parts of conversations followed by four choices, designated (A), (B), (C), and (D). Choose the one that continues or completes the conversation in a logical and culturally appropriate manner. You will have 5 seconds to answer each question.

1. (A) (B) (C) (D)   9. (A) (B) (C) (D)
2. (A) (B) (C) (D)   10. (A) (B) (C) (D)
3. (A) (B) (C) (D)   11. (A) (B) (C) (D)
4. (A) (B) (C) (D)   12. (A) (B) (C) (D)
5. (A) (B) (C) (D)   13. (A) (B) (C) (D)
6. (A) (B) (C) (D)   14. (A) (B) (C) (D)
7. (A) (B) (C) (D)   15. (A) (B) (C) (D)
8. (A) (B) (C) (D)

Listening Part Directions: Listening Selections (15%, 10 minutes)

You will listen to several selections in Chinese. For each selection, you will be told whether it will be played once or twice. You may take notes as you listen. Your notes will not be graded. After listening to each selection, you will see questions in English. For each question, choose the response that is best according to the selection. You will have 12 seconds to answer each question.

Selection 1: Announcement (Selection plays one time.)

16. Where was the sports bag found?

    A) In the classroom

    B) On the sport field

    C) In the school dining hall

    D) In the auditorium

17. Which of the following items was not in the bag?

    A) Cash

    B) Calculator

    C) Walkman

    D) Sports shoes

18. Where can the student get the lost items back?

    A) The school office

    B) Lost and Found

    C) The principal's office

    D) The teachers' office

Selection 2: Voice Message (Selection plays two times.)

19. Li Shuaishuai's mother called the teacher because

    A) she was not clear on what to talk about in her speech

    B) she was unsure about the presentation schedule

    C) she could attend the meeting

    D) her husband would give the speech instead

20. The topic of the meeting is

    A) how to improve the quality of education

    B) the Chinese culture

    C) the Chinese immigrant experience

    D) the experience of educating children

21. Which statement is NOT true?

    A) The mom does not know how much time she has for her presentation.

    B) The mom wants to know if the presentation should be in Chinese or English.

    C) The mom wonders if the students will like her presentation.

    D) The mom is not sure if she needs a written copy of her speech for students.

Selection 3: Conversation (Selection plays one time.)

22. The girl's classmate called her house because he wants to

    A) tell the girl that he is going to the party

    B) tell her that he will give her a ride to the party

    C) know if her parents would allow her to go with him

    D) know if she has the right dress to wear

23. The girl's younger brother wants to go to the party because

    A) he likes dancing

    B) he wants to go to school to have fun with his friends

    C) he is scared of being home alone

    D) he is bored by himself at home

24. Why was the girl's younger brother questioning the reason for having a party?

    A) There were no sports events.

    B) It was not a holiday or a weekend.

    C) It was not graduation day.

    D) It was not someone's birthday.

25. The girl's parents cannot send her to the party because

    A) they were at their friend's house

    B) they both work at night

    C) they were on vacation in China

    D) they were on a business trip in Shanghai

Selection 4: Instructions (Selection plays one time.)

26. Where should students go for registration?

    A) The auditorium

    B) The administration building

    C) The library

    D) The cafeteria

27. Where are student portraits taken?

    A) The auditorium

    B) The administration building

    C) The library

    D) The cafeteria

28. When should students purchase their textbooks?

    A) Before registration

    B) After registration

    C) On the first day of class

    D) The first week of school

29. What is in the packet that students receive upon registration?

    A) A calendar

    B) A yearbook

    C) Physical exam form

    D) A self portrait

30. What should students do if they paid their tuition online?

    A) Present the receipt at the accounting office

    B) Request a receipt at the auditorium

    C) Request a waiver for the registration fee

    D) Report to the administration building

Selection 5: Report (Selection plays one time.)

31. What percentage of the students turned in their survey?

    A) 85%

    B) 93%

    C) 87%

    D) 76%

32. What is the percentage of students who understand the importance of environmental protection?

    A) 67%

    B) 76%

    C) 85%

    D) 87%

33. 18% of the students

    A) think they should do more to protect the environment

    B) did not participate in the survey

    C) are motivated to protect the environment

    D) do not care about the environment

34. How many students in total participated in this survey?

    A) 120

    B) 210

    C) 2000

    D) 200

35. The majority of the students think

    A) they should correct people's bad behavior in public

    B) they only need to watch their own behavior

    C) they would help pick up waste that other people throw away

    D) it is other people's job to keep the environment clean

Part B: Reading Selections (25%, 60 minutes)

Reading Part Directions

In this part of the exam, you may move back and forth among all the questions. You will read several selections in Chinese. Each selection is accompanied by a number of questions in English. For each question, choose the response that is best according to the selection. You will have 60 minutes to answer all questions.

Read this e-mail.

[Simplified Character Version]	[Traditional Character Version]
发件人：杨东 收件人：小明 邮件主题：北京奥运会的票 邮件日期：2008年4月8日	發件人：楊東 收件人：曉明 郵件主題：北京奧運會的票 郵件日期：2009年4月8日
小明： 　　你好！你托我买北京奥运会比赛门票一事，我已帮你办好了！我一共弄到了七张兵乓球决赛的票，你们家每人一张，两张给我的朋友，另外一张是我自己的。由于此届北京奥运会门票是由国际奥组委在全世界统一分配，各国的需求远远大于所分配的数额，可以说是一票难求。特别是开幕式和闭幕式的票，比幸运大抽奖中奖都难。虽然我没能买到开幕式和闭幕式的票，但是能弄到七张兵乓球决赛的票，也是非常不容易的了。我知道你们全家都喜欢兵乓球，希望通过观摩比赛，能使你们对兵乓球运动的兴趣和球技都有所提高。 　　我父母知道你们能来北京观看奥运会，都非常高兴，他们已经把客房为你们准备好了。现在我家住的房子是两年前才搬进来的，你还没有来过。这儿离市中心不算太远，环境非常优雅，生活和交通也非常方便。从我家出门走两分钟，就有地铁直通奥运各个场馆。从早晨四点半到晚上十二点，每十五分钟一班，比自己开车或坐出租都方便。盼望你们的到来，并请代我向你父母和姐姐问好！ 杨东	小明： 　　你好！你托我買北京奧運會比賽門票一事，我已幫你辦好了！我一共弄到了七張兵乓球決賽的票，你們家每人一張，兩張給我的朋友，另外一張是我自己的。由於此屆北京奧運會門票是由國際奧組委在全世界統一分配，各國的需求遠遠大於所分配的數額，可以說是一票難求。特別是開幕式和閉幕式的票，比幸運大抽奖中獎都難。雖然我沒能買到開幕式和閉幕式的票，但是能弄到七張兵乓球決賽的票，也是非常不容易的了。我知道你們全家都喜歡兵乓球，希望通過觀摩比賽，能使你們對兵乓球運動的興趣和球技都有所提高。 　　我父母知道你們能來北京觀看奧運會，都非常高興。他們已經把客房為你們準備好了。現在我家住的房子是兩年前才搬進來的，你還沒有來過。這兒離市中心不算太遠，環境非常優雅，生活和交通也非常方便。從我家出門走兩分鐘，就有地鐵直通奧運各個場館。從早晨四點半到晚上十二點，每十五分鐘一班，比自己開車坐出租都方便。盼望你們的到來，并請代我向你父母和姐姐問好！ 楊東

1. The tickets that Yang Dong got for Xiaoming are for

    A) the final game of ping-pong

    B) Beijing Olympic semi-final game of ping-pong

    C) the opening ceremony of the Beijing 2008 Olympics

    D) the closing ceremony of the Beijing 2008 Olympics

2. The best way to get to the Olympic venues from Yang Dong's house is

    A) by walking

    B) by car

    C) by taxi

    D) by subway

3. Where does Yang Dong's family live in Beijing?

    A) In the suburb

    B) In the center of the city

    C) Near the center of the city

    D) Right next to the Olympic sites

4. How many tickets did Yang Dong get for Xiaoming and his family?

    A) 7

    B) 4

    C) 2

    D) 1

5. Which statement is FALSE according to this e-mail?

    A) Yang Dong has lived in this place for a long time.

    B) Xiaoming's family all like sports.

    C) Yang Dong's house is in a good area.

    D) Xiaoming is going to Yang Dong's house for the first time.

Read this advertisement.

[Simplified Character Version]	[Traditional Character Version]
万达计算机学校招生通告	萬達計算機學校招生通告
万达计算机学校拥有一流的教学环境和实习基地。万达师资优秀、教风严谨、设备先进，并提供校内住宿及用餐。	萬達計算機學校擁有一流的教學環境和實習基地。萬達師資優秀、教風嚴謹、設備先進，並提供校内住宿及用餐。
一、教学内容：1. 电脑基础知识 　　　　　　2. 视窗操作技术 　　　　　　3. 数据库管理 　　　　　　4. 多媒体应用技术	一、教學内容：1. 電腦基礎知識 　　　　　　2. 視窗操作技術 　　　　　　3. 數據庫管理 　　　　　　4. 多媒體應用技術
二、学制：全日制班4个月，夜校班10个月，隔日制班8个月	二、學制：全日制班4個月，夜校班10個月，隔日制班8個月
三、招收条件：面向全国招收初中和初中以上文化水平的各界人士，年龄不限	三、招收條件：面向全國招收初中和初中以上文化水平的各界人士，年齡不限
四、收费标准：学费、教材费、上机实习费，共计1350元	四、收費標準：學費、教材費、上機實習費，共計1350元
五、报名时间及方式：即日起至7月15日，可上www.wanda.com网站，或电（688）456-7788报名	五、報名時間及方式：即日起至7月15日，可上www.wanda.com網站，或電（688）456-7788報名
六、开学时间：2009年8月28日	六、開學時間：2009年8月28日
另：即日起报名的前40名学生，可享有100元的折扣。学校将向合格的毕业生颁发国家计算机技师证书，并由我校推荐、协助就业。	另：即日起報名的前40名學生，可享有100元的折扣。學校將向合格的畢業生頒發國家計算機技師證書，並由我校推薦、协助就業。

6. Which of the following courses does the school not teach?

A) Introduction to computers

B) Computer networking

C) Database management

D) Web design

7. Which of the following expenses isn't included in enrollment?

    A) Tuition

    B) Textbook

    C) Computer practice

    D) Room and board

8. Which of the following information is not mentioned in this advertisement?

    A) Full-time classes are 4 months long.

    B) Part-time classes are 8 months long.

    C) Evening classes are 10 months long.

    D) Summer classes are 8 weeks long.

9. According to the advertisement, which of the following statement is FALSE?

    A) There is a discount of ￥100 for students who enroll before August 28, 2009.

    B) The school will recommend jobs for qualified students.

    C) The school will provide boarding.

    D) The enrollment fee is ￥1350.

10. This program is open to anyone

    A) who has at least a high school diploma

    B) who has any kind of educational background

    C) who has basic computer knowledge

    D) who has at least a middle school education

Read this public sign.

[Simplified Character Version]	[Traditional Character Version]
爱护公物人人有责	愛護公物人人有責

11. What does the sign mean?

    A) Please keep away from this area.

    B) This is a public property.

    C) You will be fined for damaging this property.

    D) Everyone has the responsibility to take care of public property.

12. Where is this sign most likely seen?

    A) Near a private property

    B) At a residential area

    C) At a public park

    D) Inside a library

Read this public sign.

[Simplified Character Version]	[Traditional Character Version]
温馨提示： 步行健体、益脑、利心， 您不妨走走楼梯！	溫馨提示： 步行健體、益腦、利心， 您不妨走走樓梯！

13. Where do you see this kind of sign?

    A) At a drug store

    B) At the gym

    C) Near an elevator

    D) In an airport

14. The purpose of the sign is to

    A) suggest this medicine is good for the heart

    B) warn people who have health problems not to use the stairs

    C) warn that the stairs are not safe here

    D) remind people of the benefit of taking the stairs

Read this article.

[Simplified Character Version]	[Traditional Character Version]
### 中国武术	### 中國武術
中国武术有着悠久的历史，它不仅是中华文化的国粹，也在全世界享有盛名。武术一词在历史上有很多不同的名称：战国时期称之为"技击"，汉代出现了"武艺"一词，并延用到明末，清代初期才出现了"武术"一词，民国时称"国术"，20世纪中沿用清初的"武术"一词至今。	中國武術有著悠久的歷史，它不僅是中華文化的國粹，也在全世界享有盛名。武術一詞在歷史上有很多不同的名稱：戰國時期稱之為「技擊」，漢代出現了「武藝」一詞，並延用到明末，清代初期才出現了「武術」一詞，民國時稱「國術」，20世紀中沿用清初的「武術」一詞至今。
首先，武术是指用武的技术。它是以踢、打、摔、拿、击、刺等技击动作为主要内容，通过徒手或借助于器械的身体运动表现攻防格斗的能力。其次，武术也是体育项目，它明显区别于使人致伤致残的实用技击技术。	首先，武術是指用武的技術。它是以踢、打、摔、拿、擊、刺等技擊動作為主要內容，通過徒手或借助於器械的身體運動表現攻防格鬥的能力。其次，武術也是體育項目，它明顯區別於使人致傷致殘的實用技擊技術。
武术是特指中国武术，也有狭义和广义之分。从广义上讲，中国武术和中国功夫是一个意思。功夫是各种搏斗技巧的统称，像跆拳道、散打和摔跤等可以都可以叫做功夫。从狭义上讲，中国武术只是指中国传统的武术套路，包括太极、少林功等，而不包含摔跤和目前流行的散打。所以，确切地说，中国武术是中国功夫的一种。	武術是特指中國武術，也有狹義和廣義之分。從廣義上講，中國武術和中國功夫是一個意思。功夫是各種搏鬥技巧的統稱，像跆拳道、散打和摔跤等可以都可以叫做功夫。從狹義上講，中國武術只是指中國傳統的武術套路，包括太極、少林功等，而不包含摔跤和目前流行的散打。所以，確切地說，中國武術是中國功夫的一種。

15. The term "Martial Arts" began to be used during

    A) The Warring States Period

    B) The Han Dynasty

    C) The Ming Dynasty

    D) The Qing Dynasty

16. How many fighting styles do Martial Arts include?

    A) 3

    B) 4

    C) 5

    D) 6

17. Which sport does Chinese Martial Arts NOT include?

    A) Boxing

    B) Taichi

    C) Taiquandao

    D) Shaolingong

18. Which of the following statements is TRUE?

    A) Martial Arts are only studied by men.

    B) Martial Arts were originally a synonym for Shaolingong.

    C) Martial Arts are one type of Kongfu.

    D) Martial Arts are not considered a sport in China.

Read this announcement on a poster.

[Simplified Character Version]	[Traditional Character Version]
我校09年毕业生高考成绩高分榜	我校09年畢業生高考成績高分榜
总分最高分： 理科　　　牛　进 658 文科　　　柳　青 598 单科最高分： 理综　　　王心月 287 文综　　　远航　 235 英语　　　金明　 148 　　　　　何晓亮 148	總分最高分： 理科　　　牛　進 658 文科　　　柳　青 598 單科最高分： 理綜　　　王心月 287 文綜　　　遠航　 235 英語　　　金明　 148 　　　　　何曉亮 148

19. This notice is about the result of

    A) a final exam

    B) a college entrance exam

    C) a writing competition

    D) a school-wide proficiency test

20. What is the highest score in the humanity category?

    A) 287

    B) 658

    C) 235

    D) None of above

21. Who got the highest score of a single subject in the sciences?

    A) Niu Jin

    B) Wang Xinyue

    C) He Xiaoliang

    D) Zheng Yuan

Read this story.

[Simplified Character Version]	[Traditional Character Version]
相传在宋国，有一个农夫种了几亩地，他每天辛辛苦苦地到地里去干活儿。遇到好年景，也不过勉强吃饱穿暖，一遇灾荒，可就要忍饥挨饿了。他想过好的生活，但胆子小，人又懒，总想碰上送上门来的意外之财。 奇迹终于发生了。有一天早上，他正在田里耕地，看到周围有人在打猎。突然，他看到一只受惊的兔子剑一般地飞奔过来，不偏不倚，一头撞死在他田边的大树上，蹬蹬腿就死了。农夫赶紧把兔子捡起来，拎回家，当天晚上他就美美地饱餐了一顿。从此，他就不再种地，一天到晚等在那棵神奇的树下，等着奇迹再出现。等啊等，几天过去了，没有兔子撞过来，可是他还是不死心，一直等到地里的草长得比庄稼都高了，还是什么也没等到。因为地没耕，全荒了，最后什么收成也没有。 "守株待兔"的成语就是从这个故事来的。人们常用它来比喻不想努力，而希望获得成功的侥幸心理。	相傳在宋國，有一個農夫種了幾畝地，他每天辛辛苦苦地到地裡去幹活兒。遇到好年景，也不過勉強吃飽穿暖，一遇災荒，可就要忍饑挨餓了。他想過好的生活，但膽子小，人又懶，總想碰上送上門來的意外之財。 奇跡終於發生了。有一天早上，他正在田裡耕地，看到周圍有人在打獵。突然，他看到一隻受驚的兔子劍一般地飛奔過來，不偏不倚，一頭撞死在他田邊的大樹上，蹬蹬腿就死了。農夫趕緊把兔子撿起來，拎回家，當天晚上他就美美地飽餐了一頓。從此，他就不再種地，一天到晚等在那棵神奇的樹下，等著奇跡再出現。等啊等，幾天過去了，沒有兔子撞過來，可是他還是不死心，一直等到地裡的草長得比莊稼都高了，還是什麼也沒等到。因為地沒耕，全荒了，最後什麼收成也沒有。 「守株待兔」的成語就是從這個故事來的。人們常用它來比喻不想努力，而希望獲得成功的僥倖心理。

22. Which statement is FALSE about the farmer?

    A) He was a farmer during Qing Dynasty.

    B) He worked hard and brought his family a comfortable life.

    C) He was not a brave man.

    D) He was lazy and often dreamed of having unexpected blessings.

23. What happened the day he was working in the fields?

    A) He saw a dead bird in front of him.

    B) He saw a dead person under a tree.

    C) A terrified rabbit fled over and hit a tree.

    D) A gunshot startled him.

24. What did the farmer do with the hunted game?

    A) He took it home and tried to rescue it.

    B) He cooked and ate it.

    C) He shared the game with his neighbors.

    D) He kept it in the backyard.

25. What is NOT TRUE about the farmer after that incident?

    A) He waited under the tree everyday hoping for a miracle.

    B) He was not going to farm anymore.

    C) His wife was disappointed in him.

    D) The grains were covered with weeds.

26. What does this proverb tell people?

    A) It is better to be a hunter than a farmer.

    B) Dreams do not come true without hard work.

    C) A man needs to be brave in the face of danger.

    D) Always share your fortune with your friends.

Read this letter.

[Simplified Character Version]	[Traditional Character Version]
亲爱的妈妈：	親愛的媽媽：
您好！昨天我和妹妹给爸爸庆祝他的五十岁生日。您外出学习不在家，我和妹妹心里有些发慌，不知道用什么方法给爸爸过生日最酷，给他送什么样的礼物最好。几天前，我们俩一起商量争论了很久，最后，我们想出了一个顶好顶妙的办法：那就是给爸爸献上我们各自刚刚在学校得到的优秀学生奖状。	您好！昨天我和妹妹給爸爸慶祝他的五十歲生日。您外出學習不在家，我和妹妹心裡有些發慌，不知道用什麼方法給爸爸過生日最酷，給他送什麼樣的禮物最好。幾天前，我們倆一起商量爭論了很久，最後，我們想出了一個頂好頂妙的辦法：那就是給爸爸獻上我們各自剛剛在學校得到的優秀學生獎狀。
昨天，我跟妹妹把奖状包好，高高兴兴地给了爸爸。爸爸拿过奖状，仔细地看着，笑得合不拢嘴，然后把我俩拉到他的怀里，高兴地说："好孩子，你们最懂得爸爸的心，你们的优异成绩就是给爸爸最好的礼物！" 听了爸爸的话我们也很开心，觉得爸爸是那么的亲切。后面的事就别提了！我和妹妹给爸爸包的饺子，因为放的时间太长了，全都粘到一起了，结果煮成了一锅片儿汤。您猜爸爸怎么说？"没问题，等妈妈回来时，再请我一顿吧！"妈妈，您可千万别忘了请爸爸吃生日饭，反正我们已经替您答应了。	昨天，我跟妹妹把獎狀包好，高高興興地給了爸爸。爸爸拿過獎狀，仔細地看著，笑得合不攏嘴，然後把我倆拉到他的懷裡，高興地說：「好孩子，你們最懂得爸爸的心，你們的優異成績就是給爸爸最好的禮物！」聽了爸爸的話我們也很開心，覺得爸爸是那麼的親切。後面的事就別提了！我和妹妹給爸爸包的餃子，因為放的時間太長了，全都粘到一起了，結果煮成了一鍋片兒湯。您猜爸爸怎麼說？「沒問題，等媽媽回來時，再請我一頓吧！」媽媽，您可千萬別忘了請爸爸吃生日飯，反正我們已經替您答應了。
祝您学习顺利！早日回家！	祝您學習順利！早日回家！
女儿 丽丽敬上 2009年8月6日	女兒 麗麗敬上 2009年8月6日

27. Why did Lili write the letter?

A) She did not know how to celebrate her father's birthday.

B) She and her sister gave their dad a wonderful birthday gift.

C) To tell her mother to come home early

D) To tell her mom that she got good grades this semester

28. What Lili and her younger sister gave to their father was

    A) school report cards

    B) their graduation photos

    C) gifts they bought

    D) an award for academic excellence

29. Lili asked her mom to take her father out to dinner because

    A) the meal Lili and her sister made was too simple

    B) her mom missed the birthday celebration

    C) Lili messed up the birthday meal

    D) Lili does not have her enough money

30. Why did Lili feel uncertain about what to do for her father's birthday?

    A) Her father is a picky person.

    B) Her father doesn't care for her academic performance.

    C) She does not have experience in organizing a party.

    D) She is unsure who will come to the celebration.

Read this note.

[Simplified Character Version]	[Traditional Character Version]
欣怡：	欣怡：

这个周末，远东师范大学毕业生要自发组织一个毕业生旧物大集，就是把用不着的书本及一些生活用品集中在一起，互换或廉价甩卖。其实这个学校每年毕业生要离开母校时都会有类似的集市，但今年规模最大。听说那些外地的学生很多东西带不回家，就卖得非常便宜。你要是有兴趣，咱们可以一起去，反正不远，骑车去就行。我手上有他们的广告，上面说"无论您是初中、高中、还是大学生，只要有一些闲置物品，希望通过这样一个平台以物换物或低价转让，都可报名参加此次大集。"怎么样，想不想去凑凑热闹？咱们可以连买带卖，一举两得。快点告诉我，我都等不及了，想去的话，我们得把要卖的东西找一找，我有些样子过时的衣服，还有一些旧电器可以拿去试试。等你的信！
 	
             玉娟
    6月28日下午4点半
	這個週末，遠東師範大學畢業生要自發組織一個畢業生舊物大集，就是把用不著的書本及一些生活用品集中在一起，互換或廉價甩賣。其實這個學校每年畢業生要離開母校時都會有類似的集市，但今年規模最大。聽說那些外地的學生很多東西帶不回家，就賣得非常便宜。你要是有興趣，咱們可以一起去，反正不遠，騎車去就行。我手上有他們的廣告，上面說「無論您是初中、高中、還是大學生，只要有一些閒置物品，希望通過這樣一個平台以物換物或低價轉讓，都可報名參加此次大集。」怎麼樣，想不想去湊湊熱鬧？咱們可以連買帶賣，一舉兩得。快點告訴我，我都等不及了，想去的話，我們得把要賣的東西找一找，我有些樣子過時的衣服，還有一些舊電器可以拿去試試。等你的信！
	
	             玉娟
	    6月28日下午4點半

31. Which of the following statements is TRUE?

    A) You can only sell the items on this market.

    B) This is not the first time a market like this has been organized.

    C) To register for the event, you must be a student at the university.

    D) The event is organized by a teachers' university.

32. Which of the following statements is FALSE?

    A) Yujuan has some out-of-fashion clothes to sell.

    B) Yujuan is planning to buy and sell things.

    C) Yujuan will drive to the event.

    D) Yujuan will bring her used electronics to the market.

Read this article.

[Simplified Character Version]

读书报告

    我最近读了一本由蔡颖卿写的关于家庭教育的书，书名叫《妈妈是最初的老师》。这是一本我所看到的最好的亲子教育书。书中讲述一个母亲在台湾、曼谷、新加坡三种不同的教育环境中教养两个女儿的感人故事。

    "孩子小的时候，帮他们扎根；孩子长大了，给他们翅膀。"这是身兼数职而永远以家为主的书中女主人公最喜欢的一句名言。二十年来，她努力在不断变动的环境里让家安定下来，在旅馆住时设法自己做饭，坚持让孩子每天都能跟家人共享晚餐，因为她认为幸福蕴藏在随手可得的日常生活里。妈妈对女儿的亲情和教养女儿的心路历程都真切地表述在书中："你们像是快乐的日历，每撕一页，既不舍随之而逝的喜怒哀乐，又期待即将到来的惊喜成长，妈妈珍惜儿女们的每一个脚印，仔细端详并深深爱怜。"

    我深深地被感动了，想到了自己的妈妈，妈妈的形象无比高大起来。的确，在我的心中，妈妈不仅仅是最初的老师，也是最好的老师，是世界上最亲最伟大的人。

[Traditional Character Version]

讀書報告

    我最近讀了一本由蔡穎卿寫的關於家庭教育的書，書名叫《媽媽是最初的老師》。這是一本我所看到的最好的親子教育書。書中講述一個母親在台灣、曼谷、新加坡三種不同的教育環境中教養兩個女兒的感人故事。

    「孩子小的時候，幫他們扎根；孩子長大了，給他們翅膀。」這是身兼數職而永遠以家為主的書中女主人公最喜歡的一句名言。二十年來，她努力在不斷變動的環境裡讓家安定下來，在旅館住時設法自己做飯，堅持讓孩子每天都能跟家人共享晚餐，因為她認為幸福蘊藏在隨手可得的日常生活裡。媽媽對女兒的親情和教養女兒的心路歷程都真切地表述在書中：「你們像是快樂的日曆，每撕一頁，既不捨隨之而逝的喜怒哀樂，又期待即將到來的驚喜成長，媽媽珍惜兒女們的每一個腳印，仔細端詳並深深愛憐。」

    我深深地被感動了，想到了自己的媽媽，媽媽的形象無比高大起來。的確，在我的心中，媽媽不僅僅是最初的老師，也是最好的老師，是世界上最親最偉大的人。

33. What did the woman do to strengthen the bond between her and her daughters?

    A) She gave them everything they asked for.

    B) She bought books for them.

    C) She cooked and had family dinners with them whenever they could.

    D) She encouraged her daughters to work part time.

34. The woman believes that a mother should

    A) make sure her children eat well

    B) force her children to have dinner with the family

    C) foster her children well when they are young

    D) accept that children grow up and move on eventually

35. What is the writer's attitude towards the issue discussed in the book?

    A) A mother should be highly regarded.

    B) All mothers are similar to the character in the book.

    C) She recalled her mom was a tall woman.

    D) Each mother has her own nurturing style.

SECTION II: Free Response

Part A: Writing (Story Narration and E-mail Response)

Writing Part Directions

You will be asked to perform two writing tasks in Chinese. In each case, you will be asked to write for a specific purpose and to a specific person. You should write in as complete and as culturally appropriate a manner as possible, taking into account the purpose and the person described. In this part of the exam, the student may NOT move back and forth among questions.

Story Narration (15%, 15 minutes)

The four pictures present a story. Imagine you are writing the story to a friend. Narrate a complete story as suggested by the pictures. Give your story a beginning, a middle, and an end.

E-Mail Response (10%, 15 minutes)

Read the e-mail from someone and then type a response inside the box below.

[Simplified Character Version]	[Traditional Character Version]
发件人：高健 邮件主题：关于女朋友	发件人：高健 邮件主题：關於女朋友
表哥： 　　你好！有件事想告诉你，但是请你暂时替我保密，我有女朋友了。她人长得漂亮，也很聪明，学习又好，我们很谈得来。我最近夜里常常睡不好觉，光想着她，白天上课老打瞌睡。老师总盯着我，我一睡觉，他就提问我，同学们也常开我玩笑。我还没敢告诉我父母，因为我知道他们肯定不会同意我在高中交女朋友。我现在心理很矛盾，既不想让我父母生气，又不想中断这个关系。您是过来人，在这方面有什么高招可以指教一下？盼速回信！	表哥： 　　你好！有件事想告訴你，但是請你暫時替我保密，我有女朋友了。她人長得漂亮，也很聰明，學習又好，我們很談得來。我最近夜裡常常睡不好覺，光想著她，白天上課老打瞌睡。老師總盯著我，我一睡覺，他就提問我，同學們也常開我玩笑。我還沒敢告訴我父母，因為我知道他們肯定不會同意我在高中交女朋友。我現在心理很矛盾，既不想讓我父母生氣，又不想中斷這個關係。您是過來人，在這方面有什麼高招可以指教一下？盼速回信！

Part B: Speaking (Conversation and Cultural Presentation)

Conversation (10%, 4 minutes)

Speaking Part Directions: Conversation

You will participate in a simulated conversation. Each time it is your turn to speak, you will have 20 seconds to record. You should respond as fully and as appropriately as possible. In this part of the exam, you may NOT move back and forth among questions.

You will have a conversation with Xiaoliang, a Chinese student you met for the first time at a summer program in China, about American schools.

Cultural Presentation (15%, 7 minutes)

Speaking Part Directions: Cultural Presentation

You will be asked to speak in Chinese on a specific topic. Imagine you are making an oral presentation to your Chinese class. First, you will read and hear the topic for your presentation. You will have 4 minutes to prepare your presentation. Then you will have 2 minutes to record your presentation. Your presentation should be as complete as possible.

AP 中文模拟试题集
CHINESE LANGUAGE AND CULTURE

Set 8

SECTION I: Multiple Choice

Part A: Listening (Rejoinders and Listening Selections)

Listening Part Directions

You will answer two types of questions: rejoinders and questions based on listening selections. For all tasks, you will have a specific amount of response time. In this part of the exam, you may NOT move back and forth among questions.

Listening Part Directions: Rejoinders (10%, 10 minutes)

You will hear several short conversations or parts of conversations followed by four choices, designated (A), (B), (C), and (D). Choose the one that continues or completes the conversation in a logical and culturally appropriate manner. You will have 5 seconds to answer each question.

1. (A)   (B)   (C)   (D)
2. (A)   (B)   (C)   (D)
3. (A)   (B)   (C)   (D)
4. (A)   (B)   (C)   (D)
5. (A)   (B)   (C)   (D)
6. (A)   (B)   (C)   (D)
7. (A)   (B)   (C)   (D)
8. (A)   (B)   (C)   (D)

9. (A)   (B)   (C)   (D)
10. (A)   (B)   (C)   (D)
11. (A)   (B)   (C)   (D)
12. (A)   (B)   (C)   (D)
13. (A)   (B)   (C)   (D)
14. (A)   (B)   (C)   (D)
15. (A)   (B)   (C)   (D)

Selection 1: Announcement (Selection plays one time.)

16. How long will the exhibit be on?

    A) One day

    B) Two days

    C) Three days

    D) Two weeks

17. Where will the exhibit be?

    A) In the museum

    B) In the auditorium

    C) In the library

    D) In a large classroom

18. Which of the following statements is TRUE?

    A) The teacher assigned the students topics to work on at the beginning of the semester.

    B) The projects that the students worked on were group projects.

    C) The students chose topics related to their own culture to work on.

    D) The students worked on the exhibit for two weeks.

19. Which of the following methods did the students not employ?

    A) Writing articles

    B) Designing the display board

    C) Interviewing people

    D) Creating a PowerPoint presentation

20. Which group of people can go to the exhibit tomorrow afternoon?

    A) Parents

    B) Ninth graders

    C) Tenth graders

    D) Twelve graders

Selection 2: Conversation (Selection plays one time.)

21. The girl was in a bad mood, because

    A) her parents may get a divorce

    B) her mother left home

    C) her father is drunk all the time

    D) her mother is angry at her

22. The boy's parents are

    A) divorced

    B) separated

    C) back together again

    D) undergoing a divorce

23. Which of the following statements is FALSE?

    A) The boy's mother is even nicer to him now than before.

    B) The boy's father is an alcoholic.

    C) The girl wishes that she were not dragged into her parents' dispute.

    D) The boy tries to give the girl some advice.

24. Which of the following statements is TRUE?

    A) The girl always maintains a neutral stance toward her parents' quarreling.

    B) The girl would like her parents to vent their frustration and anger to her rather than to each other.

    C) The girl thinks her parents' problems are all her fault.

    D) The girl believes that if she tries hard she may be able to help her parents solve their problems.

Selection 3: Instructions (Selection plays two times.)

25. The man asked his mother to take care of his fish because

    A) he will be traveling to Asia

    B) he will be doing research in Asia

    C) he will be going to Europe to attend a conference

    D) he will be on an exchange program to Europe

26. The fish requires to be fed

    A) on demand

    B) three or four times a day

    C) three or four pellets a day

    D) three or four pellets each time

27. The fish tank needs to be cleaned with

    A) hot water

    B) tab water of room temperature

    C) specially treated water

    D) distilled water

28. Which of the following statements is TRUE?

    A) The man thinks his fish is very happy.

    B) The man thinks his mother is very happy.

    C) The man thinks taking care of the fish is no trouble at all.

    D) The man wants the fish to keep his mother company.

Selection 4: Voice Message (Selection plays one time.)

29. What did the girl suspect?

    A) Her friend turned off the cell phone.

    B) Her friend was in the English class when she called.

    C) Her friend was talking on the cell phone when she called.

    D) Her friend's cell phone was misplaced.

30. Which of the following statements is TRUE?

    A) The girl and her friend have to work on an English project together.

    B) The girl's mother made a dental appointment for her at four o'clock today.

    C) The girl would like her friend to go to her house at five o'clock today.

    D) The girl's friend does not like Chinese food at all.

31. The girl needs to see the dentist because

    A) she woke up with a toothache this morning

    B) her routine check-up is due

    C) her braces were a little too tight

    D) her braces were a little too loose

Selection 5: Report (Selection plays one time.)

32. How many students were in charge of the survey?

    A) Two students

    B) Three students

    C) Two groups of three students each

    D) Three groups of two students each

33. What is the percentage of the students surveyed who make cell phone calls about 25 to 30 times a day?

    A) 75%

    B) 80%

    C) 18%

    D) 45%

34. According to the survey, which of the following statements is FALSE?

    A) Most of the students' phone calls last less than one minute.

    B) Cell phones are allowed on campus.

    C) Every student's cell phone can text message as well.

    D) Only 18% of the students send more than 100 text messages a day.

35. Which of the following statements is TRUE?

    A) The students feel guilty of text messaging in class.

    B) The students all have experience sending or receiving text messages in class.

    C) The students feel that as long as the teacher is unaware of what they are doing it's alright to text message in class.

    D) The students don't think that text messaging interferes with their concentration in class.

Part B: Reading Selections (25%, 60 minutes)

Reading Part Directions

In this part of the exam, you may move back and forth among all the questions. You will read several selections in Chinese. Each selection is accompanied by a number of questions in English. For each question, choose the response that is best according to the selection. You will have 60 minutes to answer all questions.

Read this e-mail.

[Simplified Character Version]	[Traditional Character Version]
发件人：曼如 收件人：思敏 邮件主题：学校餐厅 发件日期：2009年9月18日	發件人：曼如 收件人：思敏 郵件主題：學校餐廳 發件日期：2009年9月18日
告诉你一个天大的好消息，上个学期我不是告诉过你我们学校餐厅卖的东西难吃得要命吗？经过我们再三的抗议，甚至集体拒吃，学校这个学期终于换了餐厅的老板。这个新老板的理念非常新颖，懂得怎么经营。餐厅每天更换菜单，可供选择的菜式增加了不少，不像以前不是千篇一律的三明治，就是汉堡包和热狗等垃圾食物，真让人倒胃口。另外，餐厅的蔬菜、水果，以至鸡蛋、牛奶、肉类等等，无一不是新鲜的有机食品，而且美味可口。虽然价钱比以前稍微贵了一点，但是无论是从营养、健康或口味的角度来看，我们对新餐厅都十分满意。你们学校的餐厅没有我们的酷吧？光听我描述就馋得流口水了吧？你哪天有空，非得来尝尝不可。	告訴你一個天大的好消息，上個學期我不是告訴過你我們學校餐廳賣的東西難吃得要命嗎？經過我們再三的抗議，甚至集體拒吃，學校這個學期終於換了餐廳的老闆。這個新老闆的理念非常新穎，懂得怎麼經營。餐廳每天更換菜單，可供選擇的菜式增加了不少，不像以前不是千篇一律的三明治，就是漢堡包和熱狗等垃圾食物，真讓人倒胃口。另外，餐廳的蔬菜、水果，以至雞蛋、牛奶、肉類等等，無一不是新鮮的有機食品，而且美味可口。雖然價錢比以前稍微貴了一點，但是無論是從營養、健康或口味的角度來看，我們對新餐廳都十分滿意。你們學校的餐廳沒有我們的酷吧？光聽我描述就饞得流口水了吧？你哪天有空，非得來嘗嘗不可。

1. What made the school change the cafeteria management?

    A) The school realized that the food was not tasty at all.

    B) The students went through a series of protests against the previous management.

    C) The students advocated the benefits of serving organic food.

    D) The school felt the food was too expensive before.

2. What appeals to the students about the new cafeteria?

    A) It offers a lot of fast food.

    B) The decoration is new.

    C) It's cheaper than before.

    D) It offers more varied, fresher food.

3. The students' general attitude toward the new cafeteria is

    A) satisfied

    B) critical

    C) lukewarm

    D) happy, but with suggestions for further improvement

4. What does the speaker invite the email recipient to do?

    A) Come to talk to the manager about her recipes for the food she serves

    B) Go out to a restaurant to get a break from cafeteria food

    C) Come to try the food at the new cafeteria

    D) Join the efforts to improve nutrition at the cafeteria

Read this public sign.

[Simplified Character Version]	[Traditional Character Version]
珍惜粮食，远离浪费！	珍惜糧食，遠離浪費！

5. Where would this sign most likely appear?

    A) By a water fountain

    B) At a cafeteria

    C) Next to a light switch

    D) Next to a copy machine

6. Which of the following statements is TRUE?

    A) The purpose of this sign is to encourage people to think before they act.

    B) The purpose of this sign is to encourage people to save paper.

    C) The purpose of this sign is to encourage people not to be wasteful of food.

    D) The purpose of this sign is to instruct people not to eat too much.

Read this public sign.

[Simplified Character Version]	[Traditional Character Version]
请将塑料、铝罐等废弃物品 放置回收筒内	請將塑料、鋁罐等廢棄物品 放置回收筒內

7. What is the purpose of this sign?

    A) To discourage littering of bottles and cans

    B) To request that plastic and cans be placed in recycling bins

    C) To encourage recycling of electronic waste

    D) To request that plastic and cans be placed in green garbage bins

Read this note.

[Simplified Character Version]	[Traditional Character Version]
小南： 　　刚才旅行社的林小姐打电话来，说是代你办理签证发生了一些问题。首先是你的护照有效期不到三个月，你得赶紧去延期。其次是你缴交的照片格式不对，得补交一式两张的两寸脱帽正面照片。他们还说要是你没有时间亲自去办理护照延期，他们可以代办。不过，由于现在离你预定到中国的日期只有两个月了，时间非常紧迫，签证恐怕得加急，否则来不及，然而加急必须额外再付一百五十元。她要你尽速决定，并且通知他们你打算如何处理。 　　　　　　　　　　　东梅 　　　　　　　　　4月2日上午10点	小南： 　　剛才旅行社的林小姐打電話來，說是代你辦理簽證發生了一些問題。首先是你的護照有效期不到三個月，你得起緊去延期。其次是你繳交的照片格式不對，得補交一式兩張的兩寸脫帽正面照片。他們還說要是你沒有時間親自去辦理護照延期，他們可以代辦。不過，由於現在離你預定到中國的日期只有兩個月了，時間非常緊迫，簽證恐怕得加急，否則來不及，然而加急必須額外再付一百五十元。她要你儘速決定，並且通知他們你打算如何處理。 　　　　　　　　　　　束梅 　　　　　　　　　4月2日上午10點

8. What has Dongmei just done?

    A) Spoken with a Ms. Lin from the Chinese Consulate

    B) Spoken with a Ms. Lin from a travel agency

    C) Spoken with a Ms. Lin from the passport photo shop

    D) Spoken with a Ms. Lin from the airlines

9. What is the purpose of this note?

 A) To transmit information about documents needed for Xiaonan's upcoming trip to China

 B) To transmit information about preparations to receive a delegation from China

 C) To transmit questions about what types of items are appropriate to take to China

 D) To transmit information about how to apply for a passport

10. What is wrong with Xiaonan's current documents?

 A) He has submitted a good photograph, but not a proper passport.

 B) He has not submitted a passport or photos that reflect his current age.

 C) He has submitted both a passport and photos, but both have problems.

 D) He has submitted a passport and photos, but didn't include the extra ￥150 fee.

11. Why does Ms. Lin suggest paying an extra ￥150?

 A) To expedite processing his passport application so that he can receive it in time to apply for his visa

 B) To expedite the preparation of new photos in time to submit them for his new visa application

 C) To prepare new photos of the correct dimensions so that they can be submitted in time to process the visa

 D) To expedite processing his visa application so that he can receive it before his departure date

Read this advertisement.

[Simplified Character Version]	[Traditional Character Version]
二手豪华车廉售	二手豪華車廉售
德国银色宝马，内部浅灰色系，八成新，五门七座家庭用车，立体音响，原装冷气，自动排档，三万六千公里，要价二万五，急售，有议价空间。晚上六点前请电二手车经纪李麦克：86-10-2683-9111。	德國銀色寶馬，內部淺灰色系，八成新，五門七座家庭用車，立體音響，原裝冷氣，自動排檔，三萬六千公里，要價二萬五，急售，有議價空間。晚上六點前請電二手車經紀李麥克：86-10-2683-9111。

12. What kind of vehicle is advertised for sale?

   A) A car with seven speakers and a five-disk CD player

   B) A new car with five doors and seven seats

   C) A used car with odometer reading of 36,000 kilometers

   D) A used car with manual transmission

13. Is the seller anxious to sell?

   A) Yes, because the price of 25,000 is flexible.

   B) Yes, because parking spaces in his area have become limited.

   C) No, because he can only discuss it in the daytime, when most people are at work.

   D) No, because he has engaged the services of an agent.

14. From what country does this item originate?

   A) France

   B) Italy

   C) Germany

   D) None of the above

15. Who is Li Maike?

   A) A friend of the owner

   B) The owner of a used car dealership

   C) An agent at a used car dealership

   D) A salesman for a European car dealership

16. What color is the car?

   A) Silver interior, gray exterior

   B) Gray interior, silver exterior

   C) Maroon interior, brown exterior

   D) Brown interior, gray exterior

Read this letter.

亭亭表姐：

　　你好！我上个周末从中国回来了。由于时差的问题，前两天一直日夜颠倒，白天发睏，晚上精神抖擞，我妈说我的身体以及我的心都还留在中国呢。我特别感激你鼓励我报名参加这次"寻根之旅"的活动，短短的四周带给我的不止是欢乐和喜悦，也让我留下了美好难忘的回忆。我们除了学习汉语和中华文化常识、练习武术、参观名胜古迹之外，还实际动手学习中国民族工艺制作，如剪纸、中国结、泥塑、风筝等等，也有很多机会跟来自世界各地的华裔青少年及中国当地的青少年学生交流。我还学到了一句谚语："有缘千里来相会"，有一位书法家用毛笔给我写了这一句话。我把那幅字挂在书房里，非常醒目。你下次到我们家来时，就可以欣赏到他挥洒自如的笔意了。

　　请代我问候舅舅、舅妈好！祝你健康快乐！

表妹　威威上
2010年8月20日

亭亭表姐：

　　你好！我上個週末從中國回來了。由於時差的問題，前兩天一直日夜顛倒，白天發睏，晚上精神抖擞，我媽說我的身體以及我的心都還留在中國呢。我特別感激你鼓勵我報名參加這次「尋根之旅」的活動，短短的四週帶給我的不止是歡樂和喜悅，也讓我留下了美好難忘的回憶。我們除了學習漢語和中華文化常識、練習武術、參觀名勝古蹟之外，還實際動手學習中國民族工藝製作，如剪紙、中國結、泥塑、風筝等等，也有很多機會跟來自世界各地的華裔青少年及中國當地的青少年學生交流。我還學到了一句諺語：「有緣千里來相會」，有一位書法家用毛筆給我寫了這一句話。我把那幅字掛在書房裡，非常醒目。你下次到我們家來時，就可以欣賞到他揮灑自如的筆意了。

　　請代我問候舅舅、舅媽好！祝你健康快樂！

表妹　威威上
2010年8月20日

17. What is the relationship between the letter writer and her addressee?

A) Aunt and niece

B) Sisters

C) friends

D) Cousins

18. Why does Weiwei express gratitude to Tingting?

    A) Tingting has given her advice about where to go and what to do while in the program, "Travel in Search of Roots".

    B) Tingting encouraged her to join "Travel in Search of Roots", which she greatly enjoyed.

    C) Tingting introduced her to the head of "Travel in Search of Roots", who is a noted teacher of traditional arts and crafts.

    D) Tingting told her to join "Travel in Search of Roots", and paid all of her expenses.

19. What sorts of people did she meet while in China?

    A) Young overseas Chinese from many countries, as well as young people in China

    B) Students and faculty of the schools they visited while traveling in various places in China

    C) Diverse people of many backgrounds interested in Chinese culture and language

    D) Musicians, artists, dancers, and practitioners of traditional Chinese medicine

20. In the letter, Weiwei did not mention that she had lessons of

    A) clay sculpture making

    B) Chinese culture

    C) calligraphy

    D) martial arts

21. Why does Weiwei treasure the piece of calligraphy she received while in China?

    A) It is written in a script that is extremely difficult to write, and thus rare.

    B) It is beautiful in appearance and expresses a meaning that she appreciates.

    C) It was written by a famous calligrapher whom she enjoyed meeting and conversing with.

    D) She loves its meaning: "Even 1000 miles from home, we encounter people from our hometown".

Read this article.

[Simplified Character Version]	[Traditional Character Version]

[Simplified Character Version]

文学作品里的风筝

　　中国是风筝的故乡，秋天是放风筝最好的季节。中国自古以来即有许多与风筝有关的故事。清代的著名文学家李渔，写了一个剧本，叫《风筝误》，故事的发展就是由风筝断线引出一连串误会和巧合，情节高低起伏，引人入胜。中国著名的古典小说 《红楼梦》里面也有放风筝的情节。小说中的主角之一林黛玉从小体弱多病，放风筝时，故事里的人物先是把形形色色、制作精美的风筝放到空中，有美人的、凤凰的、大雁的、蝙蝠的、螃蟹的，五颜六色，在空中飘扬飞舞、争奇斗艳，等乐了一阵子以后，再把系风筝的线剪断，说是把晦气送走，也让林黛玉的病根随着断了线的风筝飘摇而去。

[Traditional Character Version]

文學作品裡的風箏

　　中國是風箏的故鄉，秋天是放風箏最好的季節。中國自古以來即有許多與風箏有關的故事。清代的著名文學家李漁，寫了一個劇本，叫《風箏誤》，故事的發展就是由風箏斷線引出一連串誤會和巧合，情節高低起伏，引人入勝。中國著名的古典小說《紅樓夢》裡面也有放風箏的情節。小說中的主角之一林黛玉從小體弱多病，放風箏時，故事裡的人物先是把形形色色、製作精美的風箏放到空中，有美人的、鳳凰的、大雁的、蝙蝠的、螃蟹的，五顏六色，在空中飄揚飛舞、爭奇鬥豔，等樂了一陣子以後，再把系風箏的線剪斷，說是把晦氣送走，也讓林黛玉的病根隨著斷了線的風箏飄搖而去。

22. What did Li Yu write about a kite?

    A) A play about a kite that could be flown and even ridden by young children

    B) A tale about a young girl who learned to fly kites even though she was physically weak

    C) A novel about a kite contest between several members of a large, extended family

    D) A play about a kite that breaks away and leads to all sorts of accidental meetings and coincidences

23. Which of the following kite designs are NOT included in the novel "*Honglou meng*"?

    A) Bats

    B) Frogs

    C) Wild geese

    D) Crabs

24. Why do the characters in "*Honglou meng*" cut the strings to the kites they have been flying?

    A) They are frustrated that their kites are not as beautiful as some of the others.

    B) The kites are all entangled in the air, and the only way to separate them is to cut the strings and let go.

    C) They hope that by letting the kite go, the sick girl's illnesses will fly away with it.

    D) They are so exhausted by the kite contest that they want to cut off the possibility of any further involvement.

Read this poster.

[Simplified Character Version]	[Traditional Character Version]
美化环境日	美化環境日
时间：4月25日上午9时至下午3时 地点：有下列三处，请依照个人兴趣选 　　　择参加 ◆　本校花圃 ◆　圆石海滩 ◆　市立公园 活动内容：种植花草，捡拾垃圾，以期 　　　　　美化环境。 注意事项： ◆　请简便着装 ◆　带防晒油及园艺用手套 ◆　自备午餐（学校供应开水及各 　　式冷饮） ◆　若家有小型园艺工具，亦请携带 人数不拘，多多益善。请自行准时前往， 襄盛举。到达时请向各活动负责老师报 到，实际参与时数可抵社区服务时数。	時間：4月25日上午9時至下午3時 地點：有下列三處，請依照個人興趣選 　　　擇參加 ◆　本校花圃 ◆　圓石海灘 ◆　市立公園 活動內容：種植花草，撿拾垃圾，以期 　　　　　美化環境。 注意事項： ◆　請簡便著裝 ◆　帶防曬油及園藝用手套 ◆　自備午餐（學校供應開水及各 　　式冷飲） ◆　若家有小型園藝工具，亦請攜帶 人數不拘，多多益善。請自行準時前往， 共襄盛舉。到達時請向各活動負責老師報 到，實際參與時數可抵社區服務時數。

25. What is the occasion for the above announcement on the poster?

    A) Mother Earth Day (traditionally celebrated in China at the end of April)

    B) A day for beautifying one's environment

    C) A day for enhancing one's own health and beauty by beautifying the physical environment

    D) Save the Earth Day

26. Which most accurately describes the intended audience for this advertisement?

    A) The students of a school or college

    B) The neighbors of a municipal park

    C) The residents of a resort town near the ocean

    D) Homeowners with their own small gardens

27. What should the participants bring?

    A) Light, informal clothing

    B) Gardening tools if available

    C) Gloves and sunscreen

    D) All of the above

28. Which is NOT one of the locations where the work will be performed?

    A) The school garden

    B) The school sports grounds

    C) A municipal park

    D) The Yuanshi Beach

29. What will the sponsors provide to the participants?

    A) Lunch

    B) Hot drinks

    C) Soda

    D) None of the above

30. What type of transportation is advised for the participants to take to go to the three locations?

    A) Buses

    B) Bicycles

    C) Cars

    D) Not specified

Read this story.

[Simplified Character Version]	[Traditional Character Version]
孔融是东汉末年（西元二世纪）一个很博学的人，是孔子的二十世孙。他从小就很聪明，特别擅长辞令。十岁时，孔融随他父亲到了都城洛阳。当时当地的行政长官李元礼由于颇负盛名，日常拜访他的人络绎不绝，不是亲戚，就是当时享有才名的人，如果来访的人是无名之辈，守门的人照例不通报。孔融很想见见这位大学者。 　　一天，他走到李元礼的官府门前，对守门人说："我是李先生的亲戚，请给我通报。"李元礼接见了孔融，非常好奇地问他："你和我有什么亲戚关系呢？"孔融回答道："我是孔子的后代，老子李聃是你的祖先。孔子曾经向老子请教过关于礼节的问题，他们是师生关系，所以我和你说来也是世交。" 　　当时有很多宾客在座，大家都对年仅十岁的孔融的这番话感到惊奇。这时有一个叫陈韪的人来拜访李元礼，在座的宾客就将孔融刚才的言语表现告诉他。谁知陈韪深深不以为然，随口就说道："小时了了，大未必佳。"意思是说小时候纵然很聪明，长大了未必能够成材。聪明的孔融立即反驳道："我想陈先生小的时候，一定是很聪明的。"也就是暗说陈韪是个庸才。陈韪被孔融一句话难住了，半天说不出话来。	孔融是東漢末年（西元二世紀）一個很博學的人，是孔子的二十世孫。他從小就很聰明，特別擅長辭令。十歲時，孔融隨他父親到了都城洛陽。當時當地的行政長官李元禮由於頗負盛名，日常拜訪他的人絡繹不絕，不是親戚，就是當時享有才名的人，如果來訪的人是無名之輩，守門的人照例不通報。孔融很想見見這位大學者。 　　一天，他走到李元禮的官府門前，對守門人說：「我是李先生的親戚，請給我通報。」李元禮接見了孔融，非常好奇地問他：「你和我有什麼親戚關係呢？」孔融回答道：「我是孔子的後代，老子李聃是你的祖先。孔子曾經向老子請教過關於禮節的問題，他們是師生關係，所以我和你說來也是世交。」 　　當時有很多賓客在座，大家都對年僅十歲的孔融的這番話感到驚奇。這時有一個叫陳韙的人來拜訪李元禮，在座的賓客就將孔融剛才的言語表現告訴他。誰知陳韙深深不以為然，隨口就說道：「小時了了，大未必佳。」意思是說小時候縱然很聰明，長大了未必能夠成材。聰明的孔融立即反駁道：「我想陳先生小的時候，一定是很聰明的。」也就是暗說陳韙是個庸才。陳韙被孔融一句話難住了，半天說不出話來。

31. What was Kong Rong famous for?

    A) Erudition and wit

    B) As a 30th generation descendant of Confucius

    C) Filial obedience to his father

    D) None of the above

32. What did Kong Rong say to the gatekeeper to gain admittance to Li Yuanli's house?

    A) He pretended to be the descendant of Confucius.

    B) He pretended to be the son of Li's student.

    C) He pretended to be the son of an important official in the government of the time.

    D) He pretended to be a relative of Li's.

33. To what sorts of people did Li Yuanli limit his friendships?

    A) People who were famous for their talent or intelligence

    B) People who came from rich, well-established families

    C) People with whom he could discuss important matters of state

    D) People who were skilled in politics and governmental affairs

34. What is the capital of the Eastern Han Dynasty?

    A) Xi'an

    B) Luoyang

    C) Beijing

    D) Nanjing

35. Why does Chen Wei become embarrassed by Kong Rong's retort?

    A) Kong implies that Chen had gained admittance to Li's house for the wrong reasons.

    B) Kong implies that Chen is not particularly smart or talented.

    C) Kong implies that Chen has grown too old to be useful to Li.

    D) Kong implies that Chen no longer respects Li in his old age.

SECTION II: Free Response

Part A: Writing (Story Narration and E-mail Response)

Writing Part Directions

You will be asked to perform two writing tasks in Chinese. In each case, you will be asked to write for a specific purpose and to a specific person. You should write in as complete and as culturally appropriate a manner as possible, taking into account the purpose and the person described. In this part of the exam, the student may NOT move back and forth among questions.

Story Narration (15%, 15 minutes)

The four pictures present a story. Imagine you are writing the story to a friend. Narrate a complete story as suggested by the pictures. Give your story a beginning, a middle, and an end.

E-Mail Response (10%, 15 minutes)

Read this e-mail from a friend and then type a response.

[Simplified Character Version]	[Traditional Character Version]
发件人：谢明 邮件主题：暑期活动	發件人：謝明 郵件主題：暑期活動
今年暑假我有两个学习的机会，一个是到一个夏令营去打工当辅导员，有六个星期，另一个是到我家附近的大学去上两门跟电脑有关的课程，要上两个月的课。我没法儿同时做两项活动，你觉得我应该选哪项活动比较好？请你给我一些具体的建议。 谢谢！	今年暑假我有兩個學習的機會，一個是到一個夏令營去打工當輔導員，有六個星期，另一個是到我家附近的大學去上兩門跟電腦有關的課程，要上兩個月的課。我沒法兒同時做兩項活動，你覺得我應該選哪項活動比較好？請你給我一些具體的建議。 謝謝！

Part B: Speaking (Conversation and Cultural Presentation)

Conversation (10%, 4 minutes)

Speaking Part Directions: Conversation

You will participate in a simulated conversation. Each time it is your turn to speak, you will have 20 seconds to record. You should respond as fully and as appropriately as possible. In this part of the exam, you may NOT move back and forth among questions.

You will have a conversation with Jiang Ning, a passenger sitting next to you on the bus, about your experience in learning Chinese.

Cultural Presentation (15%, 7 minutes)

Speaking Part Directions: Cultural Presentation

You will be asked to speak in Chinese on a specific topic. Imagine you are making an oral presentation to your Chinese class. First, you will read and hear the topic for your presentation. You will have 4 minutes to prepare your presentation. Then you will have 2 minutes to record your presentation. You presentation should be as complete as possible.

ANSWER KEYS
试题答案

TEST SET 1   TEST SET 2

A: Listening	B: Reading	Part A: Listening	Part B: Reading
1. B	1. D	1. B	1. B
2. C	2. B	2. B	2. C
3. A	3. A	3. A	3. B
4. D	4. B	4. C	4. B
5. C	5. B	5. D	5. D
6. D	6. A	6. A	6. A
7. A	7. A	7. C	7. B
8. B	8. B	8. D	8. C
9. C	9. B	9. B	9. A
10. B	10. A	10. A	10. B
11. C	11. A	11. C	11. B
12. D	12. B	12. A	12. A
13. B	13. C	13. D	13. A
14. C	14. A	14. A	14. C
15. B	15. C	15. C	15. C
16. D	16. B	16. B	16. C
17. D	17. B	17. C	17. C
18. A	18. D	18. B	18. A
19. A	19. B	19. A	19. D
20. B	20. A	20. B	20. C
21. C	21. B	21. C	21. B
22. C	22. A	22. C	22. D
23. C	23. C	23. D	23. A
24. B	24. C	24. B	24. B
25. C	25. C	25. D	25. D
26. A	26. B	26. D	26. A
27. B	27. C	27. B	27. B
28. C	28. B	28. D	28. B
29. B	29. D	29. C	29. A
30. D	30. B	30. B	30. A
31. B	31. A	31. D	31. C
32. B	32. B	32. C	32. D
33. A	33. C	33. C	33. B
34. B	34. C	34. A	34. A
35. B	35. C	35. B	35. D

TEST SET 3

TEST SET 4

A: Listening		B: Reading		Part A: Listening		Part B: Reading	
1.	A	1.	D	1.	C	1.	C
2.	C	2.	C	2.	A	2.	D
3.	D	3.	C	3.	B	3.	B
4.	B	4.	A	4.	A	4.	C
5.	B	5.	D	5.	D	5.	A
6.	A	6.	A	6.	D	6.	C
7.	C	7.	D	7.	A	7.	A
8.	D	8.	C	8.	C	8.	C
9.	A	9.	D	9.	C	9.	B
10.	B	10.	A	10.	B	10.	B
11.	C	11.	C	11.	A	11.	B
12.	A	12.	D	12.	C	12.	B
13.	B	13.	B	13.	C	13.	A
14.	C	14.	D	14.	B	14.	D
15.	B	15.	A	15.	D	15.	C
16.	C	16.	B	16.	C	16.	B
17.	C	17.	A	17.	D	17.	C
18.	C	18.	C	18.	B	18.	D
19.	D	19.	D	19.	A	19.	A
20.	B	20.	B	20.	B	20.	B
21.	C	21.	B	21.	A	21.	C
22.	D	22.	C	22.	D	22.	B
23.	C	23.	C	23.	A	23.	A
24.	D	24.	A	24.	C	24.	C
25.	D	25.	D	25.	B	25.	C
26.	B	26.	C	26.	B	26.	C
27.	B	27.	B	27.	D	27.	D
28.	D	28.	C	28.	C	28.	C
29.	B	29.	B	29.	B	29.	A
30.	D	30.	C	30.	C	30.	D
31.	C	31.	B	31.	D	31.	D
32.	B	32.	A	32.	B	32.	B
33.	D	33.	A	33.	A	33.	A
34.	B	34.	D	34.	C	34.	C
35.	C	35.	A	35.	A	35.	B

	TEST SET 5			TEST SET 6	

A: Listening	B: Reading	Part A: Listening	Part B: Reading
1. C	1. C	1. A	1. C
2. B	2. D	2. C	2. D
3. D	3. C	3. C	3. B
4. B	4. D	4. D	4. B
5. A	5. D	5. C	5. A
6. D	6. A	6. B	6. C
7. A	7. D	7. C	7. D
8. C	8. D	8. D	8. B
9. C	9. A	9. A	9. A
10. C	10. B	10. D	10. C
11. C	11. D	11. C	11. A
12. A	12. B	12. C	12. C
13. A	13. B	13. A	13. D
14. C	14. A	14. C	14. C
15. C	15. B	15. B	15. B
16. C	16. B	16. C	16. B
17. A	17. A	17. B	17. A
18. C	18. B	18. B	18. D
19. C	19. A	19. B	19. B
20. B	20. C	20. D	20. A
21. C	21. D	21. B	21. D
22. B	22. B	22. C	22. B
23. C	23. C	23. A	23. C
24. A	24. B	24. B	24. B
25. D	25. C	25. D	25. B
26. B	26. B	26. A	26. A
27. D	27. C	27. C	27. C
28. B	28. D	28. A	28. D
29. A	29. C	29. B	29. C
30. C	30. B	30. C	30. A
31. D	31. D	31. C	31. C
32. B	32. A	32. B	32. B
33. C	33. B	33. C	33. D
34. C	34. A	34. B	34. B
35. A	35. C	35. D	35. A

TEST SET 7

A: Listening

1. D
2. A
3. C
4. B
5. C
6. B
7. B
8. B
9. C
10. D
11. B
12. A
13. B
14. D
15. B
16. B
17. B
18. A
19. A
20. C
21. C
22. B
23. D
24. B
25. D
26. B
27. C
28. D
29. C
30. A
31. B
32. B
33. A
34. D
35. B

B: Reading

1. A
2. D
3. C
4. B
5. A
6. B
7. D
8. D
9. A
10. D
11. D
12. C
13. C
14. D
15. B
16. D
17. A
18. C
19. B
20. D
21. B
22. A
23. C
24. B
25. C
26. B
27. B
28. D
29. C
30. C
31. B
32. C
33. C
34. C
35. A

TEST SET 8

Part A: Listening

1. A
2. B
3. D
4. B
5. C
6. C
7. A
8. B
9. D
10. C
11. B
12. C
13. A
14. C
15. B
16. C
17. B
18. C
19. D
20. B
21. A
22. C
23. B
24. B
25. C
26. D
27. A
28. A
29. A
30. B
31. D
32. B
33. A
34. B
35. C

Part B: Reading

1. B
2. D
3. A
4. C
5. B
6. C
7. B
8. B
9. A
10. C
11. D
12. C
13. A
14. C
15. C
16. B
17. D
18. B
19. A
20. C
21. B
22. D
23. B
24. C
25. B
26. A
27. D
28. B
29. C
30. D
31. A
32. D
33. A
34. B
35. B

Recording Scripts for Test 1

Section I: Part A: Listening

Rejoinders

Directions: You will hear several short conversations or parts of conversations followed by four choices, designated (A), (B), (C), and (D). Choose the one that continues or completes the conversation in a logical and culturally appropriate manner. You will have 5 seconds to answer each question.

(Traditional Characters)

1. 男：你收到大學錄取通知書了嗎？
   女：A）我還沒決定去哪個大學。
       B）還沒有, 都快把我急死了。
       C）大學會把通知書寄給每個學生。
       D）我從來沒去過那個大學。

   （學生答題5 秒）

2. 男：蘭蘭, 你的臉色看起來不太好。
   女：A）我這個人不喜歡化妝。
       B）我小時候比現在好看。
       C）今天我覺得不太舒服。
       D）你覺得我不漂亮嗎?

   （學生答題5 秒）

(Simplified Characters)

1. 男：你收到大学录取通知书了吗？
   女：A）我还没决定去哪个大学。
       B）还没有, 都快把我急死了。
       C）大学会把通知书寄给每个学生。
       D）我从来没去过那个大学。

   （学生答题5 秒）

2. 男：兰兰, 你的脸色看起来不太好。
   女：A）我这个人不喜欢化妆。
       B）我小时候比现在好看。
       C）今天我觉得不太舒服。
       D）你觉得我不漂亮吗?

   （学生答题5 秒）

3. 男：小姐，買單！
　　女：A）好，請稍等！
　　　　B）歡迎光臨！
　　　　C）不用客氣！
　　　　D）請慢走！

　　（學生答題5 秒）

4. 男：今年暑假你有什麼打算？
　　女：A）暑假我可能會很忙。
　　　　B）暑假時的天氣太熱了。
　　　　C）去年暑假我什麼都沒做。
　　　　D）我還沒決定做什麼呢。

　　（學生答題5 秒）

5. 女：你居然能弄到北京奧運會的門票，
　　　　真不簡單！
　　男：A）我這個人運氣是不怎麼樣。
　　　　B）我也覺得北京人很幸運。
　　　　C）能買到一張奧運會的票的確不容易。
　　　　D）奧運會能在北京舉行是中國人的驕傲。

　　（學生答題5 秒）

6. 男：昨天的歷史考試考得怎麼樣？
　　女：A）我很討厭歷史考試。
　　　　B）歷史是我最喜歡的
　　　　C）考得不好也沒什麼。
　　　　D）我覺得考得很一般。

　　（學生答題5 秒）

3. 男：小姐，买单！
　　女：A）好，请稍等.
　　　　B）欢迎光临！
　　　　C）不用客气！
　　　　D）请慢走！

　　（学生答题5 秒）

4. 男：今年暑假你有什么打算？
　　女：A）暑假我可能会很忙。
　　　　B）暑假时的天气太热了。
　　　　C）去年暑假我什么都没做。
　　　　D）我还没决定做什么呢。

　　（学生答题5 秒）

5. 女：你居然能弄到北京奥运会的门票，
　　　　真不简单！
　　男：A）我这个人运气是不怎么样。
　　　　B）我也觉得北京人很幸运。
　　　　C）能搞到一张奥运会的票的确很不容易。
　　　　D）奥运会能在北京举行是中国人的骄傲。

　　（学生答题5 秒）

6. 男：昨天的历史考试考得怎么样？
　　女：A）我很讨厌历史考试。
　　　　B）历史是我最喜欢的学科。
　　　　C）考得不好也没什么。
　　　　D）我觉得考得很一般。

　　（学生答题5 秒）

170

7. 女：我明明聞到你身上有煙味，你卻說你沒
抽煙。

　男：A）別小題大做了！

　　　B）明明根本不會抽煙！

　　　C）抽煙不是好習慣。

　　　D）你該戒煙了，抽煙對身體不好。

（學生答題5 秒）

8. 女：你平常都喜歡做些什麼運動？

　男：A）運動對人的健康有好處。

　　　B）凡是球類運動我都喜歡。

　　　C）我常常去運動。

　　　D）我從小就喜歡運動。

（學生答題5 秒）

9. 男：聽說你這幾天心情不好，怎麼啦？

　女：A）我這幾天很忙。

　　　B）這幾天天氣真糟糕！

　　　C）家裡出了點事兒。

　　　D）我好幾天都沒事做了。

（學生答題5 秒）

10. 女：你喜歡中國的北方菜還是南方菜？

　男：A）我從來沒去過南方。

　　　B）怎麼說呢？其實南北各有千秋。

　　　C）北方菜的種類沒有南方的多。

　　　D）北京菜有點鹹。

（學生答題5 秒）

7. 女：我明明闻到你身上有烟味，你却说你没
抽烟。

　男：A）别小题大做了！

　　　B）明明根本不会抽烟！

　　　C）抽烟不是好习惯。

　　　D）你该戒烟了，抽烟对身体不好。

（学生答题5 秒）

8. 女：你平常都喜欢做些什么运动？

　男：A）运动对人的健康有好处。

　　　B）凡是球类运动我都喜欢。

　　　C）我常常去运动。

　　　D）我从小就喜欢运动。

（学生答题5 秒）

9. 男：听说你这几天心情不好，怎么啦？

　女：A）我这几天很忙。

　　　B）这几天天气真糟糕！

　　　C）家里出了点事儿。

　　　D）我好几天都没事做了。

（学生答题5 秒）

10. 女：你喜欢中国的北方菜还是南方菜？

　男：A）我从来没去过南方。

　　　B）怎么说呢？其实南北各有千秋。

　　　C）北方菜的种类没有南方的多。

　　　D）北京菜有点咸。

（学生答题5 秒）

11. 男：你還在那家餐館打工嗎？

　　女：學校功課太多，所以我早就不做了。

　　男：A）餐館的工作的確很有意思。

　　　　B）我看你還是先把功課做完再去
　　　　　打工吧！

　　　　C）那麼高的工資，辭掉太可惜了。

　　　　D）那你現在在哪家餐館工作呢？

　　（學生答題5 秒）

12. 女：聽說這位歌手現在在中國很紅。

　　男：我怎麼不知道？

　　女：A）你不知道他是中國人嗎？

　　　　B）中國人很喜歡紅色。

　　　　C）你真的沒聽過中國歌曲嗎？

　　　　D）你大概不常聽音樂吧？

　　（學生答題5 秒）

13. 男：前面車堵得這麼厲害，怎麼辦呢？

　　女：真急死人了！說不定我趕不上飛機了。

　　男：A）沒關係，反正我們的車開得挺慢的。

　　　　B）我看我們還是換條道走吧。

　　　　C）我們應該給老師打個電話。

　　　　D）你幾點上班？

　　（學生答題5 秒）

14. 女：最近很少見到你，忙什麼呢？

　　男：期末考試快到了，每天都在開夜車。

　　女：A）晚上開車不安全，要小心。

　　　　B）我父母從不讓我夜裡開車。

　　　　C）還是要多休息，睡眠不足也會影
　　　　　響考試的。

　　　　D）考試怎麼會安排在晚上呢？

　　（學生答題5 秒）

11. 男：你还在那家餐馆打工吗？

　　女：学校功课太多，所以我早就不做了。

　　男：A）餐馆的工作的确很有意思。

　　　　B）我看你还是先把功课做完再去
　　　　　打工吧！

　　　　C）那么高的工资，辞掉太可惜了。

　　　　D）那你现在在哪家餐馆工作呢？

　　（学生答题5 秒）

12. 女：听说这位歌手现在在中国很红。

　　男：我怎么不知道？

　　女：A）你不知道他是中国人吗？

　　　　B）中国人很喜欢红色。

　　　　C）你真的没听过中国歌曲吗？

　　　　D）你大概不常听音乐吧？

　　（学生答题5 秒）

13. 男：前面车堵得这么厉害，怎么办呢？

　　女：真急死人了！说不定我赶不上飞机了。

　　男：A）没关系，反正我们的车开得挺慢的。

　　　　B）我看我们还是换条道走吧。

　　　　C）我们应该给老师打个电话。

　　　　D）你几点上班？

　　（学生答题5 秒）

14. 女：最近很少见到你，忙什么呢？

　　男：期末考试快到了，每天都在开夜车。

　　女：A）晚上开车不安全，要小心。

　　　　B）我父母从不让我夜里开车。

　　　　C）还是要多休息，睡眠不足也会影
　　　　　响考试的。

　　　　D）考试怎么会安排在晚上呢？

　　（学生答题5 秒）

15. 女：嗨，聽說新出的蘋果牌手機樣子特
　　　酷，功能也多，你這個舊的該淘汰
　　　了吧？

　　男：算了吧，舊的也一樣用，我還是把
　　　我父母的錢省著點兒吧。

　　女：A）你父母不喜歡蘋果牌的產品嗎？

　　　　B）你可以自己打工賺錢買呀。

　　　　C）大部分父母過日子都很省。

　　　　D）我也不太喜歡吃蘋果，太酸了。

（學生答題5 秒）

15. 女：嗨，听说新出的苹果牌手机样子特
　　　酷，功能也多，你这个旧的该淘汰
　　　了吧？

　　男：算了吧，旧的也一样用，我还是把
　　　我父母的钱省着点儿吧。

　　女：A）你父母不喜欢苹果牌的产品吗？

　　　　B）你可以自己打工赚钱买呀。

　　　　C）大部分父母过日子都很省。

　　　　D）我也不太喜欢吃苹果，太酸了。

（学生答题5 秒）

Listening Selections (15%, 10 minutes)

Directions: You will listen to several selections in Chinese. For each selection, you will be told whether it will be played once or twice. You may take notes as you listen. Your notes will not be graded. After listening to each selection, you will see questions in English. For each question, choose the response that is best according to the selection. You will have 12 seconds to answer each question.

Selection 1: Announcement

Selection plays one time.

Narrator: Now you will listen once to a public announcement.

Woman:

(Traditional Characters)

同學們請注意：

為了支援災區，學校現在正在組織一項捐衣服
獻愛心的活動。請同學們回家找一找，把家裡
人穿不著的衣服帶來交給學校。從本周開始，
每天第四節課會有同學到各教室去收集衣服，
同學們也可以自己把帶來的衣服直接放到學校
辦公室外面的箱子裡。尺寸大小不限，越多越
好，請同學們踴躍捐助。學校會在月底前把收
集到的衣服交到有關單位。謝謝大家的支持！

(Simplified Characters)

同学们请注意：

为了支援灾区，学校现在正在组织一项捐衣服
献爱心的活动。请同学们回家找一找，把家里
人穿不着的衣服带来交给学校。从本周开始，
每天第四节课会有同学到各教室去收集衣服，
同学们也可以自己把带来的衣服直接放到学校
办公室外面的箱子里。尺寸大小不限，越多越
好。请同学们踊跃捐助。学校会在月底前把收
集到的衣服交到有关单位。谢谢大家的支持！

Narrator: Now answer the questions for this selection.

(12 seconds)

(12 seconds)

(12 seconds)

(12 seconds)

Selection 2: Conversation

Selection plays one time.

Narrator: Now you will listen once to a conversation between two students.

(Traditional Characters)

男：這個星期六的晚上在學校禮堂有個舞會，
你想去嗎？

女：我對這樣的活動從來不感興趣。

男：得了吧，上次舞會你不是也去了嗎？

女：嗨，我只是湊熱鬧去了，根本沒跳舞。

男：這次舞會跟以往的不同，我保證你玩
得開心。

女：你還是找別人去吧，我實在是不想去。

男：算了算了，你這個人真不給面子。

(Simplified Characters)

男：这个星期六的晚上在学校礼堂有个舞会，
你想去吗？

女：我对这样的活动从来不感兴趣。

男：得了吧，上次舞会你不是也去了吗？

女：嗨，我只是凑热闹去了，根本没跳舞。

男：这次舞会跟以往的不同，我保证你玩
得开心。

女：你还是找别人去吧，我实在是不想去。

男：算了算了，你这个人真不给面子。

Narrator: Now answer the questions for this selection.

(12 seconds)

(12 seconds)

(12 seconds)

Selection 3: Voice message

Selection plays two times.

Narrator: Now you will listen twice to a voice message.

Man:

<table>
<tr><th>(Traditional Characters)</th><th>(Simplified Characters)</th></tr>
<tr><td>叔叔，你好！我是小明。我已經到家了。飛機早上十點半準時到達舊金山機場，我爸爸去機場接的我。謝謝您在北京招待了我那麼多天，我吃得很過癮，玩得也很開心！明年有機會我還想去北京看您。今天是學校春假的最後一天，明天我就得上學了。希望今天晚上能把時差倒過來，否則明天上課就慘了。好，有時間我再跟您聯繫。再見！</td><td>叔叔，你好！我是小明。我已经到家了。飞机早上十点半准时到达旧金山机场，我爸爸去机场接的我。谢谢您在北京招待了我那么多天，我吃得很过瘾，玩得也很开心！明年有机会我还想去北京看您。今天是学校春假的最后一天，明天我就得上学了。希望今天晚上能把时差倒过来，否则明天上课就惨了。好，有时间我再跟您联系。再见！</td></tr>
</table>

Narrator: Now listen again.

Narrator: Now answer the questions for this selection.

(12 seconds)

(12 seconds)

(12 seconds)

(12 seconds)

Selection 4: Instructions

Selection plays two times.

Narrator: Now you will listen twice to an instruction.

Man:

(Traditional Characters)

這種手機可以用來發送和接收短信，但收信人的手機必須具有同樣的功能。短信可以同時發給幾個人，收信人收到短信后可以隨時閱讀並回復。收發短信是否付費，取決於使用者所選擇的電話服務計劃。發送短信的方法很簡單：先按手機上的「短信」鍵鈕，然後輸入對方的電話號碼或姓名，再輸入您要發的信息，然後輕按「發送」鍵鈕即可。

(Simplified Characters)

这种手机可以用来发送和接收短信，但收信人的手机必须具有同样的功能。短信可以同时发给几个人，收信人收到短信后可以随时阅读并回复。收发短信是否付费，取决于使用者所选择的电话服务计划。发送短信的方法很简单：先按手机上的"短信"键钮，然后输入对方的电话号码或姓名，再输入您要发的信息，然后轻按"发送"键钮即可。

Narrator: Now listen again.

Narrator: Now answer the questions for this selection.

(12 seconds)

(12 seconds)

(12 seconds)

(12 seconds)

(12 seconds)

Selection 5: Report

Selection plays two times.

Narrator: Now you will listen twice to a report.

Woman:

(Traditional Characters)	(Simplified Characters)
下面是今明兩天我市的天氣情況。今天白天到夜間將會有中雨，部份地區會有大雨到暴雨。受冷空氣的影響，今晚大部分地區的氣溫可降至攝氏10度，明天白天氣溫會回升到攝氏22度。望大家做好防雨準備，出門請攜帶雨傘，並注意交通安全。未來幾天天氣可望轉晴，氣溫也會隨之變暖。	下面是今明两天我市的天气情况。今天白天到夜间将会有中雨，部份地区会有大雨到暴雨。受冷空气的影响，今晚大部分地区的气温可降至摄氏10度，明天白天气温会回升到摄氏22度。望大家做好防雨准备，出门请携带雨伞，并注意交通安全。未来几天天气可望转晴，气温也会随之变暖。

Narrator: Now listen again.

Narrator: Now answer the questions for this selection.

(12 seconds)

(12 seconds)

(12 seconds)

(12 seconds)

Section II: Part B: Speaking

Recording Scripts

Conversation

Directions: You will participate in a simulated conversation. Each time it is your turn to speak, you will have 20 seconds to record. You should respond as fully and as appropriately as possible.

You will have a conversation with Xiao Fan, your classmate, about your plan of SAT study during the summer vacation.

(Traditional Characters)

小凡： 聽說你準備參加一個暑假SAT補習班，
是真的嗎？
（學生答題20 秒）

小凡： 你各科成績都夠好的啦，為什麼還要去
補習呢？
（學生答題20 秒）

小凡： 我覺得只要買幾套教材，自己多做題就
可以了，沒有必要去上課。你是怎麼想
的啊？
（學生答題20 秒）

小凡： 有很多SAT補習班，你為什麼選擇那一
所離家遠的呢？
（學生答題20 秒）

小凡： 學費是多少？比其它SAT班的學費貴還
是便宜？
（學生答題20 秒）

小凡： 叫你這麼一說，我也動心了。他們有沒
有免費的講座？如果我想報名的話，都
需要做些什麼？
（學生答題20 秒）

(Simplified Characters)

小凡： 听说你准备参加一个暑假SAT补习班，
是真的吗？
（学生答题20 秒）

小凡： 你各科成绩都够好的啦，为什么还要去
补习呢？
（学生答题20 秒）

小凡： 我觉得只要买几套教材，自己多做题就
可以了，没有必要去上课。你是怎么想
的啊？
（学生答题20 秒）

小凡： 有很多SAT补习班，你为什么选择那一
所离家远的呢？
（学生答题20 秒）

小凡： 学费是多少？比其它SAT班的学费贵还
是便宜？
（学生答题20 秒）

小凡： 叫你这么一说，我也动心了。他们有没
有免费的讲座？如果我想报名的话，都
需要做些什么？
（学生答题20 秒）

Cultural Presentation

Directions: You will be asked to speak in Chinese on a specific topic. Imagine you are making an oral presentation to your Chinese class. First, you will read and hear the topic for your presentation. You will have 4 minutes to prepare your presentation. Then you will have 2 minutes to record your presentation. Your presentation should be as complete as possible.

Name a Chinese movie that has left a lasting impression on you. What aspects of Chinese culture did it present? Why did you find this movie memorable?

Recording Scripts for Test 2

Section I: Part A: Listening

Rejoinders

Directions: You will hear several short conversations or parts of conversations followed by four choices, designated (A), (B), (C), and (D). Choose the one that continues or completes the conversation in a logical and culturally appropriate manner. You will have 5 seconds to answer each question.

(Traditional Characters)

1. 女：你對這個城市熟悉嗎？
   男：A）這個城市很漂亮。
   B）我是在這兒出生、長大的。你說呢？
   C）這兒的公共汽車和地鐵都方便得很。
   D）我想在這兒住一年。

   （學生答題5 秒）

2. 女：你一直咳嗽，先喝點兒水再說吧。
   男：A）我對什麼都不過敏。
   B）哦，謝謝，我自己來。
   C）我媽媽昨天帶我去看大夫了。
   D）水和空氣對身體都很重要。

   （學生答題5 秒）

(Simplified Characters)

1. 女：你对这个城市熟悉吗？
   男：A）这个城市很漂亮。
   B）我是在这儿出生、长大的。你说呢？
   C）这儿的公共汽车和地铁都方便得很。
   D）我想在这儿住一年。

   （学生答题5 秒）

2. 女：你一直咳嗽，先喝点儿水再说吧。
   男：A）我对什么都不过敏。
   B）哦，谢谢，我自己来。
   C）我妈妈昨天带我去看大夫了。
   D）水和空气对身体都很重要。

   （学生答题5 秒）

3. 男：這條裙子漂亮是漂亮，可是太貴了。
　　　買那條便宜點兒的吧。

　　女：A）難道你買衣服就看價錢嗎？

　　　　B）我昨天也買了一條裙子。

　　　　C）這家商店從來不打折。

　　　　D）不，我覺得衣服的式樣沒有價錢
　　　　　　那麼重要。

　　（學生答題5 秒）

4. 男：你們這兒刷卡嗎？

　　女：A）我們這兒不賣生日卡。

　　　　B）刷卡非常方便。

　　　　C）對不起，我們只收現金，不收信用
　　　　　　卡。

　　　　D）我們什麼都有，您買什麼？

　　（學生答題5 秒）

5. 女：怎麼？有了女朋友就把老朋友給忘了？

　　男：A）我的女朋友跟你一樣漂亮。

　　　　B）我們交往才兩個星期呢。

　　　　C）她的地址，我忘了。

　　　　D）我沒忘，其實我這幾天太忙了，對
　　　　　　不起。

　　（學生答題5 秒）

6. 男：好不容易考完試了，小王，我們這個
　　　週末一起去慶祝慶祝吧！

　　女：A）好啊，我們上哪兒去慶祝？

　　　　B）我覺得這次考試挺容易的。

　　　　C）小王家不難找，我們週末一起去吧。

　　　　D）上個週末我們在老師家慶祝春節。

　　（學生答題5 秒）

3. 男：这条裙子漂亮是漂亮，可是太贵了。
　　　买那条便宜点儿的吧。

　　女：A）难道你买衣服就看价钱吗？

　　　　B）我昨天也买了一条裙子。

　　　　C）这家商店从来不打折。

　　　　D）不，我觉得衣服的式样没有价钱
　　　　　　那么重要。

　　（学生答题5 秒）

4. 男：你们这儿刷卡吗？

　　女：A）我们这儿不卖生日卡。

　　　　B）刷卡非常方便。

　　　　C）对不起，我们只收现金，不收信用
　　　　　　卡。

　　　　D）我们什么都有，您买什么？

　　（学生答题5 秒）

5. 女：怎么？有了女朋友就把老朋友给忘了？

　　男：A）我的女朋友跟你一样漂亮。

　　　　B）我们交往才两个星期呢。

　　　　C）她的地址，我忘了。

　　　　D）我没忘，其实我这几天太忙了，对
　　　　　　不起。

　　（学生答题5 秒）

6. 男：好不容易考完试了，小王，我们这个
　　　周末一起去庆祝庆祝吧！

　　女：A）好啊，我们上哪儿去庆祝？

　　　　B）我觉得这次考试挺容易的。

　　　　C）小王家不难找，我们周末一起去吧。

　　　　D）上个周末我们在老师家庆祝春节。

　　（学生答题5 秒）

7. 女：星期六音樂會的票聽說很難買，你買到了嗎？

　　男：A）我很想參加這次音樂會。

　　　　B）我想買兩張票，一張給你。

　　　　C）我早就上網買了。

　　　　D）沒問題，我星期六一定去。

（學生答題5 秒）

8. 男：這麼晚了，怎麼還不上床睡覺？明天一早還得上學呢。

　　女：A）今天的功課不太多，我早就做完了。

　　　　B）小明的電話號碼我不記得了。

　　　　C）明天放學後沒有籃球練習。

　　　　D）我們老師今天給的功課特別多，恐怕十二點半還做不完呢。

（學生答題5 秒）

9. 男：明天的考試，你準備好了沒有？我有一個問題，問你一下，行嗎？

　　女：A）我這個星期考試多極了，老師好像都說好同時考試似的。

　　　　B）我也有些地方不懂，我們還是一塊兒去問老師吧。

　　　　C）這次的考試挺難的，你考得怎麼樣？

　　　　D）說實在的，考得好不好，我並不在乎。

（學生答題5 秒）

7. 女：星期六音乐会的票听说很难买，你买到了吗？

　　男：A）我很想参加这次音乐会。

　　　　B）我想买两张票，一张给你。

　　　　C）我早就上网买了。

　　　　D）没问题，我星期六一定去。

（学生答题5 秒）

8. 男：这么晚了，怎么还不上床睡觉？明天一早还得上学呢。

　　女：A）今天的功课不太多，我早就做完了。

　　　　B）小明的电话号码我不记得了。

　　　　C）明天放学后没有篮球练习。

　　　　D）我们老师今天给的功课特别多，恐怕十二点半还做不完呢。

（学生答题5 秒）

9. 男：明天的考试，你准备好了没有？我有一个问题，问你一下，行吗？

　　女：A）我这个星期考试多极了，老师好像都说好同时考试似的。

　　　　B）我也有些地方不懂，我们还是一块儿去问老师吧。

　　　　C）这次的考试挺难的，你考得怎么样？

　　　　D）说实在的，考得好不好，我并不在乎。

（学生答题5 秒）

10. 男：妈，幾點了？

　　女：七點半了，你得快點兒，要不然就遲
　　　　到了。

　　男：A）哎呀，糟糕，恐怕沒時間吃早飯了。

　　　　B）今天老師會不會遲到？

　　　　C）李玫天天都遲到。

　　　　D）你快點起床吧。

　　（學生答題5 秒）

11. 女：今天來參觀的人怎麼這麼多？

　　男：是啊，比平常多多了。

　　女：A）平常參觀的人更多嗎？

　　　　B）參加舞會的人我一個都不認識。

　　　　C）啊，我知道了，今天放假，難怪人
　　　　　　這麼多。

　　　　D）你上個月去西安參觀了兵馬俑，
　　　　　　給我介紹介紹兵馬俑吧。

　　（學生答題5 秒）

12. 男：明天我們游泳比賽，你來給我們加油，
　　　　行嗎？

　　女：好啊，那你得好好兒游。

　　男：A）那當然，還用說嗎？

　　　　B）不客氣。

　　　　C）游泳比賽幾點開始？

　　　　D）我們沒油了，請你也帶點兒油來。

　　（學生答題5 秒）

10. 男：妈，几点了？

　　女：七点半了，你得快点儿，要不然就迟
　　　　到了。

　　男：A）哎呀，糟糕，恐怕没时间吃早饭了。

　　　　B）今天老师会不会迟到？

　　　　C）李玫天天都迟到。

　　　　D）你快点起床吧。

　　（学生答题5 秒）

11. 女：今天来参观的人怎么这么多？

　　男：是啊，比平常多多了。

　　女：A）平常参观的人更多吗？

　　　　B）参加舞会的人我一个都不认识。

　　　　C）啊，我知道了，今天放假，难怪人
　　　　　　这么多。

　　　　D）你上个月去西安参观了兵马俑，
　　　　　　给我介绍介绍兵马俑吧。

　　（学生答题5 秒）

12. 男：明天我们游泳比赛，你来给我们加油，
　　　　行吗？

　　女：好啊，那你得好好儿游。

　　男：A）那当然，还用说吗？

　　　　B）不客气。

　　　　C）游泳比赛几点开始？

　　　　D）我们没油了，请你也带点儿油来。

　　（学生答题5 秒）

13. 女：這個餐館的菜真地道，也不貴。下回
　　　再來吧！

　　男：地道是地道，就是辣了點兒。

　　女：A）你也這麼喜歡吃辣？跟我一樣嘛。

　　　　B）我不喜歡吃辣的東西。

　　　　C）我是這家飯館的常客。

　　　　D）哦，那下次我們還是換一家吃吧！

（學生答題5 秒）

14. 男：這幾天市立美術館有個當代名畫家的作
　　　品展，有沒有看畫的雅興？我可以先
　　　去買票。

　　女：興趣有是有，不過咱們得等下回了，
　　　那個畫展昨天已經閉幕了。

　　男：A）哎呀，結束了？可惜錯過了。

　　　　B）你對哪個畫家最有興趣？

　　　　C）只要是名畫家的畫，我都有興趣。

　　　　D）怪不得你一有空就去看畫展。

（學生答題5 秒）

15. 女：請問你們這兒有一位王先生嗎？

　　男：哪位王先生？我們這兒光是姓王的小伙
　　　子，就有五個。

　　女：A）哦，您不認識王先生？

　　　　B）是王先生要我來這兒找他的。

　　　　C）他個子跟您差不多，臉圓圓的，戴
　　　　　黑框眼鏡。

　　　　D）他約了我今天下午三點在服務台
　　　　　見面。

（學生答題5 秒）

13. 女：这个餐馆的菜真地道，也不贵。下回
　　　再来吧！

　　男：地道是地道，就是辣了点儿。

　　女：A）你也这么喜欢吃辣？跟我一样嘛。

　　　　B）我不喜欢吃辣的东西。

　　　　C）我是这家饭馆的常客。

　　　　D）哦，那下次我们还是换一家吃吧！

（学生答题5 秒）

14. 男：这几天市立美术馆有个当代名画家的作
　　　品展，有没有看画的雅兴？我可以先
　　　去买票。

　　女：兴趣有是有，不过咱们得等下回了，
　　　那个画展昨天已经闭幕了。

　　男：A）哎呀，结束了？可惜错过了。

　　　　B）你对哪个画家最有兴趣？

　　　　C）只要是名画家的画，我都有兴趣。

　　　　D）怪不得你一有空就去看画展。

（学生答题5 秒）

15. 女：请问你们这儿有一位王先生吗？

　　男：哪位王先生？我们这儿光是姓王的小伙
　　　子，就有五个。

　　女：A）哦，您不认识王先生？

　　　　B）是王先生要我来这儿找他的。

　　　　C）他个子跟您差不多，脸圆圆的，戴
　　　　　黑框眼镜。

　　　　D）他约了我今天下午三点在服务台
　　　　　见面。

（学生答题5 秒）

Listening Selections (15%, 10 minutes)

Directions: You will listen to several selections in Chinese. For each selection, you will be told whether it will be played once or twice. You may take notes as you listen. Your notes will not be graded. After listening to each selection, you will see questions in English. For each question, choose the response that is best according to the selection. You will have 12 seconds to answer each question.

Selection 1: Publie Announcement

Selection plays one time.

Narrator: Now you will listen once to a public announcement.

Woman:

(Traditional Characters)

乘坐CA3387次航班前往上海的旅客請注意：您乘坐的航班將在17點10分截止辦理登機手續。乘坐本次航班還沒有辦理登機手續的旅客，請馬上到29號櫃台辦理。

謝謝！

(Simplified Characters)

乘坐CA3387次航班前往上海的旅客请注意：您乘坐的航班将在17点10分截止办理登机手续。乘坐本次航班还没有办理登机手续的旅客，请马上到29号柜台办理。

谢谢！

Narrator: Now answer the questions for this selection.

(12 seconds)

(12 seconds)

Selection 2: Conversation

Selection plays one time.

Narrator: Now you will listen once to a conversation between two students.

(Traditional Characters)

男：小文，穿得這麼漂亮，跟男朋友約會去嗎？

女：嗨，小張，我申請了一份打工的工作，現在要去面試呢！

男：是嗎？在哪兒呀？怎麼想到要打工呢？

女：就在學校附近的一家咖啡館。要是能有一點工作經驗，對於將來申請大學或是寫履歷，都有好處。

男：所以你打工的目的不是為了掙錢呀！

女：可不是嗎？但是我媽媽老擔心打工會影響我的學習，今天出門前，還一直不讓我去呢！並且說要零花錢，跟她拿就是了。

男：父母都是這樣，他們總是認為當個學生把書念好就行了，打什麼工？

女：還好最後她同意了。哎呀，我得快點兒，遲到的話，給老闆的第一印象就糟糕了。

男：祝你順利！拿到了工資，別忘了請客喲！

女：謝謝。沒問題！回頭見！

(Simplified Characters)

男：小文，穿得这么漂亮，跟男朋友约会去吗？

女：嗨，小张，我申请了一份打工的工作，现在要去面试呢！

男：是吗？在哪儿呀？怎么想到要打工呢？

女：就在学校附近的一家咖啡馆。要是能有一点工作经验，对于将来申请大学或是写履历，都有好处。

男：所以你打工的目的不是为了挣钱呀！

女：可不是吗？但是我妈妈老担心打工会影响我的学习，今天出门前，还一直不让我去呢！并且说要零花钱，跟她拿就是了。

男：父母都是这样，他们总是认为当个学生把书念好就行了，打什么工？

女：还好最后她同意了。哎呀，我得快点儿，迟到的话，给老板的第一印象就糟糕了。

男：祝你顺利！拿到了工资，别忘了请客哟！

女：谢谢。没问题！回头见！

Narrator: Now answer the questions for this selection.

(12 seconds)

(12 seconds)

(12 seconds)

(12 seconds)

(12 seconds)

Selection 3: Instructions

Selection plays two times.

Narrator: Now you will listen twice to an instruction.

Woman:

(Traditional Characters)

謝謝您打電話來，您的電話對我們十分重要，請勿掛斷。如果您有事要跟校長商談，請按「1」字；如果您的孩子生病要請假，請按「2」字；如果您有事要我們轉達給您的孩子，請按「3」字；如果您有書想要續借，請按「4」字；如果你想知道各種運動比賽的時間、地點和結果，請按「5」字。如果是其他要事，請按「0」字。如果沒人接聽，麻煩您留下您的名字、電話及簡單的訊息，我們會盡快跟您聯絡。謝謝。

(Simplified Characters)

谢谢您打电话来，您的电话对我们十分重要，请勿挂断。如果您有事要跟校长商谈，请按"1"字；如果您的孩子生病要请假，请按"2"字；如果您有事要我们转达给您的孩子，请按"3"字；如果您有书想要续借，请按"4"字；如果你想知道各种运动比赛的时间、地点和结果，请按"5"字。如果是其他要事，请按"0"字。如果没人接听，麻烦您留下您的名字、电话及简单的讯息，我们会尽快跟您联络。谢谢。

Narrator: Now listen again.
(Repeat)

Narrator: Now answer the questions for this selection.

(12 seconds)

(12 seconds)

(12 seconds)

(12 seconds)

Selection 4: Voice message

Selection plays two times.

Narrator: Now you will listen twice to a voice message.

Woman:

(Traditional Characters)	(Simplified Characters)
媽媽，我是立立，今天早上出門的時候，我怕上學遲到，匆匆忙忙的，結果忘了把今天必須交的英文讀書報告帶到學校來了。還好英文課是今天最後一節課，希望你能及時聽到我的留言。英文讀書報告我放在書桌右邊書架上的最上層，請你盡快帶來給我。到學校的時候，就交給坐在辦公室最前邊的李小姐。還有，千萬別給我打手機，給我發個短信吧，因為我下午都有課。媽媽，拜託，拜託，對不起！謝謝！	妈妈，我是立立，今天早上出门的时候，我怕上学迟到，匆匆忙忙的，结果忘了把今天必须交的英文读书报告带到学校来了。还好英文课是今天最后一节课，希望你能及时听到我的留言。英文读书报告我放在书桌右边书架上的最上层，请你尽快带来给我。到学校的时候，就交给坐在办公室最前边的李小姐。还有，千万别给我打手机，给我发个短信吧，因为我下午都有课。妈妈，拜托，拜托，对不起！谢谢！

Narrator: Now listen again.
(Repeat)

Narrator: Now answer the questions for this selection.

(12 seconds)

(12 seconds)

(12 seconds)

(12 seconds)

Selection 5: Report

Selection plays two times.

Narrator: Now you will listen twice to a report.

Man:

<table>
<tr><td><h3>(Traditional Characters)</h3></td><td><h3>(Simplified Characters)</h3></td></tr>
<tr><td>

近年來由於電腦價格普遍降低，每個家庭一般都有電腦，並訂有網路服務，不少家長擔心子女花在網路上的時間過多，所以本台記者這個星期在學校門口、購物中心以及電影院前訪問了三百六十五位高中同學，瞭解高中生上網的情況。調查的結果顯示，將近百分之八十的學生每晚花在網上的時間平均兩個小時，百分之十八的學生花在網上的時間每晚都超過三個小時。幾乎百分之九十五的學生表示，他們父母認為他們上網的時間太多，應該多跟父母、朋友面對面溝通。但是這些學生表示，他們上網常常是為了找資料、做報告，或者跟同學討論功課上或課外活動的問題，並不是如父母以為的都是在網上玩電腦遊戲或跟朋友聊天。

</td><td>

近年来由于电脑价格普遍降低，每个家庭一般都有电脑，并订有网路服务，不少家长担心子女花在网路上的时间过多，所以本台记者这个星期在学校门口、购物中心以及电影院前访问了三百六十五位高中同学，了解高中生上网的情况。调查的结果显示，将近百分之八十的学生每晚花在网上的时间平均两个小时，百分之十八的学生花在网上的时间每晚都超过三个小时。几乎百分之九十五的学生表示，他们父母认为他们上网的时间太多，应该多跟父母、朋友面对面沟通。但是这些学生表示，他们上网常常是为了找资料、做报告，或者跟同学讨论功课上或课外活动的问题，并不是如父母以为的都是在网上玩电脑游戏或跟朋友聊天。

</td></tr>
</table>

Narrator: Now listen again.
(Repeat)

Narrator: Now answer the questions for this selection.

(12 seconds)

(12 seconds)

(12 seconds)

(12 seconds)

(12 seconds)

Section II: Part B: Speaking

Recording Scripts

Conversation

Directions: You will participate in a simulated conversation. Each time it is your turn to speak, you will have 20 seconds to record. You should respond as fully and as appropriately as possible.

You will have a conversation with Wang Zhong, your host parent, about dining at a local Chinese restaurant.

(Traditional Characters)

王中：你看看菜單，想吃什麼，就點什麼，別
　　　客氣。
　　　（學生答題20秒）

王中：他們平常上菜挺快的，今天怎麼這麼
　　　慢？你餓壞了吧？
　　　（學生答題20秒）

王中：菜來了，來，我幫你夾。多吃點。味道
　　　怎麼樣，還可以吧？
　　　（學生答題20秒）

王中：你在家時，你和家人常上館子去吃飯
　　　嗎？都吃些什麼樣口味的菜？
　　　（學生答題20秒）

王中：你媽媽會做些什麼拿手好菜？
　　　（學生答題20秒）

王中：吃飽了嗎？菜夠不夠？要不要再來點兒
　　　什麼？
　　　（學生答題20秒）

(Simplified Characters)

王中：你看看菜单，想吃什么，就点什么，别
　　　客气。
　　　（学生答题20秒）

王中：他们平常上菜挺快的，今天怎么这么
　　　慢？你饿坏了吧？
　　　（学生答题20秒）

王中：菜来了，来，我帮你夹。多吃点。味道
　　　怎么样，还可以吧？
　　　（学生答题20秒）

王中：你在家时，你和家人常上馆子去吃饭
　　　吗？都吃些什么样口味的菜？
　　　（学生答题20秒）

王中：你妈妈会做些什么拿手好菜？
　　　（学生答题20秒）

王中：吃饱了吗？菜够不够？要不要再来点儿
　　　什么？
　　　（学生答题20秒）

Cultural Presentation

You will be asked to speak in Chinese on a specific topic. Imagine you are making an oral presentation to your Chinese class. First, you will read and hear the topic for your presentation. You will have 4 minutes to prepare your presentation. Then you will have 2 minutes to record your presentation. Your presentation should be as complete as possible.

Choose one historical or contemporary Chinese figure. In your presentation, describe this person's background, what he/she has done, and explain his or her significance in China.

Recording Scripts for Test 3

Section I: Part A: Listening

Rejoinders

Directions: You will hear several short conversations or parts of conversations followed by four choices, designated (A), (B), (C), and (D). Choose the one that continues or completes the conversation in a logical and culturally appropriate manner. You will have 5 seconds to answer each question.

<table>
<tr><th>(Traditional Characters)</th><th>(Simplified Characters)</th></tr>
<tr><td>

1. 男：小紅，剛才跟你說話的那個人是誰啊？

女：A）你不認識他嗎？

B）她是你的朋友嗎？

C）那個人不是我的同學。

D）那個人很喜歡說話。

（學生答題5 秒）

</td><td>

1. 男：小红，刚才跟你说话的那个人是谁啊？

女：A）你不认识他吗？

B）她是你的朋友吗？

C）那个人不是我的同学。

D）那个人很喜欢说话。

（学生答题5 秒）

</td></tr>
<tr><td>

2. 男：昨天我沒能去看那場籃球賽，哪隊贏了？

女：A）我最不喜歡看籃球比賽了。

B）這場球賽一點兒也不精彩。

C）那還用問嗎，當然是我們班隊了。

D）那個隊沒贏。

（學生答題5 秒）

</td><td>

2. 男：昨天我没能去看那场篮球赛，哪队赢了？

女：A）我最不喜欢看篮球比赛了。

B）这场球赛一点儿也不精彩。

C）那还用问吗，当然是我们班队了。

D）那个队没赢。

（学生答题5 秒）

</td></tr>
</table>

192

3. 女：我很想找份半工做一做，免得老跟父母
　　要錢花。

　　男：A）對，跟父母要的錢是得省著花。

　　　　B）你父母不應該花你打工掙的錢。

　　　　C）我的父母花錢也很省。

　　　　D）是啊，如果自己能賺點零用錢，就
　　　　　　方便多了。

　　（學生答題5 秒）

4. 男：春假的時候你去哪兒了，怎麼連個電郵
　　都不回？

　　女：A）我春假玩兒得很開心。

　　　　B）你開玩笑吧？我根本沒收到你的
　　　　　　電郵。

　　　　C）那個地方沒有郵局，所以我沒能給
　　　　　　你回信。

　　　　D）我一到那兒，就會馬上發電郵告
　　　　　　訴你。

　　（學生答題5 秒）

5. 女：聽說去北京當交換學生的獎學金被你哥
　　哥拿到了？

　　男：A）我怎麼不知道你哥哥要去北京學習呢？

　　　　B）沒有這回事，別聽別人瞎說。

　　　　C）我也聽說從北京來的交換學生都有獎
　　　　　　學金。

　　　　D）我哥哥從來沒有去過北京。

　　（學生答題5 秒）

3. 女：我很想找份半工做一做，免得老跟父母
　　要钱花。

　　男：A）对，跟父母要的钱是得省着花。

　　　　B）你父母不应该花你打工挣的钱。

　　　　C）我的父母花钱也很省。

　　　　D）是啊，如果自己能赚点零用钱，就
　　　　　　方便多了。

　　（学生答题5 秒）

4. 男：春假的时候你去哪儿了，怎么连个电邮
　　都不回？

　　女：A）我春假玩儿得很开心。

　　　　B）你开玩笑吧？我根本没收到你的
　　　　　　电邮。

　　　　C）那个地方没有邮局，所以我没能给
　　　　　　你回信。

　　　　D）我一到那儿，就会马上发电邮告
　　　　　　诉你。

　　（学生答题5 秒）

5. 女：听说去北京当交换学生的奖学金被你哥
　　哥拿到了？

　　男：A）我怎么不知道你哥哥要去北京学习呢？

　　　　B）没有这回事，别听别人瞎说。

　　　　C）我也听说从北京来的交换学生都有奖
　　　　　　学金。

　　　　D）我哥哥从来没有去过北京。

　　（学生答题5 秒）

6. 男：咱們學校附近新開張的那家中國餐館的川菜很地道，有機會你應該去嚐一嚐。

　　女：A）我最討厭四川菜，太辣了！

　　　　B）那家餐館開的時間不太長。

　　　　C）咱們學校餐廳的川菜是很地道。

　　　　D）在學校附近開個餐館對我們來說很方便。

（學生答題5 秒）

6. 男：咱们学校附近新开张的那家中国餐馆的川菜很地道，有机会你应该去尝一尝。

　　女：A）我最讨厌四川菜，太辣了！

　　　　B）那家餐馆开的时间不太长。

　　　　C）咱们学校餐厅的川菜是很地道。

　　　　D）在学校附近开个餐馆对我们来说很方便。

（学生答题5 秒）

7. 女：我這個人很怕吵，所以我常常喜歡呆在圖書館裡看書，因為那裡最安靜，你呢？

　　男：A）很多人都喜歡去圖書館借書。

　　　　B）在圖書館學習是要安靜。

　　　　C）看來咱倆個性差不多，我也愛去圖書館看書。

　　　　D）我也覺得圖書館有時候很吵。

（學生答題5 秒）

7. 女：我这个人很怕吵，所以我常常喜欢呆在图书馆里看书，因为那里最安静，你呢？

　　男：A）很多人都喜欢去图书馆借书。

　　　　B）在图书馆学习是要安静。

　　　　C）看来咱俩个性差不多，我也爱去图书馆看书。

　　　　D）我也觉得图书馆有时候很吵。

（学生答题5 秒）

8. 女：我的朋友剛從中國回來，他說因為H1N1的事兒，在北京機場每個旅客都得測體溫，所以要好幾個小時才能出機場呢。

　　男：A）北京機場那麼大，出機場是很慢。

　　　　B）飛機怎麼晚點那麼長時間呢？

　　　　C）你朋友在北京得了流感嗎？

　　　　D）是嗎?那太麻煩了。

（學生答題5 秒）

8. 女：我的朋友刚从中国回来。他说因为H1N1的事儿，在北京机场每个旅客都得测体温，所以要好几小时才能出机场呢。

　　男：A）北京机场那么大，出机场是很慢。

　　　　B）飞机怎么晚点那么长时间呢？

　　　　C）你朋友在北京得了流感吗？

　　　　D）是吗?那太麻烦了。

（学生答题5 秒）

194

9. 男：小紅，剛五月你家怎麼就這麼熱呢？

　　女：A）老房子了，沒有空調。

　　　　B）這個房子的設備比較齊全。

　　　　C）夏天恐怕不會很熱。

　　　　D）每年都會熱上五個月。

（學生答題5 秒）

10. 女：哥哥，哪天把你的女朋友帶到家裡讓
　　　　我們看一看。

　　男：A）我覺得我的女朋友是很好看。

　　　　B）她不好意思來咱們家。

　　　　C）我一定會帶你去她家。

　　　　D）她已經帶我去過她家了。

（學生答題5 秒）

11. 男：你本來不是很喜歡化學嗎？怎麼決定上
　　　　大學以後讀英文專業呢？

　　女：其實這兩科我都喜歡，所以沒選化學專
　　　　業我也覺得有點兒可惜。

　　男：A）我也覺得科學更有意思。

　　　　B）英語的確是很難讀的專業。

　　　　C）沒關係，反正上學以後還可以改
　　　　　　專業。

　　　　D）我父母也不支持我學英文。

（學生答題5 秒）

9. 男：小红，刚五月你家怎么就这么热呢？

　　女：A）老房子了，没有空调。

　　　　B）这个房子的设备比较齐全。

　　　　C）夏天恐怕不会很热。

　　　　D）每年都会热上五个月。

（学生答题5 秒）

10. 女：哥哥，哪天把你的女朋友带到家里让
　　　　我们看一看。

　　男：A）我觉得我的女朋友是很好看。

　　　　B）她不好意思来咱们家。

　　　　C）我一定会带你去她家。

　　　　D）她已经带我去过她家了。

（学生答题5 秒）

11. 男：你本来不是很喜欢化学吗？怎么决定上
　　　　大学以后读英文专业呢？

　　女：其实这两科我都喜欢，所以没选化学专
　　　　业我也觉得有点儿可惜。

　　男：A）我也觉得科学更有意思。

　　　　B）英语的确是很难读的专业。

　　　　C）没关系，反正上学以后还可以改
　　　　　　专业。

　　　　D）我父母也不支持我学英文。

（学生答题5 秒）

12. 女：你吃過北京全聚德的烤鴨嗎？

　　男：聽說過，但還沒吃過。

　　女：A）味道好極了！跟一般的烤鴨不
　　　　　　一樣。

　　　　B）大部份中國人都不喜歡吃。

　　　　C）你真的不知道全聚德嗎？

　　　　D）很遺憾你不喜歡吃烤鴨。

（學生答題5 秒）

13. 男：這件襯衫夠便宜的啦，還猶像什麼呢？

　　女：價錢還可以，可是我穿不太合身。

　　男：A）好，我們再看看有沒有更便宜
　　　　　　的吧。

　　　　B）那我們再去別的店看看吧。

　　　　C）那家店的東西是不怎麼樣。

　　　　D）沒關係，錢不夠的話我可以借
　　　　　　給你。

（學生答題5 秒）

14. 女：好幾次游泳練習你都沒去，怎麼啦？

　　男：學校的功課太多，壓得我都喘不過氣
　　　　來了。

　　女：A）你應該去看醫生。

　　　　B）怪不得你沒去上學。

　　　　C）不能只顧學習，鍛煉身體也很重要。

　　　　D）別生氣，我也覺得老師應該多給些
　　　　　　作業。

（學生答題5 秒）

12. 女：你吃过北京全聚德的烤鸭吗？

　　男：听说过，但还没吃过。

　　女：A）味道好极了！跟一般的烤鸭不
　　　　　　一样。

　　　　B）大部份中国人都不喜欢吃。

　　　　C）你真的不知道全聚德吗？

　　　　D）很遗憾你不喜欢吃烤鸭。

（学生答题5 秒）

13. 男：这件衬衫够便宜的啦，还犹像什么呢？

　　女：价钱还可以，可是我穿不太合身。

　　男：A）好，我们再看看有没有更便宜
　　　　　　的吧。

　　　　B）那我们再去别的店看看吧。

　　　　C）这家店的东西是不怎么样。

　　　　D）没关系，钱不够的话我可以借
　　　　　　给你。

（学生答题5 秒）

14. 女：好几次游泳练习你都没去，怎么啦？

　　男：学校的功课太多，压得我都喘不过气
　　　　来了。

　　女：A）你应该去看医生。

　　　　B）怪不得你没去上学。

　　　　C）不能只顾学习，锻炼身体也很重要。

　　　　D）别生气，我也觉得老师应该多给些
　　　　　　作业。

（学生答题5 秒）

15. 男：你跟你的男朋友不是相處得挺好嗎？
　　　怎麼說分手就分手了呢？

　　女：我們其實只是一般的朋友，所以也算
　　　不上什麼分手不分手。

　　男：A）不是朋友就應該分手。

　　　　B）哦，看來大家誤會你們的關係了。

　　　　C）你男朋友長得挺好的。

　　　　D）真的沒說什麼就分手了嗎？

（學生答題5 秒）

15. 男：你跟你的男朋友不是相处得挺好吗？
　　　怎么说分手就分手了呢？

　　女：我们其实只是一般的朋友，所以也算
　　　不上什么分手不分手。

　　男：A）不是朋友就应该分手。

　　　　B）哦，看来大家误会你们的关系了。

　　　　C）你男朋友长得挺好的。

　　　　D）真的没说什么就分手了吗？

（学生答题5 秒）

Listening Selections (15%, 10 minutes)

Directions: You will listen to several selections in Chinese. For each selection, you will be told whether it will be played once or twice. You may take notes as you listen. Your notes will not be graded. After listening to each selection, you will see questions in English. For each question, choose the response that is best according to the selection. You will have 12 seconds to answer each question.

Selection 1: Conversation

Selection plays one time.

Narrator: Now you will listen once to a conversation between two students.

(Traditional Characters)

男：下週四晚上在學校召開一個關於怎樣申請
大學的諮詢會，聽說很多大學負責招生的
人都會來。我很想參加，因為有些問題我
在網上找不到答案，正好我可以趁這個機
會去問問他們。你也想去嗎？

女：我其實很想去，但是那天晚上我還有別
的事要做。麻煩你把重要的資料幫我帶
回來，或者用電子郵件發給我也行。拜
託你了！

(Simplified Characters)

男：下周四晚上在学校召开一个关于怎样申请
大学的咨询会，听说很多大学负责招生的
人都会来。我很想参加，因为有些问题我
在网上找不到答案，正好我可以趁这个机
会问问他们。你也想去吗？

女：我其实很想去，但是那天晚上我还有别
的事要做。麻烦你把重要的资料帮我带
回来，或者用电子邮件发给我也行。拜
托你了！

197

Narrator: Now answer the questions for this selection.

(12 seconds)

(12 seconds)

(12 seconds)

(12 seconds)

Selection 2: Announcement

Selection plays two times.

Narrator: Now you will listen twice to an announcement.

Woman:

(Traditional Characters)

為了慶祝教師節，中文俱樂部的同學準備在本週四舉辦一個尊師愛校的活動。中午十二點到一點，在學生中心門前將會有中國城黃河藝術團表演的中國功夫及歌舞表演，學校會為全校師生提供一份免費的中式午餐。另外，請每個學生給你最喜愛的老師寫一張卡來表示你對老師的感激，並請將卡片直接放到老師的郵箱裡。你也可以附上一份小小的禮物。謝謝大家的支持！

(Simplified Characters)

为了庆祝教师节，中文俱乐部的同学准备在本周四举办一个尊师爱校的活动。中午十二点到一点，在学生中心门前将会有中国城黄河艺术团表演的中国功夫及歌舞表演，学校会为全校师生提供一份免费的中式午餐。另外，请每个学生给你最喜爱的老师写一张卡来表示你对老师的感激，并请将卡片直接放到老师的邮箱里。你也可以附上一份小小的礼物。谢谢大家的支持！

Narrator: Now answer the questions for this selection.

(12 seconds)

(12 seconds)

(12 seconds)

Selection 3: Voice message

Selection plays two times.

Narrator: Now you will listen twice to a voice message.

Woman:

<table>
<tr><th>(Traditional Characters)</th><th>(Simplified Characters)</th></tr>
<tr><td>王老師：您好！我是李曉美。我已經告訴我媽媽我們班下周去亞洲博物館的事了，她說可以開車送我們去。我媽媽的車很大，可以坐六個人，但問題是我媽媽中午要去機場接人，她把我們送到博物館後就得先走，不能送我們回學校。其實我們幾個坐地鐵回來也很方便。您有事可以打電話跟我媽媽聯繫，她的手機號碼是（520）820-7070。再見！</td><td>王老师：您好！我是李晓美。我已经告诉我妈妈我们班下周去亚洲博物馆的事了，她说可以开车送我们去。我妈妈的车很大，可以坐六个人，但问题是我妈妈中午要去机场接人，她把我们送到博物馆后就得先走，不能送我们回学校。其实我们几个坐地铁回来也很方便。您有事可以打电话跟我妈妈联系，她的手机号码是（520）820-7070。再见！</td></tr>
</table>

Narrator: Now listen again.

Narrator: Now answer the questions for this selection.
(12 seconds)

(12 seconds)

(12 seconds)

Selection 4: Instructions

Selection plays two times

Narrator: Now you will listen once to an instruction.

Man:

(Traditional Characters)

全校師生請注意，因學校正門前面在修路，所以明天防火練習的路線有所改變。聽到防火警報時，請所有師生馬上從學校後門出去，沿著左邊的那條小路往前走，一直走到社區中心前面的草地上。各班的集合地點不變，請在那兒等候所有的同學到來。請各位老師記住帶急救包，並在集合的地點點名。

(Simplified Characters)

全校师生请注意，因学校正门前面在修路，所以明天防火练习的路线有所改变。听到防火警报时，请所有师生马上从学校后门出去，沿着左边的那条小路往前走，一直走到社区中心前面的草地上。各班的集合地点不变，请在那儿等候所有的同学到来。请各位老师记住带急救包，并在集合的地点点名。

Narrator: Now listen again.

Narrator: Now answer the questions for this selection.
(12 seconds)

(12 seconds)

(12 seconds)

(12 seconds)

Selection 5: Report

Selection plays two times.

Narrator: Now you will listen twice to a report.

(Traditional Characters)

同學們：我校一年一度的大學專業諮詢活動昨天圓滿結束了，共有十二位歷屆畢業生參加了這次活動。他們以自己的親身經歷向同學們介紹了他們所從事工作的特點，並就同學們提問給以解答。同學們都覺得這次活動使他們對許多職業增加了瞭解，這對大學專業的選擇以及未來可能從事的工作有很大的幫助。昨天沒能參加活動的同學，可以和這幾位演講者通過電郵聯繫。

(Simplified Characters)

同学们：我校一年一度的大学专业咨询活动昨天圆满结束了，共有十二位历届毕业生参加了这次活动。他们以自己的亲身经历向同学介绍了他们所从事工作的性特点，并就同学们提问给以解答。同学们都觉得这次活动使他们对许多职业增加了了解，这对大学专业的选择以及未来可能从事的工作有很大的帮助。昨天没能参加活动的同学，可以和这几位演讲者通过电邮联系。

Narrator: Now listen again.

Narrator: Now answer the questions for this selection.
(12 seconds)

(12 seconds)

(12 seconds)

Selection 6: Conversation

Selection plays one time.

Narrator: Now you will listen once to a conversation between two students.

(Traditional Characters)

男： 我下個月要去西安旅遊，最近正在準備辦簽證的事兒。以前都是我父母幫我辦，可是不巧他們都到外地開會去了。我聽說你這方面很有經驗，所以想問問你辦簽證都需要什麼手續。

女： 首先你要確定你的護照是有效的，然後你要準備一張二寸正面照片，再上網下載一份簽證申請表，填好後一起交到領事館。最後取簽證時要交$130，不管幾次入境，簽證費都是一樣的。

男： 簽證要等幾天才能取？

女： 通常是五個工作日，不過也有加急服務，但是要多付些錢。

男： 嗯，知道了，那我還是早點辦吧。
謝謝你！

女： 不客氣！

(Simplified Characters)

男： 我下个月要去西安旅游，最近正在准备办签证的事儿。以前都是我父母帮我办，可是不巧他们都到外地开会去了。我听说你这方面很有经验，所以想问问你办签证都需要什么手续。

女： 首先你要确定你的护照是有效的，然后你要准备一张二寸正面照片，再上网下载一份签证申请表，填好后一起交到领事馆。最后取签证时要交$130，不管几次入境，签证费都是一样的。

男： 签证要等几天才能取？

女： 通常是五个工作日，不过也有加急服务，但是要多付些钱。

男： 嗯，知道了，那我还是早点办吧。
谢谢你！

女： 不客气！

Narrator: Now answer the questions for this selection.

(12 seconds)

(12 seconds)

(12 seconds)

Section II: Part B: Speaking
Recording Scripts

Conversation

Directions: You will participate in a simulated conversation. Each time it is your turn to speak, you will have 20 seconds to record. You should respond as fully and as appropriately as possible.

You have been invited to have dinner with a Chinese family. You will have a conversation with a member of the family at the dinner table.

(Traditional Characters)

中國家庭：這些都是家常菜，可能做得不夠好，不知合不合你的口味？
（學生答題20秒）

中國家庭：吃得慣中餐嗎？你常吃的中餐有哪些？
（學生答題20秒）

中國家庭：你了解中國的八大菜系嗎？你最喜歡什麼地方風味的菜？
（學生答題20秒）

中國家庭：你在家裡或在中文班上學沒學過包餃了？喜歡吃餃了嗎？
（學生答題20秒）

中國家庭：美國人平常都吃什麼？
（學生答題20秒）

中國家庭：你的老家在哪兒？那兒的菜肴有什麼特色？教我做一道你的家鄉菜吧！
（學生答題20秒）

(Simplified Characters)

中国家庭：这些都是家常菜，可能做得不够好，不知合不合你的口味？
（学生答题20秒）

中国家庭：吃得惯中餐吗？你常吃的中餐有哪些？
（学生答题20秒）

中国家庭：你了解中国的八大菜系吗？你最喜欢什么地方风味的菜？
（学生答题20秒）

中国家庭：你在家里或在中文班上学没学过包饺了？喜欢吃饺了吗？
（学生答题20秒）

中国家庭：美国人平常都吃什么？
（学生答题20秒）

中国家庭：你的老家在哪儿？那儿的菜肴有什么特色？教我做一道你的家乡菜吧！
（学生答题20秒）

Cultural Presentation

Directions: You will be asked to speak in Chinese on a specific topic. Imagine you are making an oral presentation to your Chinese class. First, you will read and hear the topic for your presentation. You will have 4 minutes to prepare your presentation. Then you will have 2 minutes to record your presentation. Your presentation should be as complete as possible.

The concept of "一日為師，終身为父" ("A teacher for one day, and a father forever") has always been valued in China. In your presentation, share your thoughts on this concept, and compare and contrast it with the Western cultural attitudes toward the role of teachers, and toward education as a whole.

Recording Scripts for Test 4

Section I: Part A: Listening

Rejoinders

Directions: You will hear several short conversations or parts of conversations followed by four choices, designated (A), (B), (C), and (D). Choose the one that continues or completes the conversation in a logical and culturally appropriate manner. You will have 5 seconds to answer each question.

(Traditional Characters)	(Simplified Characters)
1. 女：今年暑假，你做了什麼有意思的事了？說來聽聽吧！ 　男：A）我暑假想去中國旅行。 　　　B）我媽媽不讓我開車上學。 　　　C）沒做什麼，整天就吃飯、睡覺。 　　　D）暑假太長了，真沒意思，怎麼辦？ 　（學生答題5 秒）	1. 女：今年暑假，你做了什么有意思的事了？说来听听吧！ 　男：A）我暑假想去中国旅行。 　　　B）我妈妈不让我开车上学。 　　　C）没做什么，整天就吃饭、睡觉。 　　　D）暑假太长了，真没意思，怎么办？ 　（学生答题5 秒）
2. 女：嗨，小王！聽說你們昨天的籃球賽贏了。 　男：A）可不是？68 比67，把我們對手給氣死了。 　　　B）我們每天放學以後都練球。 　　　C）我們今年可能連贏一場的希望都沒有。 　　　D）打籃球比踢足球容易多了。 　（學生答題5 秒）	2. 女：嗨，小王！听说你们昨天的篮球赛赢了。 　男：A）可不是？68 比67，把我们对手给气死了。 　　　B）我们每天放学以后都练球。 　　　C）我们今年可能连赢一场的希望都没有。 　　　D）打篮球比踢足球容易多了。 　（学生答题5 秒）

3.女：站在小李旁邊的那個帥哥是誰呀，是不是她的新男朋友？

男：A）小李的新男朋友是剛從華盛頓轉學到這兒的。

B）啊，哪個？哦，那是我弟弟，待會兒我幫你們介紹介紹。

C）參加晚會的人真多。

D）小李今天晚上真漂亮，喜歡她的男孩子可真不少呢。

（學生答題5 秒）

4.男：你本來不是想選電腦課的嗎？怎麼學生名單上沒有你的名字？

女：A）選是想選，但是電腦課花的時間多，我想了想，還是等下個學期功課比較不忙時再選吧。

B）我發現自己對電腦課的興趣可大著呢。

C）我打的那份工也需要電腦方面的知識。

D）我以後電腦課有問題，可以問你嗎？

（學生答題5 秒）

5.女：對不起，你音樂開得太大聲了，能不能開小聲點？我沒法兒專心看書呢。

男：A）我喜歡一邊聽音樂，一邊看書。

B）要是你不喜歡這個音樂，我可以換別的音樂。

C）不喜歡？那你可以出去。

D）哎呀，對不起，對不起，我沒注意到屋子裡還有人。

（學生答題5 秒）

3.女：站在小李旁边的那个帅哥是谁呀，是不是她的新男朋友？

男：A）小李的新男朋友是刚从华盛顿转学到这儿的。

B）啊，哪个？哦，那是我弟弟，待会儿我帮你们介绍介绍。

C）参加晚会的人真多。

D）小李今天晚上真漂亮，喜欢她的男孩子可真不少呢。

（学生答题5 秒）

4.男：你本来不是想选电脑课的吗？怎么学生名单上没有你的名字？

女：A）选是想选，但是电脑课花的时间多，我想了想，还是等下个学期功课比较不忙时再选吧。

B）我发现自己对电脑课的兴趣可大着呢。

C）我打的那份工也需要电脑方面的知识。

D）我以后电脑课有问题，可以问你吗？

（学生答题5 秒）

5.女：对不起，你音乐开得太大声了，能不能开小声点？我没法儿专心看书呢。

男：A）我喜欢一边听音乐，一边看书。

B）要是你不喜欢这个音乐，我可以换别的音乐。

C）不喜欢？那你可以出去。

D）哎呀，对不起，对不起，我没注意到屋子里还有人。

（学生答题5 秒）

6. 男：到了北京，給我們打個手機回來，別讓
我們擔心。

　　女：A）你的手機真酷，讓我瞧瞧。

　　　　B）我晚上八點會到北京。

　　　　C）現在的飛機都很準時，你不用擔心
飛機誤點。

　　　　D）那當然，一定，一定。

（學生答題5 秒）

7. 女：你的行李看起來挺重的，我來幫你提
吧！

　　男：A）不好意思，我自己來，沒問題。

　　　　B）我的行李是我媽媽幫我收拾的。

　　　　C）我的行李超重，上飛機時，罰了
五十塊錢。

　　　　D）我的行李裡裡頭有很多書。

（學生答題5 秒）

8. 男：中秋節快到了，你打算自己做月餅嗎？

　　女：A）中秋節大家都吃月餅，我也不例外。

　　　　B）我沒吃過月餅。好吃嗎？

　　　　C）我們家月餅都是在商店買的，我根本
不會做。

　　　　D）中秋節我們一起賞月、吃月餅吧。

（學生答題5 秒）

9. 女：請問，新生在哪兒辦註冊手續？

　　男：A）老生在圖書館辦註冊手續。

　　　　B）註冊手續？我已經辦好了。

　　　　C）在學生活動中心裡頭。

　　　　D）新生明天才辦註冊手續。

（學生答題5 秒）

6. 男：到了北京，给我们打个手机回来，别让
我们担心。

　　女：A）你的手机真酷，让我瞧瞧。

　　　　B）我晚上八点会到北京。

　　　　C）现在的飞机都很准时，你不用担心
飞机误点。

　　　　D）那当然，一定，一定。

（学生答题5 秒）

7. 女：你的行李看起来挺重的，我来帮你提
吧！

　　男：A）不好意思，我自己来，没问题。

　　　　B）我的行李是我妈妈帮我收拾的。

　　　　C）我的行李超重，上飞机时，罚了
五十块钱。

　　　　D）我的行李里里头有很多书。

（学生答题5 秒）

8. 男：中秋节快到了，你打算自己做月饼吗？

　　女：A）中秋节大家都吃月饼，我也不例外。

　　　　B）我没吃过月饼。好吃吗？

　　　　C）我们家月饼都是在商店买的，我根本
不会做。

　　　　D）中秋节我们一起赏月、吃月饼吧

（学生答题5 秒）

9. 女：请问，新生在哪儿办注册手续？

　　男：A）老生在图书馆办注册手续。

　　　　B）注册手续？我已经办好了。

　　　　C）在学生活动中心里头。

　　　　D）新生明天才办注册手续。

（学生答题5 秒）

10. 男：快放假了，你有什麼計劃？

　　女：我要麼到中國去玩，要麼去快餐店打
　　　　工。你呢？

　　男：A）中國各地，我都去過。

　　　　B）可能會上暑期學校。

　　　　C）我比較喜歡放寒假。

　　　　D）暑假太長了，真無聊。

　　（學生答題5　秒）

11. 女：那個新電影不錯，聽說看的人挺多的，
　　　　你看了嗎？

　　男：現在去是人擠人，過一陣子再說吧。

　　女：A）等你想看的時候，給我打個電話，
　　　　　　我們一塊兒去。

　　　　B）我們下課以後就一起去看吧。

　　　　C）沒想到看電影的人這麼多。

　　　　D）要排隊買票嗎？

　　（學生答題5　秒）

12. 男：你平常幫不幫你媽媽做家事？

　　女：我媽媽白天上班，忙得很，家裡都是
　　　　我和妹妹輪流打掃房子、倒垃圾。

　　男：A）你媽媽可真忙。

　　　　B）我父母都不上班。

　　　　C）是嗎？你媽媽有你們這樣的女兒
　　　　　　真好。

　　　　D）我媽媽很會做家事，她中國菜做得
　　　　　　特別好。

　　（學生答題5　秒）

10. 男：快放假了，你有什么计划？

　　女：我要么到中国去玩，要么去快餐店打
　　　　工。你呢？

　　男：A）中国各地，我都去过。

　　　　B）可能会上暑期学校。

　　　　C）我比较喜欢放寒假。

　　　　D）暑假太长了，真无聊。

　　（学生答题5　秒）

11. 女：那个新电影不错，听说看的人挺多的，
　　　　你看了吗？

　　男：现在去是人挤人，过一阵子再说吧。

　　女：A）等你想看的时候，给我打个电话，
　　　　　　我们一块儿去。

　　　　B）我们下课以后就一起去看吧。

　　　　C）没想到看电影的人这么多。

　　　　D）要排队买票吗？

　　（学生答题5　秒）

12. 男：你平常帮不帮你妈妈做家事？

　　女：我妈妈白天上班，忙得很，家里都是
　　　　我和妹妹轮流扫房子、倒垃圾。

　　男：A）你妈妈可真忙。

　　　　B）我父母都不上班。

　　　　C）是吗？你妈妈有你们这样的女儿
　　　　　　真好。

　　　　D）我妈妈很会做家事，她中国菜做得
　　　　　　特别好。

　　（学生答题5　秒）

208

13. 女：起來，起來，別待在家裡看電視了，
　　　我們出去走走吧！

　　男：外面下著雨呢。

　　女：A）天氣預報說明天也會下雨。

　　　　B）下雨走路要小心。

　　　　C）我們可以帶傘呀，走吧！

　　　　D）這個電視節目真好看。

（學生答題5 秒）

14. 男：你怎麼不說話？看上去好像有什麼心
　　　事似的。

　　女：我男朋友的父母請我明天晚上去他們
　　　家吃飯，這是我們第一次見面，我很
　　　緊張，不知該帶什麼樣的禮物去。

　　男：A）我緊張的時候常常說不出話來。

　　　　B）原來你煩的是這個。給你出個好
　　　　主意吧，帶一束鮮花去是再好不
　　　　過的了。

　　　　C）你吃飯時最好不要吃太多。吃太多
　　　　會給人很差的印象。

　　　　D）不用擔心送什麼禮物給我，只要你
　　　　送的，我都喜歡。

（學生答題5 秒）

13. 女：起来，起来，别待在家里看电视了，
　　　我们出去走走吧！

　　男：外面下着雨呢。

　　女：A）天气预报说明天也会下雨。

　　　　B）下雨走路要小心。

　　　　C）我们可以带伞呀，走吧！

　　　　D）这个电视节目真好看。

（学生答题5 秒）

14. 男：你怎么不说话？看上去好像有什么心
　　　事似的。

　　女：我男朋友的父母请我明天晚上去他们
　　　家吃饭，这是我们第一次见面，我很
　　　紧张，不知该带什么样的礼物去。

　　男：A）我紧张的时候常常说不出话来。

　　　　B）原来你烦的是这个。给你出个好
　　　　主意吧，带一束鲜花去是再好不过的
　　　　了。

　　　　C）你吃饭时最好不要吃太多。吃太多
　　　　会给人很差的印象。

　　　　D）不用担心送什么礼物给我，只要你
　　　　送的，我都喜欢。

（学生答题5 秒）

209

15. 女：我上個月報名申請當夏令營的輔導
員，剛剛接到了錄取通知，我樂壞
了。

男：我也被錄取了，不過我媽不讓我去，
她認為我還不夠獨立，怎麼能輔導別
人！

女：A）這次錄取的人並不多，我們可夠幸
運的。

B）我媽媽認為當輔導員不必那麼獨
立。

C）夏令營有很多好玩的活動，小孩子
肯定會非常喜歡。

D）你跟你媽媽多溝通溝通，她自然就
會改變她的想法了。

（學生答題5 秒）

15. 女：我上个月报名申请当夏令营的辅导
员，刚刚接到了录取通知，我乐坏
了。

男：我也被录取了，不过我妈不让我去，
她认为我还不够独立，怎么能辅导别
人！

女：A）这次录取的人并不多，我们可够幸
运的。

B）我妈妈认为当辅导员不必那么独
立。

C）夏令营有很多好玩的活动，小孩子
肯定会非常喜欢。

D）你跟你妈妈多沟通沟通，她自然就
会改变她的想法了。

（学生答题5 秒）

Listening Selections (15%, 10 minutes)

Directions: You will listen to several selections in Chinese. For each selection, you will be told whether it will be played once or twice. You may take notes as you listen. Your notes will not be graded. After listening to each selection, you will see questions in English. For each question, choose the response that is best according to the selection. You will have 12 seconds to answer each question.

Selection 1: Announcement

Selection plays one time.

Narrator: Now you will listen once to a public announcement.

Woman:

(Traditional Characters)	**(Simplified Characters)**
前往北京的旅客請注意：我們很抱歉地通知各位，您乘坐的MU7765次航班由於颱風來襲，風雨太大，視線不佳，不能按時起飛。在此我們深表歉意。請您先在候機廳休息，等候通知。如果您有什麼需要，請與服務台聯繫。謝謝！	前往北京的旅客请注意：我们很抱歉地通知各位，您乘坐的MU7765次航班由于台风来袭，风雨太大，视线不佳，不能按时起飞。在此我们深表歉意。请您先在候机厅休息，等候通知。如果您有什么需要，请与服务台联系。谢谢！

Narrator: Now answer the questions for this selection.

(12 seconds)

(12 seconds)

Selection 2: Conversation

Selection plays one time.

Narrator: Now you will listen once to a conversation between two students.

(Traditional Characters)

女：這家飯館你來過嗎？他們的菜怎麼樣？

男：我來是沒來過，不過，我同屋是這兒的常客，而且電視曾經報導過，報社記者也寫文章推薦。

女：是嗎？那記者說他們師傅哪些菜最拿手？

男：聽說魚香肉絲、麻婆豆腐什麼的，都十分地道，他們的水煮魚也是大家常常點的。

女：這些菜聽起來似乎都辣得很，我不太吃辣，換一家吧？

男：既來之，則安之。我們讓師傅少放辣椒，不就得了？

女：說的也是。除了辣椒以外，千萬別忘了讓他們別放味精、少放點鹽。

男：放心吧！你看，菜單上不是清清楚楚地寫著：「請安心食用，我們不用味精」？

女：好，那咱們可以點菜了吧？我餓壞了。

(Simplified Characters)

女：这家饭馆你来过吗？他们的菜怎么样？

男：我来是没来过，不过，我同屋是这儿的常客，而且电视曾经报道过，报社记者也写文章推荐。

女：是吗？那记者说他们师傅哪些菜最拿手？

男：听说鱼香肉丝、麻婆豆腐什么的，都十分地道，他们的水煮鱼也是大家常常点的。

女：这些菜听起来似乎都辣得很，我不太吃辣，换一家吧？

男：既来之，则安之。我们让师傅少放辣椒，不就得了？

女：说的也是。除了辣椒以外，千万别忘了让他们别放味精、少放点盐。

男：放心吧！你看，菜单上不是清清楚楚地写着："请安心食用，我们不用味精"？

女：好，那咱们可以点菜了吧？我饿坏了。

Narrator: Now answer the questions for this selection.

(12 seconds)

(12 seconds)

(12 seconds)

(12 seconds)

Selection 3: Instructions

Selection plays two times.

Narrator: Now you will listen twice to an instructions.

Woman:

(Traditional Characters)	(Simplified Characters)
你不用擔心，你的病沒什麼要緊，只是季節性的感冒，不是新流感，不用住院隔離觀察。我給你開兩種藥，你去藥房取藥。比較大的那種藥，一天吃三次，一次吃兩片，飯前吃，要按時吃。比較小的那種，你咳嗽不停的時候才吃，一次吃一粒，服用的時間必須間隔六個小時，一天不能超過四粒，飯前、飯後服用都可以。	你不用担心，你的病没什么要紧，只是季节性的感冒，不是新流感，不用住院隔离观察。我给你开两种药，你去药房取药。比较大的那种药，一天吃三次，一次吃两片，饭前吃，要按时吃。比较小的那种，你咳嗽不停的时候才吃，一次吃一粒，服用的时间必须间隔六个小时，一天不能超过四粒，饭前、饭后服用都可以。

Narrator: Now listen again.

Narrator: Now answer the questions for this selection.
(12 seconds)
(12 seconds)
(12 seconds)
(12 seconds)

Selection 4: Voice message

Selection plays two times.

Narrator: Now you will listen twice to a voice message.

Man:

(Traditional Characters)	(Simplified Characters)
小鵬，給你打了好幾次電話，可是一直占線，好不容易通了，你又不接。怎麼回事？你都在忙些什麼？是這樣的，我剛看到學校的告示，四月底學生會要舉辦一個才藝表演。你還記得我們去年表演的相聲是多麼受大家的歡迎嗎？想不想在畢業前再合作一次，為我們的高中生活留個美好的回憶？給我回個電話吧，我們好好好兒商量商量！雖然離演出的時間還有六個星期，但是越早準備越好，再說我們還得向王老師借說相聲的長袍，是吧？我等你回電話。	小鹏，给你打了好几次电话，可是一直占线，好不容易通了，你又不接。怎么回事？你都在忙些什么？是这样的，我刚看到学校的告示，四月底学生会要举办一个才艺表演。你还记得我们去年表演的相声是多么受大家的欢迎吗？想不想在毕业前再合作一次，为我们的高中生活留个美好的回忆？给我回个电话吧，我们好好好儿商量商量！虽然离演出的时间还有六个星期，但是越早准备越好，再说我们还得向王老师借说相声的长袍，是吧？我等你回电话。

Narrator: Now listen again.

Narrator: Now answer the questions for this selection.

(12 seconds)

(12 seconds)

(12 seconds)

(12 seconds)

(12 seconds)

Selection 5: Report

Selection plays two times.

Narrator: Now you will listen twice to a report.

(Traditional Characters)

校長、各位老師、各位同學，大家好！
現在我代表我們小組來匯報一下上學期我們調查十一、十二年級學生課餘打工的情況。一共有二百三十四位同學接受我們的電話訪問調查，其中有百分之七十的學生都有打工的經驗。百分之六十的同學平均每週工作十個小時，只有不到百分之五的學生每週打工超過二十個小時。百分之七十四的同學都表示，打工除了為了掙點兒零用錢，還為了增加一點兒工作經驗。有百分之七的學生打工是因為家境需要，課餘打工來貼補家用。這些學生一般每週打工的時間至少十五個小時。所有的同學都表示，學習比掙錢重要，如果打工影響學業的話，他們就會把工作辭掉。以上是我們的調查報告，謝謝。

(Simplified Characters)

校长、各位老师、各位同学，大家好！
现在我代表我们小组来汇报一下上学期我们调查十一、十二年级学生课余打工的情况。一共有二百三十四位同学接受我们的电话访问调查，其中有百分之七十的学生都有打工的经验。百分之六十的同学平均每周工作十个小时，只有不到百分之五的学生每周打工超过二十个小时。百分之七十四的同学都表示，打工除了为了挣点儿零用钱，还为了增加一点儿工作经验。有百分之七的学生打工是因为家境需要，课余打工来贴补家用。这些学生一般每周打工的时间至少十五个小时。所有的同学都表示，学习比挣钱重要，如果打工影响学业的话，他们就会把工作辞掉。以上是我们的调查报告，谢谢。

Narrator: Now listen again.

Narrator: Now answer the questions for this selection.

(12 seconds)

(12 seconds)

(12 seconds)

(12 seconds)

(12 seconds)

Section II: Part B: Speaking

Recording Scripts

Conversation

Directions: You will participate in a simulated conversation. Each time it is your turn to speak, you will have 20 seconds to record. You should respond as fully and as appropriately as possible.

You will have a conversation with Lin Fang, a new friend in Beijing, about the 2008 Olympics.

(Traditional Characters)

林芳：2008年的奧運，你看了吧？你是在北京看的，還是看的電視轉播？

（學生答題20秒）

林芳：請你告訴我，這次奧運會給你印象最深的是什麼？

（學生答題20秒）

林芳：在奧運的比賽項目當中，你對哪個項目最感興趣？為什麼？

（學生答題20秒）

林芳：有沒有哪個運動員是你最喜歡的？為什麼？

（學生答題20秒）

林芳：你平常是不是也參加什麼體育活動？將來想參加奧運比賽嗎？

（學生答題20秒）

林芳：你這個週末有空嗎？來我家一起看電視體育轉播，順便在我家吃個便飯，怎麼樣？

（學生答題20秒）

(Simplified Characters)

林芳：2008年的奥运，你看了吧？你是在北京看的，还是看的电视转播？

（学生答题20秒）

林芳：请你告诉我，这次奥运会给你印象最深的是什么？

（学生答题20秒）

林芳：在奥运的比赛项目当中，你对哪个项目最感兴趣？为什么？

（学生答题20秒）

林芳：有没有哪个运动员是你最喜欢的？为什么？

（学生答题20秒）

林芳：你平常是不是也参加什么体育活动？将来想参加奥运比赛吗？

（学生答题20秒）

林芳：你这个周末有空吗？来我家一起看电视体育转播，顺便在我家吃个便饭，怎么样？

（学生答题20秒）

Cultural Presentation

Choose one celebration of the Chinese festivals, such as the Spring Festival, Dragon Boat Festival, Mid-Autumn Festival, etc. In your presentation, describe the festival, how Chinese celebrate it, and explain its significance.

Recording Scripts for Test 5

Section I: Part A: Listening

Rejoinders

Directions: You will hear several short conversations or parts of conversations followed by four choices, designated (A), (B), (C), and (D). Choose the one that continues or completes the conversation in a logical and culturally appropriate manner. You will have 5 seconds to answer each question.

(Traditional Characters)	(Simplified Characters)
1. 男：你參加學校游泳隊才幾個月，就游得這麼棒，你是怎麼練的？ 女：A）我們學校的游泳隊真的很棒。 B）游泳訓練很無聊。 C）我每天早上和下午都練習兩個小時。 D）游泳的確很有意思。 （學生答題5 秒）	1. 男：你参加学校游泳队才几个月，就游得这么棒，你是怎么练的呢？ 女：A）我们学校的游泳队真的很棒。 B）游泳训练很无聊。 C）我每天早上和下午都练习两个小时。 D）游泳的确很有意思。 （学生答题5 秒）
2. 男：售貨員，我昨天買的這雙鞋質量有點問題，我想把它退了。 女：A）這雙鞋的樣子過時了，很少有人買。 B）收據帶來了嗎？ C）這雙鞋夠便宜的了，不能再打折了。 D）你還要買些什麼？ （學生答題5 秒）	2. 男：售货员，我昨天买的这双鞋质量有点问题，我想把它退了。 女：A）这双鞋的样子过时了，很少有人买。 B）收据带来了吗？ C）这双鞋够便宜的了，不能再打折了。 D）你还要买些什么？ （学生答题5 秒）

3. 男：玲玲，我好幾天沒來上學，落下了很多
　　課。可不可以借你的筆記看一下？

　　女：A) 好幾天沒見到你了。

　　　　B) 你的作業找不到了嗎？

　　　　C) 我一用完，就把筆記還給你。

　　　　D) 沒問題，就是我的筆記很亂。

　（學生答題5 秒）

4. 女：啊呀，外面下大雨了！今天的足球賽
　　恐怕得取消了。

　　男：A) 我看足球賽時一定得吃爆米花。

　　　　B) 那樣就太掃興了。

　　　　C) 不用擔心，咱們學校的足球隊肯定
　　　　　 會贏。

　　　　D) 現在喜歡足球的人越來越少了。

　（學生答題5 秒）

5. 女：嗨，下個月就要高中畢業了，想不想幫
　　學校做點什麼事表示感謝？

　　男：A) 好主意，讓我想一想。

　　　　B) 我們這幾年學到了很多東西。

　　　　C) 沒問題，我們是應該開個舞會。

　　　　D) 你猜猜學校會送畢業生什麼禮物呢？

　（學生答題5 秒）

6. 男：下週有個工作面談，我打算去買套西裝穿。

　　女：A) 穿西裝上班很得體。

　　　　B) 逛街很有意思。

　　　　C) 賣西裝的工作不好做，因為現在穿西
　　　　　 裝的人很少。

　　　　D) 現在經濟這麼差你還能有面談的機
　　　　　 會，運氣不錯啊。

　（學生答題5 秒）

3. 男：玲玲，我好几天没来上学，落下了很多
　　课。可不可以借你的笔记看一下？

　　女：A) 好几天没见到你了。

　　　　B) 你的作业找不到了吗？

　　　　C) 我一用完，就把笔记还给你。

　　　　D) 没问题，就是我的笔记很乱。

　（学生答题5 秒）

4. 女：啊呀，外面下大雨了！今天的足球赛
　　恐怕得取消了。

　　男：A) 我看足球赛时一定得吃爆米花。

　　　　B) 那样就太扫兴了。

　　　　C) 不用担心，咱们学校的足球队肯定
　　　　　 会赢。

　　　　D) 现在喜欢足球的人越来越少了。

　（学生答题5 秒）

5. 女：嗨，下个月就要高中毕业了，想不想帮
　　学校做点什么事表示感谢？

　　男：A) 好主意，让我想一想。

　　　　B) 我们这几年学到了很多东西。

　　　　C) 没问题，我们是应该开个舞会。

　　　　D) 你猜猜学校会送毕业生什么礼物呢？

　（学生答题5 秒）

6. 男：下周有个工作面谈，我打算去买套西装穿。

　　女：A) 穿西装上班很得体。

　　　　B) 逛街很有意思。

　　　　C) 卖西装的工作不好做，因为现在穿西
　　　　　 装的人很少。

　　　　D) 现在经济这么差你还能有面谈的机
　　　　　 会，运气不错啊。

　（学生答题5 秒）

7. 女：大山，你父母說英文好像沒有什麼
　　　口音。

　　男：A) 他們都是美國的第二代移民了。

　　　　B) 有些父母不會說英文。

　　　　C) 我父母英文的發音是不太標準。

　　　　D) 我父母講話聲音都很輕。

　　（學生答題5 秒）

8. 女：我們這個週末要去做義工，你有沒有
　　　空和我們一塊去？

　　男：A) 我覺得做義工很有意義。

　　　　B) 你每個星期都做義工嗎？

　　　　C) 好啊！是不是去海邊撿垃圾？

　　　　D) 我從小就喜歡做義工。

　　（學生答題5 秒）

9. 男：真倒霉！我三次駕駛考試都沒過關。

　　女：你大概太緊張了吧？要不然你肯定考
　　　得過。

　　男：A) 考試不應該緊張。

　　　　B) 你怎麼知道我不緊張呢？

　　　　C) 有一點兒，下次考試時我得放輕
　　　　　鬆點。

　　　　D) 我開得夠好的了，不用再多練了。

　　（學生答題5 秒）

7. 女：大山，你父母说英文好像没有什么
　　　口音。

　　男：A) 他们都是美国的第二代移民了。

　　　　B) 有些父母不会说英文。

　　　　C) 我父母英文的发音是不太标准。

　　　　D) 我父母讲话声音都很轻。

　　（学生答题5 秒）

8. 女：我们这个周末要去做义工，你有没有
　　　空和我们一块去？

　　男：A) 我觉得做义工很有意义。

　　　　B) 你每个星期都做义工吗？

　　　　C) 好啊！是不是去海边捡垃圾？

　　　　D) 我从小就喜欢做义工。

　　（学生答题5 秒）

9. 男：真倒霉！我三次驾驶考试都没过关。

　　女：你大概太紧张了吧？要不然你肯定考
　　　得过。

　　男：A) 考试不应该紧张。

　　　　B) 你怎么知道我不紧张呢？

　　　　C) 有一点儿，下次考试时我得放轻
　　　　　松点。

　　　　D) 我开得够好的了，不用再多练了。

　　（学生答题5 秒）

10. 女：你去過中國的雲南省嗎？聽說那個地
    方很有意思。

    男：跟我家人去過一次。那兒住著很多少
    數民族，文化非常豐富。

    女：A) 為什麼很少人住在那兒呢？

    　　B) 這個問題我不清楚。

    　　C) 這麼說我一定得去看一看。

    　　D) 雲南只有少數人很富有。

(學生答題5 秒)

11. 男：我覺得我們開錯路了，大偉家肯定沒
    這麼遠。

    女：那我們把車停在右邊那個加油站去問
    一問路吧。

    男：A) 這兒怎麼連個加油站都沒有呢？

    　　B) 我的車是今天早上剛加的油。

    　　C) 來不及了，我們這條線不能右轉。

    　　D) 加油站的右邊不讓停車。

(學生答題5 秒)

12. 男：今天我們在中文課上看了一部關於大
    熊貓的紀錄片，好看極了！

    女：你見過真正的熊貓嗎？

    男：A) 那年我去聖地亞哥動物園，看到
    了剛從中國來的大熊貓。

    　　B) 我覺得我們應該保護自然環境，
    讓熊貓有好的生存環境。

    　　C) 熊貓是瀕臨絕種的動物。

    　　D) 成龍演的那部熊貓電影真好玩兒。

(學生答題5 秒)

10. 女：你去过中国的云南省吗？听说那个地
    方很有意思。

    男：跟我家人去过一次。那儿住着很多少
    数民族，文化非常丰富。

    女：A) 为什么很少人住在那儿呢？

    　　B) 这个问题我不清楚。

    　　C) 这么说我一定得去看一看。

    　　D) 云南只有少数人很富有。

(学生答题5 秒)

11. 男：我觉得我们开错路了，大伟家肯定没
    这么远。

    女：那我们把车停在右边那个加油站去问
    一问路吧。

    男：A) 这儿怎么连个加油站都没有呢？

    　　B) 我的车是今天早上刚加的油。

    　　C) 来不及了，我们这条线不能右转。

    　　D) 加油站的右边不让停车。

(学生答题5 秒)

12. 男：今天我们在中文课上看了一部关于大
    熊猫的纪录片，好看极了！

    女：你见过真正的熊猫吗？

    男：A) 那年我去圣地亚哥动物园，看到
    了刚从中国来的大熊猫。

    　　B) 我觉得我们应该保护自然环境，
    让熊猫有好的生存环境。

    　　C) 熊猫是濒临绝种的动物。

    　　D) 成龙演的那部熊猫电影真好玩儿。

(学生答题5 秒)

221

13. 男：蘭蘭，你昨天去中國城看遊行了嗎?

　　女：我去了，人太多，簡直都擠死了。

　　男：A）幸虧我沒去，在家看電視轉播其實
　　　　　　更舒服。

　　　　B）我的天哪！擠死了幾個人呀？

　　　　C）中國城有很多旅遊的人。

　　　　D）我要是參加遊行就好了。

（學生答題5 秒）

14. 男：嗨，小麗，我昨晚做了個夢，夢見我
　　　　AP中文考試得了個5。

　　女：有意思！真是個美夢。

　　男：A）你也做過同樣的夢啊？

　　　　B）做夢沒有意思。

　　　　C）但願美夢成真。

　　　　D）我不喜歡AP中文在晚上考。

（學生答題5 秒）

15. 女：我婆婆手特巧，幾下了就能剪出個花
　　　　鳥什麼的。

　　男：剪紙是中國的傳統藝術，你應該跟你
　　　　婆婆學一學。

　　女：A）好，我讓我婆婆教你。

　　　　B）我婆婆的剪紙很酷。

　　　　C）嗯，不過看著容易，學起來難。

　　　　D）你看到我的剪刀了嗎？

（學生答題5 秒）

13. 男：兰兰，你昨天去中国城看游行了吗?

　　女：我去了，人太多，简直都挤死了。

　　男：A）幸亏我没去，在家看电视转播其实
　　　　　　更舒服。

　　　　B）我的天哪！挤死了几个人呀？

　　　　C）中国城有很多旅游的人。

　　　　D）我要是参加游行就好了。

（学生答题5 秒）

14. 男：嗨，小丽，我昨晚做了个梦，梦见我
　　　　AP中文考试得了个5。

　　女：有意思！真是个美梦。

　　男：A）你也做过同样的梦啊？

　　　　B）做梦没有意思。

　　　　C）但愿美梦成真。

　　　　D）我不喜欢AP中文在晚上考。

（学生答题5 秒）

15. 女：我婆婆手特巧，几下子就能剪出个花
　　　　鸟什么的。

　　男：剪纸是中国的传统艺术，你应该跟你
　　　　婆婆学一学。

　　女：A）好，我让我婆婆教你。

　　　　B）我婆婆的剪纸很酷。

　　　　C）嗯，不过看着容易，学起来难。

　　　　D）你看到我的剪刀了吗？

（学生答题5 秒）

Listening Selections (15%, 10 minutes)

Directions: You will listen to several selections in Chinese. For each selection, you will be told whether it will be played once or twice. You may take notes as you listen. Your notes will not be graded. After listening to each selection, you will see questions in English. For each question, choose the response that is best according to the selection. You will have 12 seconds to answer each question.

Selection 1: Announcement

Selection plays one time.

Narrator: Now you will listen once to a public announcement.

(Traditional Characters)

旅客們請注意，由於氣流的緣故，飛機顛簸得很厲害。請您馬上回到您的座位，並繫好安全帶。洗手間暫停使用。機艙乘務員也請就坐，待安全指示燈顯示後，再繼續您的工作。謝謝大家的合作。

(Simplified Characters)

旅客们请注意，由于气流的缘故，飞机颠簸得很厉害。请您马上回到您的座位，并系好安全带。洗手间暂停使用。机舱乘务员也请就坐，待安全指示灯显示后，再继续您的工作。谢谢大家的合作。

Narrator: Now answer the questions for this selection.

(12 seconds)

(12 seconds)

(12 seconds)

Selection 2: Voice message

Selection plays two times.

Narrator: Now you will listen twice to a voice message.

(Traditional Characters)

英英，我是紫薇。咱們小組星期六的活動我
去不了了。我爺爺被車撞了，星期六我得和
我父母去醫院看望他，大概很晚才能回來。
如果能把小組活動改到星期天最好了，要不
然我就只好缺席了。分給我的那部份，我一
定會完成，絕不會影響咱們小組週一的報
告。麻煩你代我向大家道個歉。有事請打我
的手機聯絡。謝謝！
再見！

(Simplified Characters)

英英，我是紫薇。咱们小组星期六的活动我
去不了了。我爷爷被车撞了，星期六我得和
我父母去医院看望他，大概很晚才能回来。
如果能把小组活动改到星期天最好了，要不
然我就只好缺席了。分给我的那部份，我一
定会完成，绝不会影响咱们小组周一的报
告。麻烦你代我向大家道个歉。有事请打我
的手机联络。谢谢！
再见！

Narrator: Now listen again.
(Repeat)

Narrator: Now answer the questions for this selection.
(12 seconds)

(12 seconds)

(12 seconds)

Selection 3: Conversation

Selection plays one time.

Narrator: Now you will listen once to a conversation between two students.

<table>
<tr><td>

(Traditional Characters)

（男）美雲，下週三學校體操隊有個選拔賽，你想去試試嗎？

（女）我是很想去，可是我的腳傷還沒全好呢，去了恐怕也選不上。你應該去啊！

（男）我覺得練體操很累，而且這學期我選的課都很難，真是有點力不從心。

（女）那你也不應該半途而廢。你從小就學體操，都練了這麼多年了，扔了太可惜了。

（男）你說的倒也是，讓我想想吧，可我還是覺得你應該去。

（女）你去我就去！

（男）好，一言為定！

</td><td>

(Simplified Characters)

（男）美云，下周三学校体操队有个选拔赛，你想要去试试吗？

（女）我是很想去，可是我的脚伤还没全好呢，去了恐怕也选不上。你应该去啊！

（男）我觉得练体操很累，而且这学期我选的课都很难，真是有点力不从心。

（女）那你也不应该半途而废。你从小就学体操，都练了这么多年了，扔了太可惜了。

（男）你说的倒也是，让我想想吧，可我还是觉得你应该去。

（女）你去我就去！

（男）好，一言为定！

</td></tr>
</table>

Narrator: Now answer the questions for this selection.

(12 seconds)

(12 seconds)

(12 seconds)

(12 seconds)

Selection 4: Instructions

Selection plays two times.

Narrator: Now you will listen twice to an instruction.

Man:

(Traditional Characters)

電腦郵寄退款說明：

　　凡是在2009年6月28至10月11日期間購買本公司電腦的客戶均可享受$50退款的優惠。郵寄日期必須是在購買日期之後的45天以內。退款所需的手續：1）購買產品的收據或網上購買的付款記錄。2）退款表格：您需在表上填寫您的姓名、住址、及聯繫電話。3）產品的型號、電腦的系列號以及郵寄公司的送貨號。請將以上材料一併寄到退款表格上所提供的地址。如資料齊全，我們會在30天內把退款支票寄給您。本優惠只限美國境內客戶。如有問題，請打我們的免費查詢電話。

電話是：1-888-666-9999。

(Simplified Characters)

电脑邮寄退款说明：

　　凡是在2009年6月28至10月11日期间购买本公司电脑的客户均可享受$50退款的优惠。邮寄日期必须是在购买日期之后的45天以内。退款所需的手续：1）购买产品的收据或网上购买的付款记录。2）退款表格：您需在表上填写您的姓名、住址、及联系电话。3）产品的型号、电脑的系列号以及邮寄公司的送货号。请将以上材料一并寄到退款表格上所提供的地址。如资料齐全，我们会在30天内把退款支票寄给您。本优惠只限美国境内客户。如有问题，请打我们的免费查询电话。

电话是：1-888-666-9999。

Narrator: Now listen again.
(Repeat)

Narrator: Now answer the questions for this selection.

(12 seconds)

(12 seconds)

(12 seconds)

(12 seconds)

Selection 5: Report

Selection plays two times.

Narrator: Now you will listen twice to a report.

(Traditional Characters)

上海氣象台於2009年7月12日18時08分發佈雷電黃色預警信號：預計1到3小時內本市自西向東會有雷電活動，可能造成雷電災害事故。政府及相關部門會按照規定做好防雷工作，市民應密切注意天氣，盡量避免戶外活動。如有事故發生，請撥打120或999求助。

(Simplified Characters)

上海气象台于2009年7月12日18时08分发布雷电黄色预警信号：预计1到3小时内本市自西向东会有雷电活动，可能造成雷电灾害事故。政府及相关部门会按照规定做好防雷工作，市民应密切注意天气，尽量避免户外活动。如有事故发生，请拨打120或999求助。

Narrator: Now listen again.
(Repeat)

Narrator: Now answer the questions for this selection.

(12 seconds)

(12 seconds)

(12 seconds)

(12 seconds)

(12 seconds)

Section II: Part B: Speaking

Recording Scripts

Conversation

Directions: You will participate in a simulated conversation. Each time it is your turn to speak, you will have 20 seconds to record. You should respond as fully and as appropriately as possible.

You will have a conversation with Li Long, a Chinese student you met on the Great Wall, about your experiences in China.

(Traditional Characters)	(Simplified Characters)
李龍：很高興認識你，你的中文講得這麼好，還有點北京口音，你在北京生活過嗎？ （學生答題20秒）	李龙：很高兴认识你，你的中文讲得这么好，还有点北京口音，你在北京生活过吗？ （学生答题20秒）
李龍：我看你登長城很輕鬆，你大概經常運動吧？你都喜歡些什麼運動？ （學生答題20秒）	李龙：我看你登长城很轻松，你大概经常运动吧？你都喜欢些什么运动？ （学生答题20秒）
李龍：你們外國人是怎樣理解“不到長城非好漢”這句話的呢？ （學生答題20秒）	李龙：你们外国人是怎样理解“不到长城非好汉”这句话的呢？ （学生答题20秒）
李龍：這次中國之行你還打算去哪些地方？ （學生答題20秒）	李龙：这次中国之行你还打算去哪些地方？ （学生答题20秒）
李龍：北京有很多有名的小吃，你都吃過哪些？ （學生答題20秒）	李龙：北京有很多有名的小吃，你都吃过哪些？ （学生答题20秒）
李龍：過一段時間我要去美國旅遊，可以給我介紹一些好玩的地方嗎？ （學生答題20秒）	李龙：过一段时间我要去美国旅游，可以给我介绍一些好玩的地方吗？ （学生答题20秒）

Cultural Presentation

Directions: You will be asked to speak in Chinese on a specific topic. Imagine you are making an oral presentation to your Chinese class. First, you will read and hear the topic for your presentation. You will have 4 minutes to prepare your presentation. Then you will have 2 minutes to record your presentation. Your presentation should be as complete as possible.

Choose one contemporary Chinese celebrity (athlete, musician, actor, politician, etc.) and describe the reason for his or her popularity, his or her achievements, and any influence he or she has had on Chinese culture at large or on your life.

Recording Scripts for Test 6

Section I: Part A: Listening

Rejoinders

Directions: You will hear several short conversations or parts of conversations followed by four choices, designated (A), (B), (C), and (D). Choose the one that continues or completes the conversation in a logical and culturally appropriate manner. You will have 5 seconds to answer each question.

(Traditional Characters)

1. 男：我們家的洗衣機、烘乾機都壞了，這
　　幾天又一直下雨，衣服乾不了，真討厭。
　女：A）你可以來用我們家的。
　　　B）下雨才好呢，要不然，今年夏天就
　　　　　缺水了。
　　　C）你不洗衣服嗎？
　　　D）我們家的衣服都是我洗的。

（學生答題5 秒）

2. 女：小林的生日晚會，你要是不去，那我也
　　不去。
　男：A）他去年的生日晚會邀請了很多的親朋
　　　　好友。
　　　B）你知道哪些人去了嗎？
　　　C）我是因為第二天有考試才不去的，你
　　　　　沒什麼事，還是去吧！
　　　D）小林再過三天就十八歲了。

（學生答題5 秒）

(Simplified Characters)

1. 男：我们家的洗衣机、烘干机都坏了，这
　　几天又一直下雨，衣服干不了，真讨厌。
　女：A）你可以来用我们家的。
　　　B）下雨才好呢，要不然，今年夏天就
　　　　　缺水了。
　　　C）你不洗衣服吗？
　　　D）我们家的衣服都是我洗的。

（学生答题5 秒）

2. 女：小林的生日晚会，你要是不去，那我也
　　不去。
　男：A）他去年的生日晚会邀请了很多的亲朋
　　　　好友。
　　　B）你知道哪些人去了吗？
　　　C）我是因为第二天有考试才不去的，你
　　　　　没什么事，还是去吧！
　　　D）小林再过三天就十八岁了。

（学生答题5 秒）

3. 男：今天晚上的電視節目不是球賽，就是
　　　動畫，沒什麼好看的。
　　女：A）現在的電視節目都做得不錯。
　　　　B）我妹妹現在在學習動畫的製作，聽
　　　　　　說挺有意思的。
　　　　C）那你怎麼還一直坐在電視機前面
　　　　　　盯著電視看呢？
　　　　D）今天下午的球賽非常精彩，你去看
　　　　　　了沒有？

（學生答題5 秒）

4. 女：我們前兩天剛搬進了新家，這回我可
　　　有自己的房間了。
　　男：A）我家離學校很近，非常方便。
　　　　B）你喜歡跟你妹妹住同一個房間嗎？
　　　　C）我們應該常常把自己的房間打掃
　　　　　　打掃、收拾收拾。
　　　　D）太好了。你們是自己搬的家，還
　　　　　　是請搬家公司幫的忙？

（學生答題5 秒）

5. 男：這種藥還不錯，你試試看！
　　女：A）我已經試過五、六種藥了，都沒用，
　　　　　　明天還得再去看醫生。
　　　　B）我沒有健康保險，所以從不去看醫
　　　　　　生，也不吃藥。
　　　　C）謝謝你的關心，希望吃了這個藥病
　　　　　　就好了。
　　　　D）我家附近的藥店也不錯。

（學生答題5 秒）

3. 男：今天晚上的电视节目不是球赛，就是
　　　动画，没什么好看的。
　　女：A）现在的电视节目都做得不错。
　　　　B）我妹妹现在在学习动画的制作，听
　　　　　　说挺有意思的。
　　　　C）那你怎么还一直坐在电视机前面盯
　　　　　　着电视看呢？
　　　　D）今天下午的球赛非常精彩，你去看
　　　　　　了没有？

（学生答题5 秒）

4. 女：我们前两天刚搬进了新家，这回我可
　　　有自己的房间了。
　　男：A）我家离学校很近，非常方便。
　　　　B）你喜欢跟你妹妹住同一个房间吗？
　　　　C）我们应该常常把自己的房间打扫
　　　　　　打扫、收拾收拾。
　　　　D）太好了。你们是自己搬的家，还
　　　　　　是请搬家公司帮的忙？

（学生答题5 秒）

5. 男：这种药还不错，你试试看！
　　女：A）我已经试过五、六种药了，都没用，
　　　　　　明天还得再去看医生。
　　　　B）我没有健康保险，所以从不去看医
　　　　　　生，也不吃药。
　　　　C）谢谢你的关心，希望吃了这个药病
　　　　　　就好了。
　　　　D）我家附近的药店也不错。

（学生答题5 秒）

6. 女：你出門以前，先幫我把碗、盤洗了吧！
   男：A）我比較喜歡洗車。
       B）哎呀，碗、盤那麼多，等我回來再說吧！
       C）我要出門去買東西。
       D）碗、盤在哪兒？我不知道。

（學生答題5 秒）

7. 女：你要是真想吃，就吃吧，但是減肥失敗了，可別怪別人喲！
   男：A）好了，好了，我吃就是了，何必怪我呢？
       B）哪有這樣的事？為了你減肥，我就不能吃東西了？
       C）要說不怕胖是假的，但是美食當前，胖就胖吧，吃了再說。
       D）你這麼胖下去，怎麼得了？

（學生答題5 秒）

8. 男：今年這個棒球隊表現傑出，尤其是他的當家投手，很少人打得到他的球。
   女：A）籃球賽比棒球賽精彩多了。
       B）真沒想到你棒球打得這麼好，你是怎麼練的？
       C）他們的打擊不行，所以今年常常輸球。
       D）他可值錢呢，聽說一年可以賺上兩百萬美金。

（學生答題5 秒）

6. 女：你出门以前，先帮我把碗、盘洗了吧！
   男：A）我比较喜欢洗车。
       B）哎呀，碗、盘那么多，等我回来再说吧！
       C）我要出门去买东西。
       D）碗、盘在哪儿？我不知道。

（学生答题5 秒）

7. 女：你要是真想吃，就吃吧，但是减肥失败了，可别怪别人哟！
   男：A）好了，好了，我吃就是了，何必怪我呢？
       B）哪有这样的事？为了你减肥，我就不能吃东西了？
       C）要说不怕胖是假的，但是美食当前，胖就胖吧，吃了再说。
       D）你这么胖下去，怎么得了？

（学生答题5 秒）

8. 男：今年这个棒球队表现杰出，尤其是他的当家投手，很少有人打得到他的球。
   女：A）篮球赛比棒球赛精彩多了。
       B）真没想到你棒球打得这么好，你是怎么练的？
       C）他们的打击不行，所以今年常常输球。
       D）他可值钱呢，听说一年可以赚上两百万美金。

（学生答题5 秒）

232

9. 男：沒想到這次考試會這麼難，恐怕我會
      不及格。

   女：你父母會罵你嗎？

   男：A）那倒不至於，不過，我自己會挺
          難過的。

      B）希望下星期的考試容易些。

      C）我父母希望我考上名牌大學。

      D）我父母經常嘮叨，說我不用功，可
          是我不聽他們的。

   （學生答題5 秒）

10. 女：你今年生日過得怎麼樣？

    男：哎，別提了，收到了兩件一模一樣
        的禮物。

    女：A）你今年生日是怎麼過的？

       B）你今年多大了？

       C）我非常喜歡你送我的生日禮物。

       D）那你可以拿到商店去退換呀。

   （學生答題5 秒）

11. 男：這個學期的課外活動，你決定參加什
        麼了沒有？

    女：我對羽毛球和網球都非常感興趣，
        還不知道該選什麼才好。

    男：A）我可以跟你一起練習。

       B）別說了，我也不行。

       C）你看看球隊練習的時間再決定吧。

       D）羽毛球隊、網球隊，我都參加過。

   （學生答題5 秒）

9. 男：没想到这次考试会这么难，恐怕我会
      不及格。

   女：你父母会骂你吗？

   男：A）那倒不至于，不过，我自己会挺难
          过的。

      B）希望下星期的考试容易些。

      C）我父母希望我考上名牌大学。

      D）我父母经常唠叨，说我不用功，可
          是我不听他们的。

   （学生答题5 秒）

10. 女：你今年生日过得怎么样？

    男：哎，别提了，收到了两件一模一样
        的礼物。

    女：A）你今年生日是怎么过的？

       B）你今年多大了？

       C）我非常喜欢你送我的生日礼物。

       D）那你可以拿到商店去退换呀。

   （学生答题5 秒）

11. 男：这个学期的课外活动，你决定参加什
        么了没有？

    女：我对羽毛球和网球都非常感兴趣，
        还不知道该选什么才好。

    男：A）我可以跟你一起练习。

       B）别说了，我也不行。

       C）你看看球队练习的时间再决定吧。

       D）羽毛球队、网球队，我都参加过。

   （学生答题5 秒）

12. 女：這家商店在大減價，我們進去看看有
什麼便宜的。

男：打折的衣服常常大小不合適，樣子也
不好。

女：A）我最喜歡打折的時候買東西了。

B）這家商店難得大減價，你不買點
兒嗎？

C）那也不見得。

D）你看，打七折呢，真便宜。

（學生答題5 秒）

13. 男：對不起，我來晚了，路上堵車，平
常十分鐘的路，足足開了一個小時。

女：怎麼了，又有人發生車禍了？

男：A）大概是吧，有兩輛車停在馬路中
間，旁邊圍著四、五個警察。

B）一發生車禍，保險費馬上就跟著
漲了。

C）現在開車的人沒什麼耐心，車禍
比前幾年頻繁多了。

D）我的車平常挺快的，大概是出了什
麼毛病了，過兩天得送廠去修修。

（學生答題5 秒）

12. 女：这家商店在大减价，我们进去看看有
什么便宜的。

男：打折的衣服常常大小不合适，样子也
不好。

女：A）我最喜欢打折的时候买东西了。

B）这家商店难得大减价，你不买点
儿吗？

C）那也不见得。

D）你看，打七折呢，真便宜。

（学生答题5 秒）

13. 男：对不起，我来晚了，路上堵车，平常
十分钟的路，足足开了一个小时。

女：怎么了，又有人发生车祸了？

男：A）大概是吧，有两辆车停在马路中
间，旁边围着四、五个警察。

B）一发生车祸，保险费马上就跟着
涨了。

C）现在开车的人没什么耐心，车祸
比前几年频繁多了。

D）我的车平常挺快的，大概是出了什
么毛病了，过两天得送厂去修修。

（学生答题5 秒）

234

14. 女：你看那隻貓，多可愛啊，真想求媽媽讓我養一隻貓，可是我知道她絕對不會答應的。

　　男：你又沒問，怎麼知道你媽媽絕對不會答應？

　　女：A）因為對貓過敏的人一天到晚打噴嚏。

　　　　B）因為我們家鄰居也有一隻貓，常常上我們家來玩兒。

　　　　C）因為我媽媽嫌貓髒，也怕傢具被貓抓壞了。

　　　　D）因為我每天都花很多時間上網看貓的圖片。

（學生答題5 秒）

14. 女：你看那只猫，多可爱啊，真想求妈妈让我养一只猫，可是我知道她绝对不会答应的。

　　男：你又没问，怎么知道你妈妈绝对不会答应？

　　女：A）因为对猫过敏的人一天到晚打喷嚏。

　　　　B）因为我们家邻居也有一只猫，常常上我们家来玩儿。

　　　　C）因为我妈妈嫌猫脏，也怕家具被猫抓坏了。

　　　　D）因为我每天都花很多时间上网看猫的图片。

（学生答题5 秒）

15. 女：小陳，是你呀，這麼巧！

　　男：啊，小茵，你不是說最近挺忙的嗎，今天怎麼有空逛商場呢？

　　女：A）今天是什麼日子，商場擠得人山人海的。

　　　　B）母親節快到了，我想給媽媽挑個別緻的禮物。

　　　　C）要是買的東西不合適，這個商場讓不讓顧客退換？

　　　　D）聽說這個商場的工作人員買東西有很好的折扣。

（學生答題5 秒）

15. 女：小陈，是你呀，这么巧！

　　男：啊，小茵，你不是说最近挺忙的吗，今天怎么有空逛商场呢？

　　女：A）今天是什么日子，商场挤得人山人海的。

　　　　B）母亲节快到了，我想给妈妈挑个别致的礼物。

　　　　C）要是买的东西不合适，这个商场让不让顾客退换？

　　　　D）听说这个商场的工作人员买东西有很好的折扣。

（学生答题5 秒）

Listening Selections (15%, 10 minutes)

Directions: You will listen to several selections in Chinese. For each selection, you will be told whether it will be played once or twice. You may take notes as you listen. Your notes will not be graded. After listening to each selection, you will see questions in English. For each question, choose the response that is best according to the selection. You will have 12 seconds to answer each question.

Selection 1: Public Announcement

Selection plays one time.

Narrator: Now you will listen once to a public announcement.

Woman:

(Traditional Characters)

各位旅客請注意！本列車的終點站上海就要到了，請您拿好隨身攜帶的行李，準備下車。要前往南京的旅客，請到三號月台轉乘到南京的火車；前往蘇州的旅客，請到五號月台等候上車。謝謝各位旅客搭乘本次列車，若有服務不周的地方，請包涵，並請多多指教。

(Simplified Characters)

各位旅客请注意！本列车的终点站上海就要到了，请您拿好随身携带的行李，准备下车。要前往南京的旅客，请到三号月台转乘到南京的火车；前往苏州的旅客，请到五号月台等候上车。谢谢各位旅客搭乘本次列车，若有服务不周的地方，请包涵，并请多多指教。

Narrator: Now answer the questions for this selection.
(12 seconds)

(12 seconds)

Selection 2: Conversation

Selection plays one time.

Narrator: Now you will listen once to a conversation between two students.

(Traditional Characters)

男：明明，後天晚上的畢業舞會你去嗎？

女：去是肯定會去的，可是不知道該穿哪件衣服。這兩天功課忙，又沒有時間去買衣服。

男：你上次參加小莉生日舞會時穿的那件連衣裙不是挺好的嗎？既漂亮，又合適。

女：哪件？

男：就是那件藍底兒帶小白花兒的。

女：那件啊，不行，那件是我姐姐的。上次跟她借，結果呢，喝咖啡時不小心，灑了幾滴在上頭。我姐姐簡直氣炸了，一連三天一句話都不跟我說。

男：你姐姐脾氣那麼大啊？

女：不管她了！你說我該怎麼辦？

男：那跟小平借吧！她的衣服多，個子又跟你差不多，你穿肯定合身。

女：好吧！那我現在就給她打電話。

(Simplified Characters)

男：明明，后天晚上的毕业舞会你去吗？

女：去是肯定会去的，可是不知道该穿哪件衣服。这两天功课忙，又没有时间去买衣服。

男：你上次参加小莉生日舞会时穿的那件连衣裙不是挺好的吗？既漂亮，又合适。

女：哪件？

男：就是那件蓝底儿带小白花儿的。

女：那件啊，不行，那件是我姐姐的。上次跟她借，结果呢，喝咖啡时不小心，洒了几滴在上头。我姐姐简直气炸了，一连三天一句话都不跟我说。

男：你姐姐脾气那么大啊？

女：不管她了！你说我该怎么办？

男：那跟小平借吧！她的衣服多，个子又跟你差不多，你穿肯定合身。

女：好吧！那我现在就给她打电话。

Narrator: Now answer the questions for this selection.

(12 seconds)

(12 seconds)

(12 seconds)

(12 seconds)

(12 seconds)

Selection 3: Instructions

Selection plays two times.

Narrator: Now you will listen twice to an instruction.

Woman:

(Traditional Characters)

凡是本市居民或在本市就讀的學生都可申請借
書證。如果是本市的學生，你需要帶學生證，
另外帶兩張一寸的脫帽黑白照片，親自到市立
圖書館的櫃台辦理。如果不是學生，除了帶兩
張照片以外，你還必須帶一個上面有本市地址
的信封，以及一種身份證明文件，例如駕照或
護照，也可託別人代辦。我們當天辦，當天就
發證，當天就可以借書。

(Simplified Characters)

凡是本市居民或在本市就读的学生都可申请借
书证。如果是本市的学生，你需要带学生证，
另外带两张一寸的脱帽黑白照片，亲自到市立
图书馆的柜台办理。如果不是学生，除了带两
张照片以外，你还必须带一个上面有本市地址
的信封，以及一种身份证明文件，例如驾照或
护照，也可托别人代办。我们当天办，当天就
发证，当天就可以借书。

Narrator: Now listen again.
(Repeat)

Narrator: Now answer the questions for this selection.

(12 seconds)

(12 seconds)

(12 seconds)

(12 seconds)

Selection 4: Voice message

Selection plays two times.

Narrator: Now you will listen twice to a voice message.

Woman:

(Traditional Characters)

爸爸，對不起，剛剛教練說，因為這個週末就
要比賽了，可是我們練習得還不夠好，所以他
要我們留下來再多練一個小時，要不然比賽的
結果可能不太理想。我們羽毛球隊隊友對這次
的比賽都非常重視，希望能獲得冠軍，所以大
家都很樂意地留下來練習。本來我練了球是要
坐公共汽車回家的，但是如果我坐車回家，就
趕不上七點的小提琴課了。能不能麻煩您六點
半來接我？謝謝。我們學校正門口見。

(Simplified Characters)

爸爸，对不起，刚刚教练说，因为这个周末就
要比赛了，可是我们练习得还不够好，所以他
要我们留下来再多练一个小时，要不然比赛的
结果可能不太理想。我们羽毛球队队友对这次
的比赛都非常重视，希望能获得冠军，所以大
家都很乐意地留下来练习。本来我练了球是要
坐公共汽车回家的，但是如果我坐车回家，就
赶不上七点的小提琴课了。能不能麻烦您六点
半来接我？谢谢。我们学校正门口见。

Narrator: Now listen again.
(Repeat)

Narrator: Now answer the questions for this selection.

(12 seconds)

(12 seconds)

(12 seconds)

(12 seconds)

Selection 5: Report

Selection plays two times.

Narrator: Now you will listen twice to a report.

Man:

(Traditional Characters)

校長、各位老師、各位同學，大家好！
我是王大為，代表學生會來匯報我們這次交通
工具問卷調查的結果。我們總共發出五百份問
卷，收回四百五十份，謝謝所有參與問卷調查
的同學。百分之六十的同學自己上下學，完全
不用父母接送。百分之二十五的學生上學、放
學都是靠父母開車接送。剩餘的百分之十五有
時候自己上下學，有時候父母開車接送。自己
上下學的同學，有的坐校車，有的坐公共汽
車，有的騎車，有的走路，還有的自己開車。
有父母接送的同學比自己上下學的同學遲到的
比例高得多。他們表示，遲到的原因往往不在
他們身上，而是因為父母的動作太慢。我的報
告結束，謝謝。

(Simplified Characters)

校长、各位老师、各位同学，大家好！
我是王大为，代表学生会来汇报我们这次交通
工具问卷调查的结果。我们总共发出五百份问
卷，收回四百五十份，谢谢所有参与问卷调查
的同学。百分之六十的同学自己上下学，完全
不用父母接送。百分之二十五的学生上学、放
学都是靠父母开车接送。剩余的百分之十五有
时候自己上下学，有时候父母开车接送。自己
上下学的同学，有的坐校车，有的坐公共汽
车，有的骑车，有的走路，还有的自己开车。
有父母接送的同学比自己上下学的同学迟到的
比例高得多。他们表示，迟到的原因往往不在
他们身上，而是因为父母的动作太慢。我的报
告结束，谢谢。

Narrator: Now listen again.
(Repeat)

Narrator: Now answer the questions for this selection.

(12 seconds)

(12 seconds)

(12 seconds)

(12 seconds)

(12 seconds)

Section II: Part B: Speaking

Recording Scripts

Conversation

Directions: You will participate in a simulated conversation. Each time it is your turn to speak, you will have 20 seconds to record. You should respond as fully and as appropriately as possible.

You will have a conversation with Chen Chong, the community service director, about your applying for volunteering to tutor English to the new immigrant Chinese students at the local elementary schools.

(Traditional Characters)

陳沖：你為什麼對幫助小學生英文有興趣？
  （學生答題20秒）

陳沖：你以前做過義工嗎？有沒有輔導英文或
  其他的教學經驗？
  （學生答題20秒）

陳沖：如果小朋友上課不聽話，你會怎麼辦？
  （學生答題20秒）

陳沖：你會怎樣提升孩童學習英語的興趣？
  （學生答題20秒）

陳沖：我們的上課時間是星期一到星期五下午
  三點半到晚上六點，星期六上午八點到
  下午五點。你一個星期哪幾天，從幾點
  到幾點可以來輔導孩童學習？
  （學生答題20秒）

陳沖：你覺得課外來輔導小學生學英文，對你
  學校的功課會有什麼影響？
  （學生答題20秒）

(Simplified Characters)

陈冲：你为什么对帮助小学生英文有兴趣？
  （学生答题20秒）

陈冲：你以前做过义工吗？有没有辅导英文或
  其他的教学经验？
  （学生答题20秒）

陈冲：如果小朋友上课不听话，你会怎么办？
  （学生答题20秒）

陈冲：你会怎样提升孩童学习英语的兴趣？
  （学生答题20秒）

陈冲：我们的上课时间是星期一到星期五下午
  三点半到晚上六点，星期六上午八点到
  下午五点。你一个星期哪几天，从几点
  到几点可以来辅导孩童学习？
  （学生答题20秒）

陈冲：你觉得课外来辅导小学生学英文，对你
  学校的功课会有什么影响？
  （学生答题20秒）

Cultural Presentation

Choose one "成语故事"(「成語故事」), such as "守株待兔"、"画龙点睛"、"自相矛盾"、"亡羊补牢"、"拔苗助长"、"南辕北辙"、"望梅止渴"、"买椟还珠"、"夜郎自大"、"滥竽充数",(「守株待兔」、「畫龍點睛」、「自相矛盾」、「亡羊補牢」、「拔苗助長」、「南轅北轍」、「望梅止渴」、「買櫝還珠」、「夜郎自大」、「濫竽充數」)etc. In your presentation, describe the original story of the expression, what the expresions means, and give an example to explain how the expression is used.

Recording Scripts for Test 7

Section I: Part A: Listening

Rejoinders

Directions: You will hear several short conversations or parts of conversations followed by four choices, designated (A), (B), (C), and (D). Choose the one that continues or completes the conversation in a logical and culturally appropriate manner. You will have 5 seconds to answer each question.

(Traditional Characters)

1. 男：唉，這幾天因為選大學專業的事兒跟我父母吵了一架，他們不同意我報考的專業，可明天申請表就得交了，我真不知怎麼辦才好。

   女：A) 填寫大學申請表很費時間。

   B) 我聽說生物專業很難念，也許你應該尊重你父母的意見。

   C) 哦，既然如此，那你就再考慮幾天吧，反正不急。

   D) 我覺得你應該心平氣和地再跟你父母好好談談。

   （學生答題5 秒）

(Simplified Characters)

1. 男：唉，这几天因为选大学专业的事儿跟我父母吵了一架，他们不同意我报考的专业，可明天申请表就得交了，我真不知怎么办才好。

   女：A) 填写大学申请表很费时间。

   B) 我听说生物专业很难念，也许你应该尊重你父母的意见。。

   C) 哦，既然如此，那你就再考虑几天吧，反正不急。

   D) 我觉得上你应该心平气和地再跟你父母好好谈谈。

   （学生答题5 秒）

2. 女：今天上中文課時，老師教我們打太極拳，挺有意思的，可是不太好學。

   男：A) 我也學過，其實難倒是不難，我這個人就是沒耐性。

   B) 我們的中文課也挺有意思的，就是有時聽不太懂。

   C) 慢性子的人學不了太極拳。

   D) 打太極拳的確是又難又沒意思。

   （學生答題5 秒）

3. 男：婷婷，你昨晚看體育新聞了嗎？中國女子跳水隊又拿到了一塊金牌。

   女：A) 哎呀，怎麼搞的？

   B) 世界游泳錦標賽是在羅馬舉行的。

   C) 真的嗎？中國跳水隊太了不起了！

   D) 看了，他們踢得很辛苦，好不容易才進了一個球。

   （學生答題5 秒）

4. 女：樂樂，你去夏令營那麼長時間怎麼一直都沒跟我聯繫呢？

   男：A) 你說得沒錯，夏令營的時間是有兒有點太長了。

   B) 那個地方既不能上網，也不能打電話。

   C) 我們在夏令營交了很多新朋友，過得很快樂。

   D) 時間過得真快，夏令營很快就要結束了。

   （學生答題5 秒）

2. 女：今天上中文课时，老师教我们打太极拳，挺有意思的，可是不太好学。

   男：A) 我也学过，其实难倒是不难，我这个人就是没耐性。

   B) 我们的中文课也挺有意思的，就是有时听不太懂。

   C) 慢性子的人学不了太极拳。

   D) 打太极拳的确是又难又没意思。

   （学生答题5 秒）

3. 男：婷婷，你昨晚看体育新闻了吗？中国女子跳水队又拿到了一块金牌。

   女：A) 哎呀，怎么搞的？

   B) 世界游泳锦标赛是在罗马举行的。

   C) 真的吗？中国跳水队太了不起了！

   D) 看了，他们踢得很辛苦，好不容易才进了一个球。

   （学生答题5 秒）

4. 女：乐乐，你去夏令营那么长时间怎么一直都没跟我联系呢？

   男：A) 你说得没错，夏令营的时间是有儿有点太长了。

   B) 那个地方既不能上网，也不能打电话。

   C) 我们在夏令营交了很多新朋友，过得很快乐。

   D) 时间过得真快，夏令营很快就要结束了。

   （学生答题5 秒）

5. 女：嗨，算上新來的那個印度同學，咱們
班現在一共有從11個不同國家來的學
生了。

男：A) 每個國家的人都有自己的語言。

B) 印度離中國比美國離中國近。

C) 咱們班都快成一個小聯合國了。

D) 我從來沒有去過印度。

（學生答題5 秒）

6. 男：一看你家牆上掛的那些字畫，就知道你
爸爸的毛筆字功底很深，你知道他是怎
麼學的嗎？

女：A) 毛筆字是中國傳統文化藝術的一種
形式，很多外國人也喜歡學。

B) 聽奶奶說我爸爸像我這麼大時就開
始學了。

C) 我爸爸字畫的水平，一般人比不了。

D) 有些人是跟老師學，有些人是自
學的。

（學生答題5 秒）

7. 女：嗨，漢語橋美英中學生夏令營不是在北
京嗎？你怎麼跑山東去了呢？

男：A) 山東是個旅遊的好地方，我很喜歡。

B) 不都是去北京，有去山東的，還有
去上海的。

C) 山東離北京可遠了，我們是坐飛機
去的。

D) 夏令營活動在中美青少年之間架起
了一座友誼的橋樑。

（學生答題5 秒）

5. 女：嗨，算上新来的那个印度同学，咱们
班现在一共有从11个不同国家来的学
生了。

男：A) 每个国家的人都有自己的语言。

B) 印度离中国比美国离中国近。

C) 咱们班都快成一个小联合国了。

D) 我从来没去过印度。

（学生答题5 秒）

6. 男：一看你家墙上挂的那些字画，就知道你
爸爸的毛笔字功底很深，你知道他是怎
么学的吗？

女：A) 毛笔字是中国传统文化艺术的一种
形式，很多外国人也喜欢学。

B) 听奶奶说我爸爸像我这么大时就开
始学了。

C) 我爸爸字画的水平，一般人比不了。

D) 有些人是跟老师学，有些人是自
学的。

（学生答题5 秒）

7. 女：嗨，汉语桥美英中学生夏令营不是在北
京吗？你怎么跑山东去了呢？

男：A) 山东是个旅游的好地方，我很喜欢。

B) 不都是去北京，有去山东的，还有
去上海的。

C) 山东离北京可远了，我们是坐飞机
去的。

D) 夏令营活动在中美青少年之间架起
了一座友谊的桥梁。

（学生答题5 秒）

8. 女：以後上課時你可千萬別給我發短信了，
　　　弄得我心神不定的，今天差點兒被老師
　　　發現。

　　男：A）如果你上課時覺得不舒服，要馬上
　　　　　告訴老師。

　　　　B）謝謝你提醒我，以後咱們上課應該
　　　　　專心點兒。

　　　　C）發短信在青少年中很流行，因為比
　　　　　發電郵方便。

　　　　D）要是我早知道你心情不好，我一定
　　　　　會給你發短信的。

（學生答題5 秒）

9. 男：咱們學校外語系上週組織的那個演出，
　　　你去看了嗎？我們班唱周傑倫歌
　　　的那個同學，得了一等獎。

　　女：A）周傑倫的確唱得不錯，得一等獎是
　　　　　應該的。

　　　　B）我不信周傑倫會到你們學校來表演。

　　　　C）我去看了，那個同學唱得是很棒，
　　　　　而且他的歌兒也選得好。

　　　　D）這個學期我沒選外語課，因爲我的
　　　　　學分已經夠了。

（學生答題5 秒）

8. 女：以后上课时你可千万别给我发短信了，
　　　弄得我心神不定的，今天差点儿被老师
　　　发现。

　　男：A）如果你上课时觉得不舒服，要马上
　　　　　告诉老师。

　　　　B）谢谢你提醒我，以后咱们上课应该
　　　　　專心點兒。

　　　　C）发短信在青少年中很流行，因为比
　　　　　发电邮方便。

　　　　D）要是我早知道你心情不好，我一定
　　　　　会给你发短信的。

（学生答题5 秒）

9. 男：咱们学校外语系上周组织的那个演出，
　　　你去看了吗？我们班唱周杰伦歌
　　　的那个同学得了一等奖。

　　女：A）周杰伦的确唱得不错，得一等奖是
　　　　　应该的。

　　　　B）我不信周杰伦会到你们学校来表演。

　　　　C）我去看了，那个同学唱得是很棒，
　　　　　而且他的歌儿也选得好。

　　　　D）这个学期我没选外语课，因为我的
　　　　　学分已经够了。

（学生答题5 秒）

10. 女：大偉，你今天走路看起來怪怪的？怎
    麼了？

    男：昨天踢足球把腳扭傷了，不過醫生說
    沒大事兒，休息幾天就好了。

    女：A）這麼多天還沒好啊？

    　　B）今天放學後我們一起去游泳，好嗎？

    　　C）我也是個足球迷，不過我沒你踢
    得好。

    　　D）那這幾天上下學要不要我接送你
    一下？

    （學生答題5 秒）

11. 男：媽媽，我還有半個鐘頭就練完球了，
    今天晚飯我們可不可以吃韭菜餡兒
    餃子？

    女：我正包著呢！等你回來時就差不多包
    完了。

    男：A）我不喜歡吃蒸包子，咱們家最近
    老吃包子。

    　　B）太好了！我都快餓死了！

    　　C）餃子做起來很麻煩，但吃起來
    很香。

    　　D）北方人都很喜歡吃餃子。

    （學生答題5 秒）

10. 女：大伟，你今天走路看起来怪怪的，怎
    么了？

    男：昨天踢足球把脚扭伤了，不过医生说
    没大事儿，休息几天就好了。

    女：A）这么多天还没好啊？

    　　B）今天放学后我们一起去游泳，好吗？

    　　C）我也是个足球迷，不过我没你踢
    得好。

    　　D）那这几天上下学要不要我接送你
    一下？

    （学生答题5 秒）

11. 男：妈妈，我还有半个钟头就练完球了，
    今天晚饭我们可不可以吃韭菜馅儿
    饺子？

    女：我正包着呢！等你回来时就差不多包
    完了。

    男：A）我不喜欢吃蒸包子，咱们家最近
    老吃包子。

    　　B）太好了！我都快饿死了！

    　　C）饺子做起来很麻烦，但吃起来
    很香。

    　　D）北方人都很喜欢吃饺子。

    （学生答题5 秒）

12. 男：老師，我這學期一直很努力，可是成績就是上不去，您看我是哪方面的問題？

女：光靠努力還不夠，也要注意學習方法，我覺得你課後應該多複習。

男：A）知道了，我放學回家後要多花點時間複習。

B）謝謝你，我一定努力學習中文和中國的文化。

C）我覺得一個學生的學習成績是很重要的。

D）我們應該活到老學到老。

（學生答題5 秒）

13. 女：樂樂，媽媽在學校門口等了都快半個小時了，以後放了學快點兒出來。

男：A）我放學已經半個小時了，您怎麼才到呢？

B）對不起，今天學生會有事兒，耽誤了一會兒。

C）您怎麼來的這麼晚呢？

D）您用了半個多小時才開到學校，是不是路上塞車啊？

（學生答題5 秒）

14. 男：嗨，小玲，差點沒認出你來。今天怎麼想起穿旗袍上學了？

女：今天中文課有一個關於中國傳統服裝的報告，我就把我媽媽的旗袍穿來了。

男：A）中國有五千年的悠久歷史。

B）現在的中國人已經不太穿旗袍了。

C）旗袍是中國傳統服裝的一種。

D）這身打扮肯定會給你們的報告增加不少色彩。

（學生答題5 秒）

12. 男：老師，我这学期一直很努力，可成績就是上不去，您看我是哪方面的问题？

女：光靠努力还不够，也要注意学习方法，我觉得你课后应该多复习。

男：A）知道了，我放学回家后要多花点时间复习。

B）谢谢你，我一定努力学习中文和中国的文化。

C）我觉得一个学生的学习成績很重要的。

D）我们应该活到老学到老。

（学生答题5 秒）

13. 女：乐乐，妈妈在学校门口等了都快半个小时了，以后放了学快点儿出来。

男：A）我放学已经半个小时了，您怎么才到呢？

B）对不起，今天学生会有事儿，耽误了一会儿。

C）您怎么来的这么晚呢？

D）您用了半个多小时才开到学校，是不是路上塞车啊？

（学生答题5 秒）

14. 男：嗨，小玲，差点没认出你来。今天怎么想起穿旗袍上学了？

女：今天中文课有一个关于中国传统服装的报告，我就把我妈妈的旗袍穿来了。

男：A）中国有五千年的悠久历史。

B）现在的中国人已经不太穿旗袍了。

C）旗袍是中国传统服装的一种。

D）你这身打扮肯定会给你的报告增加不少色彩。

（学生答题5 秒）

15. 女：馬東，你發現沒有，最近我們學校餐廳的飯菜好像越來越豐盛了。

男：真是英雄所見略同，我也覺得飯菜種類多了很多。

女：A）我這個人中餐西餐都喜歡吃。

B）這說明學校很重視我們的身體健康。

C）飯菜好的學校不一定是好學校。

D）價錢便宜是好事，我可以省下錢來買書。

（學生答題5 秒）

15. 女：马东，你发现没有，最近我们学校餐厅的饭菜好象越来越丰盛了。

男：真是英雄所见略同，我也觉得饭菜种类多了很多。

女：A）我这个人中餐西餐都喜欢吃。

B）这说明学校很重视我们的身体健康。

C）饭菜好的学校不一定是好学校。

D）价钱便宜是好事，我可以省下钱来买书。

（学生答题5 秒）

Listening Selections (15%, 10 minutes)

Directions: You will listen to several selections in Chinese. For each selection, you will be told whether it will be played once or twice. You may take notes as you listen. Your notes will not be graded. After listening to each selection, you will see questions in English. For each question, choose the response that is best according to the selection. You will have 12 seconds to answer each question.

Selection 1: Announcement

Selection plays one time.

Narrator: Now you will listen once to a public announcement.

(Traditional Characters)

同學們請注意：

　　昨天下午，有人在學校操場上撿到一個藍色的運動袋，裡面有一套運動服、一雙球鞋、一個隨身聽、幾本書和一個錢包，還有少量現金。請丟失此物的同學速到校辦公室認領。

(Simplified Characters)

同学们请注意：

　　昨天下午，有人在学校操场上捡到一个蓝色的运动袋，里面有一套运动服、一双球鞋、一个随身听、几本书和一个钱包，还有少量现金。请丢失此物的同学速到校办公室认领。

Narrator: Now answer the questions for this selection.

(12 seconds)

(12 seconds)

(12 seconds)

Selection 2: Voice message

Selection plays two times.

Narrator: Now you will listen twice to a voice message.

(Traditional Characters)

王老師：您好！我是您中文三班學生李帥帥的媽媽。帥帥回家跟我提到您班上要組織一個討論會，想請家長去講講我們在美國奮鬥的經歷和感受。我和我先生都非常願意參加這次討論會，但是有幾個問題想問問您，比如，每個家長可以講多長時間，用中文還是用英文講，是否需要我們把講稿事先給每個學生印一份等等。麻煩您有時間給我回個電話：(415)541-6969。

謝謝！

(Simplified Characters)

王老师：您好！我是您中文三班学生李帅帅的妈妈。帅帅回家跟我提到您班上要组织一个讨论会，想请家长去讲讲我们在美国奋斗的经历和感受。我和我先生都非常愿意参加这次讨论会，但是有几个问题想问问您，比如，每个家长可以讲多长时间，用中文还是用英文讲，是否需要我们把讲稿事先给每个学生印一份等等。麻烦您有时间给我回个电话：(415)541-6969。

谢谢！

Narrator: Now listen again.

Narrator: Now answer the questions for this selection.

(12 seconds)

(12 seconds)

(12 seconds)

Selection 3: Conversation

Selection plays one time.

Narrator: Now you will listen once to a conversation between a girl and her younger brother.

(Traditional Characters)

男：姐姐，剛才你的一個同學打電話找你。他說今晚你們學校有舞會，你要去做他的舞伴兒。

女：他還說什麼啦？

男：他說等你準備好了，就馬上給他打個電話，他會開車來接你。

女：知道了，謝謝你。

男：可不可以帶我一起去啊？我一個人在家真無聊。

女：哎呀，我真希望爸媽去上海開會時把你也帶著。好了好了，趕緊準備吧。

男：為什麼今天學校有舞會呢？今天既不是週末，也不是什麼節日。

女：你去了就知道了，快換衣服吧，別囉嗦了！

(Simplified Characters)

男：姐姐，刚才你的一个同学打电话找你。他说今晚你们学校有舞会，你要去做他的舞伴儿。

女：他还说什么啦？

男：他说等你准备好了，就马上给他打个电话，他会开车来接你。

女：知道了，谢谢你。

男：可不可以带我一起去啊？我一个人在家真无聊。

女：哎呀，我真希望爸妈去上海开会时把你也带着。好了好了，赶紧准备吧。

男：为什么今天学校有舞会呢？今天既不是周末，也不是什么节日。

女：你去了就知道了，快换衣服吧，别啰嗦了！

Narrator: Now answer the questions for this selection.

(12 seconds)

(12 seconds)

(12 seconds)

(12 seconds)

Selection 4: Instructions

Selection plays two times.

Narrator: Now you will listen twice to an instruction.

Man:

(Traditional Characters)

東華大學關於新生辦理入學手續的說明

歡迎各位同學來到東華大學學習，為方便各位同學辦理入學手續，請按照以下程序辦理：

　　入學手續的辦理時間為2009年8月28日，地點在學校行政大樓一樓。首先，要到新生註冊中心辦理入學登記手續，向學校提交入學通知書，同時領取新生選課手冊、校服和體檢表格。然後，請大家在財務辦公室繳納學費。已在網上預交學費的同學，請把收據交給財務辦公室。最後，請大家到圖書館拍照，製作住宿卡並辦理住宿手續。入學後的第一週請到學校書店購買教科書。祝願各位同學在東華大學度過美好的大學時光。

(Simplified Characters)

东华大学关于新生办理入学手续的说明

欢迎各位同学来到东华大学学习，为方便各位同学办理入学手续，请按照以下程序办理：

　　入学手续的办理时间为2009年8月28日，地点在学校行政大楼一楼。首先，要到新生注册中心办理入学登记手续，向学校提交入学通知书，同时领取新生选课手册，校服和体检表格。然后，请大家在财务办公室缴纳学费。已在网上预交学费的同学，请把收据交给财务办公室。最后，请大家到图书馆拍照，制作住宿卡并办理住宿手续。入学后的第一周请到学校书店购买教科书。祝愿各位同学在东华大学度过美好的大学时光。

Narrator: Now listen again.
(Repeat)

Narrator: Now answer the questions for this selection.

(12 seconds)

(12 seconds)

(12 seconds)

(12 seconds)

Selection 5: Report

Selection plays two times.

Narrator: Now you will listen twice to a report.

Man:

(Traditional Characters)

大家好！

　　我代表我們小組的四名同學向大家匯報一下我們這次就環所展開的調查活動的結果。本次調查共發放問卷223份，收回問卷率為90%，85%的學生對問卷進行了認真填寫。調查結果顯示76%以上的學生已認識到環境保護的重要性，並會主動監督自己的行為。18%的同學認為他們的環保意識還可以，但做得還不夠，6%的同學覺得他們沒有什麼環保意識，並承認有破壞環境的行為。當問到如果在公共場所看到有人亂扔垃圾他們該怎麼做時，87%的同學說他們明明知道不對，也不會去管別人，認為只要自己不去扔就行了。9%的同學說他們會告訴那些人把垃圾撿起來，4%的同學覺得無所謂，反正有清潔工處理垃圾。

以上是我們小組的調查報告，謝謝大家！

(Simplified Characters)

大家好！

　　我代表我们小组的四名同学向大家汇报一下我们这次就环所展开的调查活动的结果。本次调查共发放问卷223份，收回问卷率为90%，85%的学生对问卷进行了认真填写。调查结果显示76%以上的学生已认识到环境保护的重要性，并会主动监督自己的行为。18%的同学认为他们的环保意识还可以，但做得还不够，6%的同学觉得他们没有什么环保意识，并承认有破坏环境的行为。当问到如果在公共场所看到有人乱扔垃圾他们该怎么做时，87%的同学说他们明明知道不对，也不会去管别人，认为只要自己不去扔就行了。9%的同学说他们会告诉那些人把垃圾捡起来，4%的同学觉得无所谓，反正有清洁工处理垃圾。

以上是我们小组的调查报告，谢谢大家！

Narrator: Now listen again.

Narrator: Now answer the questions for this selection.

(12 seconds)

(12 seconds)

(12 seconds)

(12 seconds)

(12 seconds)

Section II: Part B: Speaking

Recording Scripts

Conversation

Directions: You will participate in a simulated conversation. Each time it is your turn to speak, you will have 20 seconds to record. You should respond as fully and as appropriately as possible.

You will have a conversation with Xiaoliang, a Chinese student you met for the first time at a summer program in China, about American schools.

(Traditional Characters)	(Simplified Characters)
小亮：聽說美國的學校聚會特別多，你們學校是這樣嗎？ （學生答題20秒）	小亮：听说美国学校的聚会特别多，你们学校是这样吗？ （学生答题20秒）
小亮：一般來說，學校爲什麼有聚會呢？ （學生答題20秒）	小亮：一般来说，学校为什么有聚会呢？ （学生答题20秒）
小亮：聚會通常都有哪些形式？你們都做些什麼？ （學生答題20秒）	小亮：聚会通常都有哪些形式？你们都做些什么？ （學生答题20秒）
小亮：你覺得參加聚會對於你的學習、生活有什麼影響？ （學生答題20秒）	小亮：你觉得参加聚会对于你的学习、生活有什么影响？ （学生答题20秒）
小亮：聽說美國不允許青少年喝酒，如果學生在聚會上喝了酒，學校會怎麼處理？ （學生答題20秒）	小亮：听说美国不允许青少年喝酒，如果学生在聚会上喝了酒，学校会怎么处理？ （学生答题20秒）
小亮：咱們暑期班最後一天有個文化交流聚會，我們可以一起表演個節目，你有什麼好主意嗎？ （學生答題20秒）	小亮：咱们暑期班最后一天有个文化交流聚会，我们可以一起表演个节目，你有什么好主意吗？ （学生答题20秒）

254

Cultural Presentation (15%, 7 minutes)

Please describe the culinary diversity in China in terms of the various food styles and geographic regions. Choose one specific culinary style, and talk about its popular dishes, commonly used ingredients, and unique cooking techniques.

Recording Scripts for Test 8

Section I: Part A: Listening

Rejoinders

Directions: You will hear several short conversations or parts of conversations followed by four choices, designated (A), (B), (C), and (D). Choose the one that continues or completes the conversation in a logical and culturally appropriate manner. You will have 5 seconds to answer each question.

(Traditional Characters)

1. 男：趕快把電視打開，現在正轉播世界盃籃球賽呢！

   女：A）你今天就歇著吧，咱們家的電視壞了。

   B）我現在看的這個節目可精彩呢，我不想看什麼籃球賽。

   C）比賽什麼時候開始？

   D）想不想出去練籃球？明天不是有比賽嗎？

   （學生答題5秒）

(Simplified Characters)

1. 男：赶快把电视打开，现在正转播世界杯篮球赛呢！

   女：A）你今天就歇着吧，咱们家的电视坏了。

   B）我现在看的这个节目可精彩呢，我不想看什么篮球赛。

   C）比赛什么时候开始？

   D）想不想出去练篮球？明天不是有比赛吗？

   （学生答题5秒）

2. 女：你急什麼啊？瞧你滿頭大汗的。

   男：A）唉呀，熱死了，熱死了！我買一瓶
         礦泉水！

       B）我的登機證不見了，剛才還在這兒。

       C）這兒的夏天就是這樣，常常熱得讓
         人滿頭大汗。

       D）我今天的作業早就做好了，所以我
         一點也不急。

   （學生答題5秒）

3. 男：這是昨天買的那部電腦的收據，收好，
      別丟了。

   女：A）大家都說那個牌子的電腦質量很
         好，售後服務也很不錯。

       B）你把收據擺到哪兒去了？怎麼轉眼
         就不見了？

       C）這個收據是誰簽的名？我一點都看
         不出來。

       D）你儘管放心，連十年前的收據我都
         保存得好好的。

   （學生答題5秒）

4. 女：大大超市旁邊新開了一家中國飯館，電
      視廣告上說這個星期六中午最早到的
      一百名顧客免費招待自助餐，咱們要不
      要去碰碰運氣？

   男：A）既然你做東，我當然去。

       B）那星期六得一早就去排隊了，值
         得嗎？

       C）自助餐最好是能吃多少才拿多少，
         拿多了吃不完，實在浪費。

       D）這家飯館很會招待人，服務特別
         好，我們運氣不錯。

   （學生答題5秒）

2. 女：你急什么啊？瞧你满头大汗的。

   男：A）唉呀，热死了，热死了！我买一瓶
         矿泉水！

       B）我的登机证不见了，刚才还在这儿的。

       C）这儿的夏天就是这样，常常热得让
         人满头大汗。

       E）我今天的作业早就做好了，所以我
         一点也不急。

   （学生答题5秒）

3. 男：这是昨天买的那部电脑的收据，收好，
      别丢了。

   女：A）大家都说那个牌子的电脑质量很
         好，售后服务也很不错。

       B）你把收据摆到哪儿去了？怎么转眼
         就不见了？

       C）这个收据是谁签的名？我一点都看
         不出来。

       E）你尽管放心，连十年前的收据我都
         保存得好好的。

   （学生答题5秒）

4. 女：大大超市旁边新开了一家中国饭馆，电
      视广告上说这个星期六中午最早到的
      一百名顾客免费招待自助餐，咱们要不
      要去碰碰运气？

   男：A）既然你做东，我当然去。

       B）那星期六得一早就去排队了，值
         得吗？

       C）自助餐最好是能吃多少才拿多少，
         拿多了吃不完，实在浪费。

       E）这家饭馆很会招待客人，服务特别
         好，我们运气不错。

   （学生答题5秒）

5. 男：你的選課表還少了導師簽字，註冊組恐怕不會接受。

　女：A）這位導師開的課都極受學生的歡迎。

　　　B）註冊組這個星期忙著學生選課的事，不會給我簽字的。

　　　C）我的導師這兩天出城開會去了，怎麼辦？

　　　D）我的導師認為我選的課太多了，要我少選一門。

　　（學生答題5秒）

6. 女：你們這個小區公共設施非常齊全，在這兒生活很方便吧？

　男：A）這個小區的房子看起來都差不多，相當高級。

　　　B）我們家住十六層，視野非常好。

　　　C）只可惜沒有游泳池，未免美中不足。

　　　D）這兒的住戶都有正當工作。

　　（學生答題5秒）

7. 男：你高中畢業後，打算工作還是上大學？

　女：A）我早就申請到學校了。

　　　B）其實工作賺多少錢並不重要，夠用就行了。

　　　C）我沒有什麼工作經驗，履歷不容易寫。

　　　D）畢業以後，我會常和朋友聯繫。

　　（學生答題5秒）

5. 男：你的选课表还少了导师的签字，注册组恐怕不会接受。

　女：A）这位导师开的课都极受学生的欢迎。

　　　B）注册组这个星期忙着学生选课的事，不会给我签字的。

　　　C）我的导师这两天出城开会去了，怎么办？

　　　D）我的导师认为我选的课太多了，要我少选一门。

　　（学生答题5秒）

6. 女：你们这个小区公共设施非常齐全，在这儿生活很方便吧？

　男：A）这个小区的房子看起来都差不多，相当高级。

　　　B）我们家住十六层，视野非常好。

　　　C）只可惜没有游泳池，未免美中不足。

　　　D）这儿的住户都有正当的工作。

　　（学生答题5秒）

7. 男：你高中毕业以后，打算工作还是上大学？

　女：A）我早就申请到学校了。

　　　B）其实工作赚多少钱并不重要，够用就行了。

　　　C）我没有什么工作经验，履历不容易写。

　　　D）毕业以后，我会常和朋友联系。

　　（学生答题5秒）

8. 男：你一天到晚坐在電腦前，不怕腰酸背痛嗎？最好不時站起來走走。

　　女：A）腰酸背痛得去看醫生，太麻煩了。

　　　　B）你的建議真好，就怕我一專心工作就忘了。

　　　　C）我的電腦桌是特別設計的，手指不容易受傷。

　　　　D）我們可以上網去查電腦和腰酸背痛有什麼關係。

　　（學生答題5秒）

9. 女：小白上課的時候常常跟我遞條子。

　　男：A）條子短是短，但是都很有趣。

　　　　B）難得這次他記得把作業帶來了。

　　　　C）原來他健康狀況不好，難怪常常請病假。

　　　　D）你不怕老師發現嗎？

　　（學生答題5秒）

10. 男：美國好大學比比皆是，我不瞭解我媽媽為什麼一定要我跟別人去擠所謂的名牌大學。

　　女：A）除非你的功課太差，否則你不用擔心上不了大學。

　　　　B）名牌大學的校園人很擠嗎？

　　　　C）那你的心理負擔可重了，是吧？

　　　　D）這個大學的教授素質和教學設備都比別的大學好。

　　（學生答題5秒）

8. 男：你一天到晚坐在电脑前，不怕腰酸背痛吗？最好不时站起来走走。

　　女：A）腰酸背痛得去看医生，太麻烦了。

　　　　B）你的建议真好，就怕我一专心工作就忘了。

　　　　C）我的电脑桌是特别设计的，手指不容易受伤。

　　　　D）我们可以上网去查电脑和腰酸背痛有什么关系。

　　（学生答题5秒）

9. 女：小白上课的时候常常跟我递条子。

　　男：A）条子短是短，但是都很有趣。

　　　　B）难得这次他记得把作业带来了。

　　　　C）原来他健康状况不好，难怪常常请病假。

　　　　D）你不怕老师发现吗？

　　（学生答题5秒）

10. 男：美国好大学比比皆是，我不了解我妈妈为什么一定要我跟别人去挤所谓的名牌大学。

　　女：A）除非你的功课太差，否则你不用担心上不了大学。

　　　　B）名牌大学的校园人很挤吗？

　　　　C）那你的心理负担可重了，是吧？

　　　　D）这个大学的教授素质和教学设备都比别的大学好。

　　（学生答题5秒）

11. 女：真氣人，屋裡的空調又壞了。

男：天氣這麼熱，趕緊找工人來修吧！

女：A）咱們家的空調開關在哪兒？

B）已經打了電話了，可是他們今天沒空，明天下午才能來。

C）把溫度調高點兒吧，可以節省點兒電費。

D）修車廠的工人都忙得很，找他們來修，恐怕得等上一陣子。

（學生答題5秒）

12. 男：你這是什麼打扮？男不男、女不女的，穿出去像話嗎？

女：爸，這你就不懂了，這叫流行。我走了，bye bye。

男：A）我和你媽年輕的時候，也都挺講究流行的。

B）我對流行再熟悉不過了。

C）你今天不把你那身衣服換下來，就別出門。

D）你現在不聽流行音樂了嗎？也好，我耳朵樂得清淨。

（學生答題5秒）

13. 女：你怎麼悶悶不樂的，有什麼心事嗎？

男：我跟我女朋友為了一點小事兒鬧翻了，現在覺得挺後悔的。

女：A）與其一個人在這兒後悔，還不如給她打個電話賠個不是吧。

B）哦，你的女朋友有新男朋友了？

C）你說的話要算話，別說了又後悔了。

D）你何必後悔呢？你的個性這麼開朗，人緣又好，大家都喜歡你。

（學生答題5秒）

11. 女：真气人，屋里的空   了。

男：天气这么热，赶紧   人来修吧！

女：A）咱们家的空调开关在哪儿？

B）已经打了电话了，可是他们今天没空，明天下午才能来。

C）把温度调高点儿吧，可以省点儿电费。

D）修车厂的工人都忙得很，找他们来修，恐怕得等上一阵子。

（学生答题5秒）

12. 男：你这是什么打扮？男不男、女不女的，穿出去像话吗？

女：爸，这你就不懂了，这叫流行。我走了，bye bye。

男：A）我和你妈年轻的时候，也都挺讲究流行的。

B）我对于流行再熟悉不过了。

C）你今天不把你那身衣服换下来，就别出门。

D）你现在不听流行音乐了吗？也好，我耳朵乐得清净。

（学生答题5秒）

13. 女：你怎么闷闷不乐的，有什么心事吗？

男：我跟我女朋友为了一点小事儿闹翻了，现在觉得挺后悔的。

女：A）与其一个人在这儿后悔，还不如给她打个电话赔个不是吧。

B）哦，你的女朋友有新男朋友了？

C）你说的话要算话，别说了又后悔了。

D）你何必后悔呢？你的个性这么开朗，人缘又好，大家都喜欢你。

（学生答题5秒）

14. 男：從十年級以來，老師生怕我們閒著似的，每天給我們的作業寫都寫不完。

女：那你怎麼有足夠的時間睡覺呢？

男：A）所以小白上課常打瞌睡，挨老師罵。

B）明天要考試，我今天晚上得熬夜準備，沒時間睡覺。

C）所以我上課的時候常常累得眼睛都睜不開。

D）作業太多了，幾點可以上床睡覺呢？

（學生答題5秒）

15. 女：現在父母要求孩子全面發展，既要學習好，又要琴棋書畫樣樣都行，真不容易。

男：有些父母對孩子的期望值太高了。

女：A）這就叫愛之深，責之切啊。

B）這就叫望子成龍、望女成鳳啊。

C）這就叫養子不教父之過啊。

D）這就叫天下無不是的父母啊。

（學生答題5秒）

14. 男：从十年级以来，老师生怕我们闲着似的，每天给我们的作业写都写不完。

女：那你怎么有足够的时间睡觉呢？

男：A）所以小白上课常打瞌睡，挨老师骂。

B）明天要考试，我今天晚上得熬夜准备，没时间睡觉。

C）所以我上课的时候常常累得眼睛都睁不开。

D）作业太多了，几点可以上床睡觉呢？

（学生答题5秒）

15. 女：现在父母要求孩子全面发展，既要学习好，又要琴棋书画样样都行，真不容易。

男：有些父母对孩子的期望太高了。

女：A）这就叫爱之深，责之切啊。

B）这就叫望子成龙、望女成凤啊。

C）这就叫养子不教父之过啊。

D）这就叫天下无不是的父母啊。

（学生答题5秒）

Listening Selections

Directions: You will listen to several selections in Chinese. For each selection, you will be told whether it will be played once or twice. You may take notes as you listen. Your notes will not be graded. After listening to each selection, you will see questions in English. For each question, choose the response that is best according to the selection. You will have 12 seconds to answer each question.

Selection 1: Public Announcement

Selection plays one time.

Narrator: Now you will listen once to a public announcement.

Woman:

<table>
<tr><td>(Traditional Characters)</td><td>(Simplified Characters)</td></tr>
<tr><td>各位同學！從明天早上八點起到大後天下午四點止，十一年級的學生將在大禮堂展示他們歷史課的作品。他們這次的展覽，主要是他們這兩個月研究、訪談的成果。他們每個人在學期初選定一個跟他們自己的文化有關的題目，然後找資料、照片、寫文章，並設計自己的展示板。就我所知，每個學生都很認真努力，如期完成這個項目，他們也從中學習到了很多。為了方便各位同學的參觀活動，學校決定明天早上開放給家長參觀，明天下午九年級學生，後天十年級，大後天十二年級，各年級可按時前往觀覽。</td><td>各位同学！从明天早上八点起到大后天下午四点止，十一年级的学生将在大礼堂展示他们历史课的作品。他们这次的展览，主要是他们这两个月研究、访谈的成果。他们每个人在学期初选定一个跟他们自己的文化有关的题目，然后找资料、照片、写文章，并设计自己的展示板。就我所知，每个学生都认真努力，如期完成这个项目，他们也从中学习到了很多。为了方便各位同学的参观活动，学校决定明天早上开放给家长参观，明天下午九年级学生，后天十年级，大后天十二年级，各年级可按时前往观览。</td></tr>
</table>

Narrator: Now answer the questions for this selection.

(12 seconds)

(12 seconds)

(12 seconds)

(12 seconds)

(12 seconds)

Selection 2: Conversation

Selection plays one time.

Narrator: Now you will listen once to a conversation between two students.

<table>
<tr><td>

(Traditional Characters)

男：蘭蘭，心情不好啊，怎麼看起來這麼
鬱悶？

女：哎，我爸爸、媽媽最近在鬧離婚，家裡氣
氛非常糟糕，我真不想回家。

男：我可以瞭解你的感覺。去年我媽媽離家出
走的那幾個星期，我爸爸整天不停地喝
酒，醉了就摔杯子，還罵我，拿我出氣。

女：我都不知道你們家這些事，你當時怎麼沒
跟我說呢？後來呢？

男：後來我媽媽又回來了，家才又有了家的樣
子，我媽媽甚至比以前更關心我，爸爸也
把酒戒了。

女：唉！我不懂為什麼大人鬧不愉快，非得把
小孩扯進去不可？我都不知道該聽誰的。

男：依照我的經驗，你最好什麼話都別說，要
不然，他們可能會生你的氣，拿你出氣。

女：哎，我寧可他們生我的氣，要是他們把氣
都出在我身上，從此就和好、不離婚了，
那不是很值得嗎？

</td><td>

(Simplified Characters)

男：兰兰，心情不好啊，怎么看起来这么
郁闷？

女：哎，我爸爸、妈妈最近在闹离婚，家里气
氛非常糟糕，我真不想回家。

男：我可以了解你的感觉。去年我妈妈离家出
走的那几个星期，我爸爸整天不停地喝
酒，醉了就摔杯子，还骂我，拿我出气。

女：我都不知道你们家这些事，你当时怎么没
跟我说呢？后来呢？

男：后来我妈妈又回来了，家才又有了家的样
子，我妈妈甚至比以前更关心我，爸爸也
把酒戒了。

女：唉！我不懂为什么大人闹不愉快，非得把
小孩扯进去不可？我都不知道该听谁的。

男：依照我的经验，你最好什么话都别说，要
不然，他们可能会生你的气，拿你出气。

女：哎，我宁可他们生我的气，要是他们把气
都出在我身上，从此就和好、不离婚了，
那不是很值得吗？

</td></tr>
</table>

Narrator: Now answer the questions for this selection.

(12 seconds)

(12 seconds)

(12 seconds)

(12 seconds)

Selection 3: Instructions

Selection plays two times.

Narrator: Now you will listen twice to an instruction.

Woman:

(Traditional Characters)

媽媽，謝謝您不嫌麻煩、答應照顧我的熱帶魚。我去歐洲開會的這段時間，您就多費心了。小瓶裡的魚食，一天餵兩次或三次都行，每次餵三、四顆，千萬別給太多，因為魚是給多少吃多少，可能會撐死。魚缸的水每七天換一次，先把水龍頭的水調到室溫，把一些水放到一個乾淨的碗裡，用漁網把魚撈起來，放到碗裡，再把魚缸裡的水倒掉，用熱水沖洗魚缸和魚缸裡的石頭，最後把魚缸加七、八分滿，再滴一、兩滴大瓶裡的營養水，就可以把魚放回魚缸裡了。媽媽，看到魚在水裡游來游去非常快樂的樣子，您肯定也非常快樂的。

(Simplified Characters)

妈妈，谢谢您不嫌麻烦、答应照顾我的热带鱼。我去欧洲开会的这段时间，您就多费心了。小瓶里的鱼食，一天喂两次或三次都行，每次喂三、四颗，千万别给太多，因为鱼是给多少吃多少，可能会撑死。鱼缸的水每七天换一次，先把水龙头的水调到室温，把一些水放到一个干净的碗里，用渔网把鱼捞起来，放到碗里，再把鱼缸里的水倒掉，用热水冲洗鱼缸和鱼缸里的石头，最后把鱼缸加七、八分满，再滴一、两滴大瓶里的营养水，就可以把鱼放回鱼缸里了。妈妈，看到鱼在水里游来游去非常快乐的样子，您肯定也会非常快乐的。

Narrator: Now listen again.
(Repeat)

Narrator: Now answer the questions for this selection.

(12 seconds)

(12 seconds)

(12 seconds)

(12 seconds)

264

Selection 4: Voice message

Selection plays two times.

Narrator: Now you will listen twice to a voice message.

Woman:

<table>
<tr><th>(Traditional Characters)</th><th>(Simplified Characters)</th></tr>
<tr><td>

慧心，我是可文。你的手機大概是關機了吧？響了一聲就跳到你的語音信箱了，希望你能及時聽到我的留言。我們原先不是預定明天放學後一起留在學校討論英文小說的問題嗎？很不巧，早上起床的時候，牙套有點鬆了，剛才我媽媽打電話來，說是幫我預約了今天四點去看牙醫。要是方便，明天五點到我家來吧！我們可以那時候再一起討論英文課業上的問題，你也可以順便在我家吃晚飯，我媽媽會做你最喜歡的紅燒獅子頭。盡快給我回電或發個短信吧。

</td><td>

慧心，我是可文。你的手机大概是关机了吧？响了一声就跳到你的语音信箱了，希望你能及时听到我的留言。我们原先不是预定明天放学后一起留在学校讨论英文小说的问题吗？很不巧，早上起床的时候，牙套有点松了，刚才我妈妈打电话来，说是帮我预约了今天四点去看牙医。要是方便，明天五点到我家来吧！我们可以那时候再一起讨论英文课业上的问题，你也可以顺便在我家吃晚饭，我妈妈会做你最喜欢的红烧狮子头。尽快给我回电或发个短信吧。

</td></tr>
</table>

Narrator: Now listen again.
(Repeat)

Narrator: Now answer the questions for this selection.

(12 seconds)

(12 seconds)

(12 seconds)

Selection 5: Report

Selection plays two times.

Narrator: Now you will listen twice to a report.

Man:

<table>
<tr><th>(Traditional Characters)</th><th>(Simplified Characters)</th></tr>
<tr><td>

老師、同學們，大家好！

現在我代表我們的三人小組來匯報一下我們這次手機問卷調查的結果。我們一共發出三百份問卷，收回二百九十份。所有答卷的同學都有手機，其中百分之七十五的同學每天打的手機次數在二十五到三十次之間。百分之八十的同學認為他們每次通話的時間都不到一分鐘，完全是短話短說。所有同學的手機也都能發短信，有百分之十八的同學表示，他們平均一天發的短信超過一百個。雖然學校不准學生在校園使用手機，但是三分之一的學生承認，他們都曾有在上課時收發過短信的經驗，而且認為只要不被老師發現，並沒有什麼大不了的。以上是我們小組的報告，謝謝。

</td><td>

老师、同学们，大家好！

现在我代表我们的三人小组来汇报一下我们这次手机问卷调查的结果。我们一共发出三百份问卷，收回二百九十份。所有答卷的同学都有手机，其中百分之七十五的同学每天打的手机次数在二十五到三十次之间。百分之八十的同学认为他们每次通话的时间都不到一分钟，完全是短话短说。所有同学的手机也都能发短信，有百分之十八的同学表示，他们平均一天发的短信超过一百个。虽然学校不准学生在校园使用手机，但有三分之一的学生承认，他们都曾有在上课时收发过短信的经验，而且认为只要不被老师发觉，并没有什么大不了的。以上是我们小组的报告，谢谢。

</td></tr>
</table>

Narrator: Now listen again.
(Repeat)

Narrator: Now answer the questions for this selection.

(12 seconds)

(12 seconds)

(12 seconds)

(12 seconds)

Section II: Part B: Speaking

Recording Scripts

Conversation

Directions: You will participate in a simulated conversation. Each time it is your turn to speak, you will have 20 seconds to record. You should respond as fully and as appropriately as possible.

You will have a conversation with Jiang Ning, a passenger sitting next to you on the bus, about your experience in learning Chinese.

(Traditional Characters)

姜寧：你來中國多久了？是來學習的嗎？
　　　（學生答題20秒）

姜寧：你中文說得這麼好，學了幾年了？在哪
　　　兒學的？你是怎麼對中文產生興趣的？
　　　（學生答題20秒）

姜寧：你覺得中文難不難學？你有沒有什麼學
　　　中文的有趣經驗？
　　　（學生答題20秒）

姜寧：我現在正在學英文，你說我要怎麼做才
　　　能把英文學好？
　　　（學生答題20秒）

姜寧：除了學習以外，你平常都做些什麼？
　　　（學生答題20秒）

姜寧：跟你聊天真有意思，我能不能跟你做個
　　　朋友？我們以後怎麼聯繫？
　　　（學生答題20秒）

(Simplified Characters)

姜宁：你来中国多久了？是来学习的吗？
　　　（学生答题20秒）

姜宁：你中文说得这么好，学了几年了？在哪
　　　儿学的？你是怎么对中文产生兴趣的？
　　　（学生答题20秒）

姜宁：你觉得中文难不难学？你有没有什么学
　　　中文的有趣经验？
　　　（学生答题20秒）

姜宁：我现在正在学英文，你说我要怎么做才
　　　能把英文学好？
　　　（学生答题20秒）

姜宁：除了学习以外，你平常都做些什么？
　　　（学生答题20秒）

姜宁：跟你聊天真有意思，我能不能跟你做个
　　　朋友？我们以后怎么联系？
　　　（学生答题20秒）

Cultural Presentation

Directions: You will be asked to speak in Chinese on a specific topic. Imagine you are making an oral presentation to your Chinese class. First, you will read and hear the topic for your presentation. You will have 4 minutes to prepare your presentation. Then you will have 2 minutes to record your presentation. Your presentation should be as complete as possible.

Choose one of your favorite Chinese writers, ancient or contemporary. In your presentation, describe this writer's background, name one of his/her most famous works and introduce its form and content, and explain the writer's significance in the history of Chinese literature.